Predestined
Journey

Predestined Journey

Man's Responsibility in God's Plan

by the messenger of wisdom
PEGGY HOF CORRIGAN

ARPress
ILLUMINATING IDEAS
EMPOWERING VOICES

ARPress
45 Dan Road Suite 5
Canton MA 02021

Hotline: 1(888) 821-0229
Fax: 1(508) 545-7580

Ordering Information:
Quantity sales. Special discounts are available on quantity purchases by corporations, associations, and others. For details, contact the publisher at the address above.

Printed in the United States of America.

ISBN-13:   Softcover   979-8-89356-821-9
            eBook   979-8-89356-822-6

Library of Congress Control Number: 2024906123

Table of Contents

Purposes of Predestined Journey

Sound the Alarm as the Watchman on the Wall
1. Revealing Hidden Mysteries
2. Treasure Chest Jewels
  o Principle of Time
  o Principle of Order
  o Principle of Obedience
  o Principle of the Seed
3. Exposing the Delicacies of the Counterfeit

1. The Family Unit
 All God's Secrets are Found Hidden from the Wise and Prudent
 Bondage to a Lie Producing Unbelief
 Job, the Man Most Judged and Misunderstood
 A man of his word is highly valued!
 God has No Secrets from a Humble, Righteous Man
 God Will Fill my Treasure Chest

2. Pride is the Root Cause

3. Repentance, Forgiveness, and Restoration

Study Guide

Additional Biblical addresses can be found in the Predestined Journey study guide in the back section of this book.

"Predestined Journey" by Peggy Hof-Corrigan is a profound Christian commentary that delves into the complexities of modern life and the enduring struggle to align one's path with God's will. Through insightful reflections and unwavering devotion to biblical principles, Hof-Corrigan invites readers on a transformative journey towards spiritual enlightenment and divine understanding.

Key Themes and Messages: At its core, "Predestined Journey" serves as a beacon of faith, illuminating the eternal truths found within the Word of God. Hof-Corrigan courageously tackles controversial topics such as a free will choice and abortion with a refreshing blend of honesty and compassion. Through her meticulous exploration of scripture, she challenges readers to confront the moral dilemmas of our time and discern the righteous path amidst a world plagued by moral relativism.

The book's central message revolves around the necessity of surrendering to God's divine plan and relinquishing control over our lives. Hof-Corrigan emphasizes the dangers of succumbing to sin, idolatry, and misplaced trust in mortal beings. Instead, she encourages readers to cultivate a deeper relationship with God, allowing His wisdom to guide their decisions and actions.

Strengths and Unique Qualities: One of the standout strengths of "Predestined Journey" lies in Hof-Corrigan's ability to blend theological insights with practical wisdom. Her writing resonates with authenticity and sincerity, drawing readers into a heartfelt dialogue with God's Word. Through powerful observations and impassioned rhetoric, she dismantles the barriers of ignorance and fosters a spirit of introspection and self-discovery.

Furthermore, Hof-Corrigan's unwavering commitment to biblical truth sets her apart as a beacon of moral clarity in an age of moral ambiguity. Her bold stance on contentious issues demonstrates a steadfast allegiance to God's commandments, inspiring readers to embrace their faith with conviction and purpose.

Tailored Presentation: For Christian readers seeking spiritual guidance and biblical wisdom, "Predestined Journey" offers a compelling narrative infused with timeless truths and transformative insights. Hof-

Corrigan's profound reflections on the challenges of contemporary life resonate deeply with individuals navigating the complexities of faith and morality.

Moreover, for skeptics and seekers alike, the book serves as a thought-provoking exploration of the human condition and the eternal quest for meaning and purpose. Hof-Corrigan's nuanced perspective invites readers from all walks of life to engage in a dialogue about the nature of truth, morality, and the divine.

In essence, "Predestined Journey" is not merely a book but a transformative odyssey towards spiritual enlightenment and divine revelation. Peggy Hof-Corrigan's profound insights and unwavering faith serve as a guiding light in a world shrouded in darkness, beckoning readers to embark on a journey of faith, hope, and redemption.

PREDESTINED JOURNEY
MAN' RESPONSIBILITY IN
GOD'S PLAN

Peggy Hof-Corrigan
Messenger of Wisdom

FULLY REVISED AND EXPANDED
2nd edition

About The Author

Peggy Hof-Corrigan met and married her wonderful husband Patrick Corrigan in Entebbe, Uganda Africa in May of 2007. Their intense love for Jesus Christ and their school experience at Charis Bible College was the common link in their marriage made in heaven. After returning from Africa in 2008, God began to blend them together. Their relationship began as oil and water, however the love of Jesus soon found the weak cords within each of us and replaced them with His cords of love, trust, and strength. Today those cords of three are binding us to His will, His plans and His purpose.

Peggy's desire to write this book began in the beginning of 2000 in a little apartment in Kentucky. After many attempts, with each one ending up in the trash, the hope was deferred and the possibility became less visible and almost one of those dreams that become hazy as the day wears on. Years passed, and she had no prompting from the Holy Ghost to try again. Then in early November 2015, Patrick and Peggy were on their way home from a shopping trip in the nearby city when Peggy heard the Lord speak the name, "Planned Parenthood," and knew that was the referencing point for their book. Confirmation came the following week, when they saw on the evening news that the building housing the organization, known as Planned Parenthood, in Colorado Springs, Colorado, was the site of a horrific shooting.

Peggy and Patrick believe nothing is by accident and that all things work together for the good to those who love the Lord and who are called according to His purpose. Please do not misquote me; I did not say the shooting was a good thing. However, for me it was a Word from the Lord--to the Messenger of Wisdom--to light the fire and sound the alarm. This is an alarm call, if you will. Wake up, it is time for you to decide, acknowledge, and take responsibility for the choices you have made.

Between Peggy and Patrick, they have five living children, ten grandchildren, four foster grandchildren , and many great-grandchildren.

Ministry in the Word is their passion. Peggy loves to teach, her treasure chest of wisdom, understanding and knowledge has only been tapped. She encourages others to search the Scriptures for in them you will find the answer to all your questions.

Unless stated otherwise, all scripture references come from the Kings James Foundation Study Bible translation of the Bible, copyright 2015 (year), Thomas Nelson (publishers).

Dedication

Predestined Journey is dedicated to TRUTH and to all those who choose to ask, seek, and find the best thing.

To the overcomers who refused to settle for what the world might refer to as "delicacies of the counterfeit." Daniel, Shadrach, Meshach, and Abednego, after being taken into bondage, were placed in the king's court, and refused to compromise their integrity for the sake of pagan gods.

The servants of the king set before them all the royal delicacies: meats, drinks and sweets, the very best their world had to offer. However, they were taught by wise men of the Torah what to put into their bodies to give them life and longevity, and what to abstain from, that would make them weak and mindless. Therefore, they refused all the counterfeit treats and requested the simple, plain, healthy foods and drinks of the time. In the end, they were found to be genuine, real, transparent, with no color added to their loyalty or sincerity, being true and absolute in nature and character. Even though they were under bondage to those who changed their Hebrew names to pagan names, they knew who their true parents were, and their covering never changed.

Truth is only found as we hunger and thirst for it. Truth is only received when we understand where Truth comes from and from whom Truth comes.

Let us take a short side trip to *Webster's College Dictionary* and look up the word **"TRUTH."** "The true or actual state of a matter; conformity with fact or reality; verified or indisputable fact, proposition, principle, or the like." Truth is transparent, no color added; "the state or character of being true; actual existence; and ideal or fundamental reality apart from and transcending perceived experience." You might go as far as to say with total conviction that it is Absolutely Truth.

Acknowledgments

Patrick, my husband and I are indeed thankful for each other. We waited patiently for God's perfect will, His plans for us, in His time and order. For it has been with great love for the Word of God, and thousands of hours spent in study and prayer, that with humble hearts we can offer you a treasure chest filled with many of the hidden treasures from the mysteries of God. We give all the glory to God, who is the originator and revelator of His Word.

We praise our Lord and Savior, Jesus Christ, for the inheritance of a full measure of faith and the gift of grace.

We offer our deepest thanks to you, the reader, and to our Lord in whom we sow our seeds.

Preface: by Peggy Hof-Corrigan

Predestined Journey
By The Messenger of Wisdom

The book Predestined Journey began with the question of, "Where did the term planned parenthood originate from?" I am just a few years ahead of the baby boomers, and in my early years the term "planned parenthood" referred to men and women who were planning on having children and were putting aside savings so that they could pay their medical bills during and after the birth of their child. It was a time of deciding how many children to have according to their ability to provide for them from birth through college.

Planned Parenthood in the nineteenth century has a completely different meaning. Therefore, we have written this book to explain the Truth of planned parenthood and how that relates to every human's journey past, present and future.

Biblically based, Predestined Journey explains planned parenthood, how it began, who began it, and our responsibility in God's creative plans. It is a book containing flavors that you most likely have never tasted anywhere else. The primary ingredient "Absolute Truth" will be the most costly and sought-after ingredient used throughout the entirety of this book.

Today we (the Church family) are in the latter years of our predestined journey. As we look back our concern is for all the overcomers in the body of believers and just as the Apostle Paul stated in 2 Colossians 2:1-23 For I would that ye knew what great conflict I have for you, **and *for* them at Laodicea**, and for as many as have not seen my face in the flesh. The majority of those of you who are reading this book have never seen my face nor will you until we stand in Eternity Future.

Revelations 3 **To the Church in Laodicea**

Revelation 3:14-17 And unto the angel of the church of the Laodiceans write; These things saith the Amen, the faithful and true witness, the beginning of the creation of God; I know thy works, that thou art neither cold nor hot: I would thou wert cold or hot. So then because thou art lukewarm, and neither cold nor hot, I will spue thee out of my mouth. **Because thou sayest, I am rich, and increased with goods, and have need of nothing; and knowest not that thou art wretched, and miserable, and poor, and blind, and naked:**

The Apostle Paul was speaking of the same Church in Laodicea that Jesus spoke of in the book of Revelations. The Apostle Paul could see the problem that Jesus saw and was trying to help all of them and also us the believers. I have heard so many ask of the Lord to give them eyes to see and ears to hear what the Spirit says to the believers. This is a time where the Word of God has been explained but not accurately or biblically. Let us have spiritual eyes and ears.

Mark 11:12-14 And on the morrow, when they were come from Bethany, he was hungry:

(Jesus clearly said that He hungered only for Spiritual food, not natural food. So, what do you think He really hungered for? He knew His time was near and He could read the hearts of His followers. Clearly they did not understand the spiritual aspect of the parables that He had tried so hard to explain to them, He was going to be crucified, hung on a tree and they only saw the miracles He did as just signs and wonders. Even Satan could do signs and wonder. He did when Moses presented Aaron's rod and it turned into a serpent, frogs covered the land and the rivers ran red with blood. They knew He was the Son of God, the Messiah by human reasoning, but not as Abraham knew the LORD, or Elijah and Elisha knew the LORD. They saw Him as only a man, yes, He was a special man but they did not see Him as their Savior and their Lord, the Christ. We will study how important time is in the Kingdom of God.

When Jesus saw the fig tree, he knew it was not the season for the fruit to be ripe. This fig tree, was the only fig tree in the whole place, does that not seem strange to you? It was not disobedient and it was not defiant because it was there; Yes, the fig tree was there, in the right place at the right time, yet the lesson of this tree was not going to be understood, because the disciples spiritual eyes were not open, once again Jesus is using an object in the natural to show us the reality of Truth. This was not because its time was not yet, it was because of His time.)

And seeing a fig tree afar off having leaves, he came, if haply he might find anything thereon: and when he came to it, he found nothing but leaves; for the time of figs was not yet. And Jesus answered and said unto it, **No man eat fruit of thee hereafter forever**. And his disciples heard *it*.

When Jesus came to His brothers and sisters, the Children of Israel, He had hoped that they would receive Him. However, history has proven for over two thousand years they did not recognize who He was even though from before His birth He was showing the world the leaves were on the tree, and He hungered for them to UNDERSTAND why the LORD had sent Him. He called for them to come to Him just as the fig tree called to Jesus and the disciples to come and eat, but without faith there will be no fruit in season or out of season. He hoped they would be hungry for the fig fruit of understanding that He was bring them. But they had not. Just as the fig tree stood alone, Jesus had stood alone. Now, Jesus saw that His time was drawing to an end and they still were not understanding His purpose.

Jesus was on this earth for thirty three years, ONE TIME and one time only would man have the Son of God in the flesh to eat from, Remember He said, "if you do not eat of my body and drink of my blood you cannot be my disciple," and many were repulsed by the thought and went away. Thirty Three years He stood as that fig tree, offering Himself to the world, and no one hungered for Him in His season. He knew once He was resurrected and they received the Holy Ghost they would be hungry, however, they missed their season of opportunity to walk by faith, now they would go through a very difficult time after His death with fear, unbelief, loss and persecution. All that could have been avoided if they would have understood the spiritual aspect of His time and order when He was with them.

And in the morning, as they passed by, they saw the fig tree dried up from the roots.

Some times we have to see it to believe it, Thomas could not believe the Master was really alive until he put his hands in the nail holes. It is better to have faith for the fruit of our healing, and praise Him than to wait to see it with our natural understanding (eye of human reasoning) and praise Him. Missing our appointed time of opportunity costs that fruit (or the roots) to dry up.

Mark 11:21 And Peter calling to remembrance saith unto him, Master, behold, the fig tree which thou cursedst is withered away.

No where can I find Jesus ever cursing anything or anyone. He came to make alive not to kill, or to curse. Could Peter have misunderstood why that tree was dead from the roots? Timing has everything to do with the outcome of God's Word. In the following scriptures Jesus explains why that fig tree would die. Its purpose was not met, I eat figs often so I know the fig tree was not cursed. Mark 11:23 (If I speak to the mountain believing, using the faith of God, it will have to move out of the way. It does not mean the mountain will crumble and disintegrate, it simply UNDERSTANDS and moves.) Our words have great power, we have been given the same power and authority Jesus had then if we believe. Had there been hunger, their faith would have spoken to the fig tree to feed them and it would have been faithful to the Words of Creativity and the figs would have appeared.

More revelation of The Fig Tree will be explained in Chapter 1 and 7, because it has great importance.

Invitation:
Predestined Journey is a book you will never forget. You will love its spice and zest; which will become an acquired taste that will quickly wake up your **spiritual** taste buds for the whole truth of life in the Word of God that has been hidden underneath the disguise of perception.

Word of Wisdom -- Never go through a door uninvited. "You can expect to get bit!"

Please enter through this door that is covered by the blood of Jesus, now open to you as you read through the book called *Predestined Journey* with an open mind.

When you finish reading Predestined Journey you will have to ask yourselves, could these treasured truths be real, and if they are real, are they eternal? Then there is the question, why was I not told the absolute truth, when the truth would have made my journey through life light and easy and given it a sense with purpose. The LORD tells us in Jeremiah 29:11 For I know the thoughts that I think toward you, saith the LORD, thoughts of peace, and not of evil, to give you an expected end.

I have always said, "I can handle whoever, or whatever, is outside in the dark, if I know what it is that is out there." God gives us word pictures in all 66 books of the Bible to help us decipher His Word, and to help keep us on the right path.

The Word of God is Absolute Truth!

2 Timothy 3:16, 17 All scripture is given by inspiration of God, and is profitable for doctrine, for reproof, for correction, for instruction in righteousness: That the man of God may be perfect, thoroughly furnished unto all good works.

Proverbs 30:5, 6 Every Word of God is pure; He is a shield to those who put their trust in Him. Do not add to His Words, lest He reprove you and you be found a liar.

I absolutely love this passage in Proverbs 30:5 "Every Word of God is pure." I have a very dear friend whom I love as a woman of God. She was not only a sister in Christ to me in my early years, she has mentored me since 1971 indirectly, now, she went home to be with her bridegroom several years ago. It is to her I owe my hunger for the full stature of Jesus Christ. Throughout this book, we will refer often to the seed principles she sowed into my life. When I was but a spiritual baby, she shared her knowledge with me and taught me that I needed understanding before I could understand the knowledge given me through the study of the bible through tapes and books and as my pastor when I could get to her congregation. She taught me that the fear of the LORD was the beginning of wisdom and without it I would go nowhere. One of the first scriptures she said I had to memorize was 2 Timothy 3:16 and 17. She taught me to respect the entire Word of God as absolute truth and not to take any of it for granted.

Frequently, I have been told there are passages in the Old and New Testaments that are not profitable for our doctrine today, or that God is only a God who loves us with His kindness and goodness, which is the truth, *however*, that is not absolute truth. He loves us with not only kindness, goodness and mercy; He loves us by disciplining us with His love through reproof and correction. The LORD is a jealous God; He is a wrathful LORD who got angry with His Creation because they were not obedient. 2Kings 22:13 Go ye, enquire of the LORD for me, and for the people, and for all Judah, concerning the words of this book that is found: for great is the wrath of the LORD that is kindled against us, because our fathers have not hearkened unto the words of this book, to do according unto all that which is written concerning us. The LORD loves those who are obedient to His Word and who fear the LORD and reverence God. Exodus 32:11 And Moses besought the LORD his God, and said, LORD, why doth thy wrath wax hot against thy people, which thou hast brought forth out of the land of Egypt with great power, and with a mighty hand? However, He is not happy with those who are disrespectful of His messengers. 2Chronicals 36:16 But they mocked the messengers of God, and despised his words, and misused his prophets, until the wrath of the LORD arose against his people, till *there* was no remedy.

Let us note here that there is no difference between the wrath of the LORD which is found in the Old Testament and the wrath of God which is found only in the New Testament.

He sent His Only Begotten Son Jesus Christ in to the world of the human race so that through His Blood we could be covered and forgiven of all that causes Heavenly Father and God to have a reason and need to become angry and wrathful. He sent us the Holy Ghost to bring us understanding of the Father and the Son and to comfort us in times of trouble and to instruct us in all righteousness. I know many people bypass the words in Proverbs, yet they are words of wisdom. Every Word written in the Bible covers great territories and has no boundaries. His Word is eternal, with no beginning and no ending. In the book of Revelation, we are warned not to add to or take away from His Word.

His Word is spoken, written, felt, transferred, transmitted, and stored. It is seen in the fire, ice, snow, hail, rain, and wind. Mankind has tried to change the Word of God, however, they cannot. They have tried to destroy it, and they cannot. Try as they have, men cannot add to the Word of God, nor can they take away from it and make it last, because He absolutely will not allow it to be changed in any way, therefore it will always stand the test.

From Genesis through Revelation in the Holy Bible, no principle, doctrine, belief, or concept will stand on its own and function properly. Like a table, the Word of God has four legs; if you take one of them away, the table will not be complete and will easily be toppled over. God hung the universe and everything in it to be balanced. Therefore, none of the subjects mentioned in this book will stand when tested with His weights and measures of truth if one side is compromised. The Word of God is laid out in the form of a cross; it has four sides; the earth has four sides, east, north, south, and west. In our world today there is the belief or concept that we can build a church on a doctrine or a movement and it is complete, increased in goods and have need of nothing. Denominations and organizations are like books. There is a ton of them and they are missing legs, none are complete. They cannot be complete if they are not balanced, the Word of God says we know in part, the tomorrows are still hidden from our view until we reach that time and order.

There are many today who do not know, or simply do not want to know. Regardless of the motive, they do not know the difference between a "revelation" (insight or an idea that may be of God, or of man, or of the devil) and the Revelation (revealed Word) of God. The revealed Word of God comes through man inspired by the Holy Ghost. The Word of God has been spoken and prophesied in all sixty-six books of the Bible, referred to as the Scriptures, or the Holy Bible. It takes all sixty-six books, and every word in those books to make you, your church, your denomination or organization balanced.

There are many books written which claim to be divinely given, yet are written from the same childlike perception seen in a children's book on Creation or Noah's Ark. *The LORD God never has and never will do anything or give any directions in His Word that are not complete.* It is the casual or gullible individual with an unknowing lack of desire about the whole Scripture that will settle for the half-truths, the Christian world has offered us that result in confusion and eventual destruction and death of the Absolute Truth.

According to historical research by other biblical scholars, it is recorded that in Jesus' time there were Old Testament scrolls in existence which were held in the tight clutches of the scribes and Pharisees. Yet in the sixty-four times Jesus quotes from the Old Testament, not once does He quote book, address, verse, or passage, Jesus was to fulfill the promises of God to His Creation. So why should the author of this book be any different? Taking a guess, the counterfeit law, and all those who stand in the shoes of Eve at the foot of the Tree of knowledge of right and wrong, say I am different or better yet difficult because I want to see with fresh eyes and enjoy the whole picture of all the trees in the Garden, from the Tree of Life, the Tree of Knowledge and the Tree of Understanding and simply walk out the scriptures and promises that our Lord and Savior fulfilled.

The Messenger of Wisdom would like to leave you to ponder a moment.
The skeptic swore, "There is no God! No God! —I can do anything I want! I'm more animal than human; so-called human intelligence escapes me. I flunked 'wisdom.' I see no evidence of a holy God. Has anyone ever seen anyone climb into Heaven and take charge? Grab the winds and control them? Gather the rains in his bucket? Stake out the ends of the earth? Just tell me His name, tell me the names of His sons. Come on now—tell me!"

The believer replied, "Every promise of God proves true; He protects everyone who runs to Him for help. So don't second-guess Him; He might take you to task and show up your lies." And then he prayed, "God, I'm asking for two things before I die; don't refuse me— Banish lies from my lips and liars from my presence." (Proverbs 30:1-8 MSG)

Word of Wisdom -- the skeptic is one who questions the validity, authenticity, or truth of something purposing to be factual. Wisdom is to take time to question every word posed to you, and avoid the serpents beckoning, they will lead you to unrighteous judgment and blasphemy.

Introduction from the Messenger of Wisdom/the Watchman on the Wall

As the author of this book, my hope and prayer is that you will not only enjoy the information offered you, but you will allow the information to become jewels of revelation knowledge so you can fill your treasure chest with gold, silver and the twelve precious stones of understanding. If you do not have a treasure chest yet, do not worry. Moses did not have the little basket that was his salvation or the Ark of the Covenant until needed. When needed God provided and then God coated them with blood to seal in what was precious to Him and to seal out the enemies of death. No one begins with a full seed barn. We all begin with a small sack and as you place your seeds of revelation in the sack, one day you will find the soil and the need to plant as the seeds multiply you will find you have many sacks, then the master of the seed will build for you a beautiful seed barn to hold all your sacks until it is planting season. Please use your time of studying the scripture to journal all the hidden jewels of revelation that hop out of my seed barn into your seed sack.

Remember, it is the delight of the enemy to steal, kill and destroy the seed before it ever gets to the sack. He does that through a spirit of unbelief. However, if you choose to believe all scriptures are given you for your doctrine, to correct, reprove, and instruct you, then you will fight the good fight of faith. However, if, due to your traditions and customs you are not willing to put all that you think you know on the shelf and walk the walk of the cross, for sure the enemy will steal, kill and destroy all of your seeds, and there will be no time for planting or harvesting.

Word of Wisdom -- do not cast your pearls before the swine, nor discard your uncut jewel into the trash, but rather place all uncut jewels in a jar on the warming rack. One day you will find your uncut jewels will have been washed smooth by your tears of love for the Creator, and they will sparkle with His love revelation for His Absolute Truth.

Truth, fiction, science fiction, or a little of all three will depend upon individual perception?

The Word of the Lord came again to me, saying, "Son of man, say to the prince of the underworld (Lucifer), thus says the Lord GOD: Because your heart is lifted up (in pride) and you have said and thought, I am a God, I sat in the seat of God, in the heart of the seas (abyss, bottomless pit, i.e., Hell), which in my perfect time will hurl itself over you, drowning you and all your horses (carnal strengths and courage) and chariots (abilities), because you are only a weak, feeble, made of earth (ash and dust) man and not God, though you imagine yourself to be almost more than mortal with your mind, as the mind of God; indeed, you compare and imagine yourself wiser than the prophets of old who could foretell My purpose, and plans revealed through visions and dreams. Know this, you who walk in the darkness of deception and think that there is no secret hidden from you. Because you follow after your own wisdom, understanding and trickery, by peddling your counterfeit goods you have gotten your riches and powers and have filled your treasure chests with jewels, gold and silver, your heart is proud and lifted up. Therefore, thus says the Lord GOD: Because you have imagined your mind as the mind of God having My thoughts, which are always for your good, and My plans and purposes, which are only suitable for Myself, I am going to bring death and destruction upon your seed. (taken from Ezekiel 28:1-)

The previous message of wisdom leaves us with many questions, and with every question we should ask and expect an answer.

Question number one is: Who is the prince of the underworld? <u>Lucifer, Satan, the Devil!</u>
Question number two is: Why are the secrets of the LORD hidden from those who choose to walk in darkness? <u>"PRIDE!"</u>
Question number three is: How is God going to bring death and destruction upon the seeds of the ones who walk in darkness? <u>"Destroys them!"</u>
Question number four is: Why is God going to bring death and destruction upon the seeds of those who walk in darkness? <u>"Rebellion!"</u>
Question number five is: Who is the Lord referring to in the very last sentence of the introduction, <u>"Everyone who rejects the love of the Truth of salvation (life) and views him/her selves as Gods."</u>

The man of God suffers destruction or ruin because of the lack of Wisdom, Understanding and Knowledge. Truth is, we know not the secrets of God, because we choose not to believe the truth that is written, or we sweep it under the table, believing it is not for us today. (Ref. Luke 11:9) We are way too busy reading what we believe rather than believing what we read and studying to show ourselves approved unto God and then just accepting by faith the simple fact of what the Word says. Human reasoning completely wipes out the reasoning of God. The Word refers to those who suffer destruction or ruin as foolish ones because of the lack of knowledge. They have the same origin, foundation, and blueprint, as those who had no interest in finding out the hidden facts about Creation. Eternity Past, Eternity Present, and Eternity Future, they choose to bypass the more structured path and have chosen to stay babies; it is so much easier to drink the milk than to have to chew the meat.

It is no wonder that even Bible scholars skip over the hidden truths written in the Word of God. I have always wondered why the cookbook section in the bookstores are so large when so few women amongst our younger generation use cookbooks? They rely on the directions on the boxes and bags of the microwave meals they are preparing for those they say they love. Families seldom sit down to a well-prepared meal, taking the time to bless the food that has been provided and prepared for them, and then while they eat, enjoy the company and fellowship of those at the table with them. Technology such as microwaves, television, telephones, and computers have made communication so fast that relationships are impersonal and a thing of the past. Communication and relationships have been drowned by the seas of indifference. While those that feed the flock of God, use sermons prepared by others or artificial intelligence, so as to offer continuity amongst the organized church. Very little natural or spiritual organic, raw, or home-grown foods are served at the family table or the church table. I believe it is safe to say, "We are a society of tainted eaters."

I am not sure if you or I will ever know all the secrets of God in their fullness until we reside again in the original Eden, the Garden of God.

CHAPTER 1

1. The Family Unit.

2. All God's Secrets are Found Hidden from the Wise and Prudent!
(Lord, how is it that thou wilt manifest Thyself unto us, and not unto the world?)

I would like to begin this first chapter by introducing and talking about the Principles of Time and Order. However, I entitled this chapter as The Family Unit all God's secrets are found hidden from the wise and prudent. As I studied the Word of God, I discovered words and names had been changed depending on the translation, however, when I would look up definitions in the Blue Letter or Strongs concordances I soon found the absence of time, order and disinformation in all the translations except the King James Bible. Meanings are relayed through the word or name given a situation, place, person or thing. If the name is wrong the definition is generally wrong which will lead us down a path of untruths.

Years ago, I found myself in a mental facility because of depression. It was a very useful time for me to seek the Lord as never before, I had very few distractions, no television, no radio, no phone services and no visitors. Even though it was not completely silent, the few sounds and voices were as it was behind a wall. Since I do not believe in accidents or coincidences that must mean I believe that everything has a time and an order and since I believe that the LORD is sovereign and head over all things, he must be in charge of all time and order. At least that is my understanding as life began to unfold during my days in a cool almost to quite room all by myself. Now was when my senses of smell, sight, and hearing began to wake up and I could hear the voice of the Lord clearly, and not only could I hear him because he told me, my spiritual vision or we might call it the imagination woke up as He showed me the principles of how the natural was a type and shadow of the spiritual. He showed me the order a cabbage grew in and when it was time for it to be eaten. In many incidences time and order can be reversed, however within the God head it is never reversed The Father has His role, God/Holy Ghost has his role and the Lord Jesus Christ has his role. He told me how and why they created the family and the order and importance of the family unit; He showed me the role of the father, the mother, and the son. Therefore, I would like to begin this book with the family unit. Remember the natural is a type and shadow of the spiritual. Therefore, we begin by looking at the man whom LORD God created first. We know he was created in their likeness and image of them! This is key to understanding why the family unit is as we find it today, man, woman, and child.

Genesis 1 shows us that the term them begins with God, Elohim--God is in the ordinary sense: but specifically used in the plural here thus, God is seen as the supreme God. The second sense or form Eloah is rare and refers to deity. God is the type and shadow of the mother in the family, in the home she has a place that no one else can step into. She is the organizer in the family and the home. She is the teacher, the comforter, it was through her that life was created and birthed. It is the mother that brings understanding. The mother is the one who provides the nutritional needs for the entire family. The kitchen is her domain. If you want to communicate with the mother you will have to go to where she is most useful, the kitchen. We pray for wisdom and we know that the Christ is all Wisdom, however we need understanding; understanding comes through the Holy Ghost, Once the disciples went to the upper room and were filled with the Holy Ghost, they understood the LORD'S Kingdom plans and purposes.

God is a name that is used a lot. According to E-Sword, we find it occurs 2601 times in the Kings James Version of the Bible. The name LORD or Jehovah is the self-Existent or eternal one and is used 6521 times in the Kings James Version of the Bible. In Genesis 3 we find the two names together, LORD God indicating that both the LORD and God was responsible in the beginning of Creation. The TSK cross reference in the app E-Sword gives us this word of wisdom. All beginnings must begin with God. Always put God first. The first stone in every building, our first thought every morning, the first aim and purpose of all activity. Begin the book of the year with God, and you will end it with the glory of the New Jerusalem.

We are going to talk about who God is and why our Bibles begin with God.

Most Christian faiths believe in the Trinity, Father, Son and Holy Ghost; however, this version of the Trinity leaves the name of God out, or does it??? This is a key question in the family unit.

Genesis 2:4-7 These *are* the generations of the heavens and of the earth when they were created, in the day that the LORD God made the earth and the heavens, And every plant of the field before it was in the earth, and every herb of the field before it grew: for the LORD God had not caused it to rain upon the earth, and *there was* not a man to till the ground. But there went up a mist from the earth, and watered the whole face of the ground. And the LORD God formed man of the dust of the ground, and breathed into his nostrils the breath of life; and man became a living soul.

Here we see that it took both the LORD and God to create the heavens and the earth.

In the spiritual realm the LORD Jehovah is the Father. Jesus referred to the LORD as our Father who at that time was in Heaven. Jesus did not refer to God anywhere in the Lord's prayer. It was up to God to answer their prayers, and meet their needs, however it was up to the Father, the LORD to provide for them according to His Will, He was and is the LORD of Seed Time and Harvest. He has always been and will always be and His Word is the final Word. Matthew 6:14,15 For if ye forgive men their trespasses, your heavenly Father will also forgive you: But if ye forgive not men their trespasses, neither will your Father forgive your trespasses.

It is the Father that is the barer of the seed, in the natural and spiritual. The LORD is the Lord of the Seed Time and Harvest. In the natural, the father is the seed barer, he set the rules, he is the provider, and he is the one who is the judge, it is up to him to meet out rewards and punishments. But yet there was God the creator, the beginning of the creation of God, the one who organized Genesis from the beginning. The LORD did not do it all by Himself. He had a helpmate. Therefore, which all of creation every male was given a female, his counterpart, his help meet. One who believed just like he believed, and could carry his seed to its completion, birth it and then lead it and guide it according to its bent to maturity. LORD God are the original parents in our predestined journey and are the ones who gets the credit for planned parenthood.

Man must operate out of his faith and his total dependence on his LORD and God. Personally, I have to hide in my cave from time to time, so that I can spend time with God, in complete separation from the world and all the noise, clutter and clammer asking Him to change me and give me an enlarged heart of gratitude for the natural world I live in, my husband, my children, my family, my work, my friends, my home and most of all, for my LORD, God and His faithfulness in all things. It is my greatest desire that everything I do, everything I say, everywhere I go and everything I hope for will bring honor and glory to God. However, the reality is I am a human being who has every evil demon trying to sneak into my back door.

All God's Secrets are Found Hidden from the Wise and Prudent!
(Lord, how is it that thou wilt manifest Thyself unto us, and not unto the world?)

I shared my book writing adventure with an acquaintance a few years ago, and he seemed surprised that I would be able to write a book and have a goal of getting it published. He said, "You have to know what you are talking about before you can put it into print!" This is so very true. So, does that mean, if I am very smart, computer savvy, and think I know it all, that I have no demons (such as anger, rebellion, fear, rejection, unbelief), and in my perception know what I am talking about and how to take what I am talking about from thought to pen and paper, then and only then I will be qualified to write and publish a book? Or perhaps it might be of value to write from the viewpoint of one who is searching the only mind that knows the beginning from the end of every thought, from the truths that He has hidden within my seed sack, then to write what He speaks as seed word that has grown up into a twig, a leaf and then a fruit that has reproduced seed after its kind to be shared with others that have a seed sack of like kind. Note here I said, "a seed sack of like kind," because if your seed sack is not like mine, you will most likely reject the seeds I am sowing. You see one of God's first commands in Genesis was that His Creation reproduce after its own kind.

Should we humbly ask for knowledge, and understanding from the mind of the LORD God for His plans and purposes for us in every circumstance and situation known to man? For it is written to all the overcomers of the enemies of the flesh, the pride of life, lust of the flesh, jealousy, envy, strife, greed, etc., which so easily beset us, to stand fast and allow Him to make us strong, and He will gift us the desires of our heart. For it is God who prepares us for the jobs set before us, be it writing a book or standing in the pulpit, being a mother, father, or a truck driver.

▶ **Bondage to a lie producing unbelief!**
Recently I read a story about a young man, whom one of the disciples of Christ recalled. Back in the day, while being taught the truth about the deception of what freedom really meant, a young man replied to his teacher, "We are Abraham's seed and were never in bondage to anyone. Why do you say, 'you will be made free'?" (See John 8:30-37)

Either this young man had never heard, or he simply chose not to listen to the stories told by his ancestors of their many battles with the enemies, of their homeland and the encounters with slavery. Or he simply chose to forget the truth and only remembered his perception of the past. Either way, the truth is that he was in bondage to a lie, which produced unbelief.

It might be difficult for us to think of ourselves as being in bondage to anyone, however, can you imagine being in bondage to a doctrine that is not completely truth? It may have some truth in it, yet it is not completely the truth. Or the lie might be a family tradition that has been handed down from generation to generation that is absolutely pagan. Its foundation is based on a belief learned from men or woman like the young man in the previous paragraph, yet because we do not know the truth of its origin, we keep it going. Truth is not always positive; it can be negative! Truth is not always happy; it can be sad! Truth is not always good; it can be bad! Truth is never based on our perception alone of what we saw, heard, smelled, tasted, or felt, until it is stood up alongside the Word of God to be measured by the origin of all matter.

In a court of law, when the prosecutor questions the witnesses, there is always what is called, "the burden of proof." More than one witness establishes proof. The Word of God says, "From the mouth of two or more witnesses." Truth is found during a process of discovery. Some believed the things that were spoken, and some believed not. **Freedom** is a wonderful gift and must be earned by those who, for whatever reason, find themselves in some form of bondage. No person or thing can own you unless you allow him, her, or it to claim ownership rights.

Unbelief is the twin to pride. One cannot be in pride unless they are in unbelief of the truth and are in a state of delusional grandeur. If the young man who knew his identity was of Abraham's seed, had listened to the truth taught in the Torah of God about Abraham and his seed, he would have understood the lesson being taught to him by the teacher. He would have understood about bondage and would have answered the teacher in truth instead of a lie. The young man would have never dared question the teacher with an arrogant (proud) attitude, had his seed not been tarnished by those whom he was following.

One of the Ten Commandments is to honor your father and your mother that your life might be fruitful and long on this earth. Deuteronomy 11:1 Therefore thou shalt love the LORD thy God, and keep his charge, and his statutes, and his judgments, and his commandments, always.

Word of Wisdom -- Do not be deceived: Evil company corrupts good habits.

God's plan for people was to allow them to be born as babies in the natural and grow into the full stature of a man or woman slowly, and in the proper time and order, so that when they were old, they could look back and say it was all good. God did this for the man named Jesus the Messiah and Teacher. We will share many hidden secrets about the origin of man and about the origin of many of those the LORD God created in Eternity Past.

▶ Job, the man most judged and misunderstood!

The man named Job found that even he was not beyond the testing of his LORD at the hand of Satan.

Pride leads us to believe our thoughts are more credible than a God we cannot touch or see. Pride is the original seed from which all sin sprang! The seed, regardless of its size, is the origin or the very beginning, a tangible object that brought forth all of God's creations.

Job lost everything he valued, including his status in his country, yet when he accepted his imperfections, and as I might say, "His nothingness," and entered into a place of humility, repentance, and praise before the LORD, he found complete restoration.

Job discovered that he did not have a healthy relationship with his God, and through that revelation he soon was able to see how his relationship with his family and the world around him was also just an illusion. What he believed to be true was not true at all; it was just his perception of what he believed to be true.

Remember now that in the very beginning of our book, I told you there would be many of God's secrets revealed as we journeyed through this book. Those of you who can accept the truth, acknowledge the truth, and live the truth; the truth will set you free. The journey will not only bring light and life to you spiritually, it will also bring you naturally to a place that Job found himself at the end of his very best day.

Job thought that he was doing the will of God, he loved his family and was trying to protect them and keep them from the consequences of evil. There were many problems with Job's life style, however, the first one was Job did not know the LORD of the harvest. What you sow you will reap. Seed time and harvest was one of the first principal lessons that Jesus taught the disciples. The Word of God tells us that Job was perfect and upright and one that feared God and eschewed evil. He feared God however he did not fear the LORD. Now Satan could not come before God so he came in the back door to get to Job. Job 1:6-9 Now there was a day when the sons of God came to present themselves before the LORD, and Satan came also among them. And the LORD said unto Satan, Whence comest thou? Then Satan answered the LORD, and said, From going to and fro in the earth, and from walking up and down in it. And the LORD said unto Satan, Hast thou considered my servant Job, that *there* is none like him in the earth, a perfect and an upright man, one that feareth God, and escheweth evil? Then Satan answered the LORD, and said, Doth Job fear God for nought? Hast not thou made an hedge about him, and about his house, and about all that he hath on every side? thou hast blessed the work of his hands, and his substance is increased in the land.

The LORD of the Harvest took down the hedge that was about Job's house and the house of his family. All died except Job and his wife naturally. He lost his children whom he worshiped and scarified for. He lost his reputation, lively hood, servants, animals and lands. His wife came to him with hatred in her heart and told Job to curse God and die. Job died in ways most of us cannot even imagine and yet he did not die spiritually. Once he died to himself, he was able to hear what the prophet was telling him, once his eyes were opened, he was able to find the truth.

Can we find this story in our natural lives? We are told in 2 Timothy that all scripture is given by the inspired word of God and is profitable for our doctrine, reproof, correction and instruction. Therefore, we need to see why Job's story is so very important to the growth and development of not only our natural relationship with the Father LORD and the mother God. OH, don't get bent out of your religious shape. You have to see that we were all created in their likeness and image. Therefore, since the natural family has a father, mother, and child. That is the order of the family unit.

▶ **A man of his word is highly valued!**

Job began his journey of life before there was the laws of Moses, therefore he was not held to the same level of accountability that Abraham, Isaac or Jacob was. And then we come to the backside of the cross; that is where we find the Apostles and of course you and I. It is written, "To whom much is given, much is required." (Ref. Luke 12:48)

We find a man named King Solomon, who began his life as the son of King David. When Solomon grew into manhood, he was chosen to succeed his father and was crowned the king of a great nation. Solomon was very young, and even though he had great wealth in the natural and was highly valued, he lacked wisdom to rule the nation. Therefore, when the LORD God asked him, "What is the one thing you most desire?" Solomon said, "Wisdom." So, wisdom it was, and Solomon began his kingship with a full measure of wisdom. He was the wisest man who ever lived. He wrote Proverbs chapters 1-29. The book of Proverbs is thought to be the book of principles, or we might say the principles of the book of truths. Yet as Solomon grew physically in stature, his pride grew right alongside his natural ability to use wisdom in making his kingly decisions. Eventually, pride overtook wisdom, and in the end, Solomon wrote the book called Ecclesiastes, declaring that all was vanity and vexation to the body, soul, and spirit.

Solomon found his popularity to be a detriment, and in the latter years of his life, he discovered the value of solitude. He discovered little to be better than more, and quiet to be better than racket and great noise. We cannot think proper thoughts or say the proper words when our minds are filled with the clutter of man's reasoning.

Solomon's experience was much like Job's; they both received their natural reward of wealth and popularity before they realized the principle of humility and repentance, a lesson they both received at the ends of their lives.

Job began with much; however, due to the lack of godly wisdom, understanding and the fear of the LORD, he lost all at the beginning of his story. Therefore, in the end of Job's trial, he found favor with the LORD and was rewarded twice for everything he lost.

Our principle here is learning what it takes to recognize the fear of the LORD. Job had it in the beginning of his ways, however, somewhere along the way he found himself in the same position of many of us, putting our family, friends, business, ministry before God, taking no account of the facts that there is the LORD and taking that seat as their savior and God. God knew what He had for Job, for He sees the beginning and the end therefore, Job was tested and tried, and in the end he finished well.

It is the plan of Satan to mature the seeds of pride and unbelief (these are the seeds God must destroy) that were sown in the hearts and the souls of men before they were formed in the womb of the woman, so that as the man grows into natural maturity, pride will grow in equal measure. Pride and unbelief were the roots of Job's fall; pride and unbelief were the root cause of Lucifer's fall. <u>Then we come to the Watchman on the Wall, who for centuries has warned all of mankind through the Word of God that pride and unbelief will result in the fall of everything that man calls "his own."</u>

In this day and time, most people would respond to Job by saying, "Oh, don't be so hard on yourself. I would have done the same things you did. After all, look at what you have lost." However, because Solomon was given much, and because of the fame and fortune of his father David, we might equate it to grace. In the eyes of God, we are all viewed as individuals, and will stand before God not based on the merits of our father, but based on our own words and deeds. Maybe the view of our society today would equate Solomon, and not hold him accountable for his reckless behavior with women and wealth, based on affluenza, as He did not know the consequences of sowing and reaping. Therefore, he would not be accountable for his idolatry, yet this is not God view. No more than giving grace to Adam and Eve for their attitude of rebellion and disobedience. In the New Testament we find two people in the book of Acts, Ananias and Sapphira who through acts of pride, selfishness, and greed lied to God, and died at the feet of Peter. In all the lives of the people mentioned above there was the absence of the fear of the LORD.

One might ask, what kind of God would do this to a man who (Ref. Job 1:1) was blameless and upright and one who (reverently) feared God, and abstained from and shunned evil (because it was wrong)? The conclusion that one should come to is; a God that is a righteous judge. In the books of Haggai and Zechariah, we find that the beginning of a thing is much easier than the end of that thing. Yet we are often told that the end of a thing is better than the beginning. Moral and physical growth and development has what the medical profession calls "growing pains." Who better than the Creator to see what is needed for our growth, for He is one who will always balance pleasure and pain! What a blessing it was for Job who in the end was able to offer gratitude and praise to the LORD, to repent of his pride and self-righteousness, and to forgive himself and those who offended and judged him un-righteously because he saw with the eye of revelatory understanding. Job had only used one of his five senses, his hearing in the natural (I had heard of You only by the hearing of the ear). (Ref. Job 42:5) Have you ever heard someone say as they listened to you tell them a story, "I see that!" How could they see anything? All that they had were the words of a story. Here is a jewel for our treasure chest—word pictures.

"We are told to shun evil, because it was wrong. (Proverbs 3:7) Be not wise in thine own eyes: fear the LORD, and depart from evil. (Ref. Proverbs 8:13) The fear of the LORD is to hate evil: pride, and arrogance, and the evil way, and the forward mouth, do I hate." Evil is not only defined as bad it is described as grief or grievous, distress, misery, trouble, sorrow, affliction, adversity, calamity, and displeasure. From H7489; Hebrew-- rah, raw-aw' Strong's Exhaustive Concordance. I will be referring to evil frequently and will list it as misery, woe, affliction, and pain. These word descriptions concur with the definitions from the Hebrew word rah, raw-aw'.

We can go to church from our birth unto death, and live under the Word of God, but until God opens our spiritual eye and ear, and allows all of Him to be seen with transparency and heard with clarity in our spiritual being, we will not have that personal relationship with our Lord of Lords and our King of Kings. We can accept Christ as our Savior, know all about what He did, who He is, and not allow Him to possess all of us. In opening our spiritual eye and ear of understanding, we will find the answer to knowing God through His Only Begotten Son, Jesus Christ. By not knowing who we are in Christ, or who Christ is in us, we miss the complete cycle of God's reason for the earthly eternal present journey experience of man.

For many years, I professed to be a Christian. I went to church. I tried to do all the right stuff -- you know, dress right, drink right, and eat right; all of those outward cleansings of the cup rituals which prove to the rest of the Christian world that I am "sanctified." Then the tests began and I discovered I was without revelation wisdom, knowledge, and understanding. Oh, I had head knowledge, but I lacked heart knowledge, and the only understanding I had come out of my carnal sense of human reasoning. It was spoken by Moses saying, the children of Israel were impressed with what they saw and heard, but their hearts were unchanged. I was a clean cup of outward pride, and an inward cup of self-righteous judgment. That was why I had so many questions, for if I had understood this, I could have used the very same methods of acquiring wisdom given to King Solomon. I could have simply asked my Heavenly Father for it, and then waited patiently for Him to give me the answers I so needed. However, like Job, my learning came through many hard knocks, as did my knowing that I was full of self-righteous pride, selfishness and self-centeredness and was in for many hours on my knees. That is why I can write this book based on truth, and not my perception of biblical facts that I perceived to be truth. Most likely you are in the same shoes as Job and I were in, and I know it is your greatest desire to end well.

My hope is that you are beginning to have questions about your life, and what is going on in the world today. That is why you are reading this book, you are searching for answers to questions you either just cannot find, or you do not have the time and experience to dig out of the pages of Scriptures holding the answers. I believe that every problem has a solution, and that solution can be found in that little black book Christianity calls, the Holy Bible.

Job could say the things he said about God being good and never being the problem. However, not until he got to the end of himself, where he could see with his spiritual eye of understanding, could he know in his heart the words he spoke were true and everlasting. It is written, this comes when we have been tested and tried (like gold), and can come through as Job did, as an overcomer. The inward manifestation of wealth always comes before we see the outward rewards revealed. As a man thinks in his heart, so is he, so I am told.

First comes the thought, and then comes the seed (from the father). That seed is then planted in the ground of your heart (the mother). Remember, even though the thought came first, that thought had an origin. So where did the thought come from? For Adam female (Eve), the thought came from unbelief. However, she did not believe the words she had been told by Adam male, or maybe the thought came by suggestion, also known as coercion. After all, the serpent put out a suggestion, and after thinking about the possibility that her Creator might be withholding the best from her, or maybe she was just bored with the trees, fruits, and leaves she was eating, she decided to exercise her free will and try something new. Regardless, the thought came from somewhere and it fell into soil that allowed it to grow into an action. It wasn't that the fruit on the Tree of Knowledge of Good and Evil was bad. The evil was that Eve bore witness to the testimony of her heart. She did not respect God's time and order.

Let us take a short side trip to **Webster's College Dictionary** and look up the word **"TRUTH."** "The true or actual state of a matter; conformity with fact or reality; verified or indisputable fact, proposition, principle, or the like." Truth is transparent, no color added; "the state or character of being true; actual existence; and ideal or fundamental reality apart from and transcending perceived experience." You might go as far as to say with total conviction that it is Absolutely Truth.

Word of Wisdom--Without the fear of the LORD, familiarity can lead to a faults sense of identity.

Know this: regardless of where the thought originated, we are the receiver or rejecter, so the responsibility or the outcome cannot be scapegoated off on anyone or anything else. We must also understand there are many types of ground. For it is written that there is rocky ground, shallow ground, and fertile ground. (Ref. Matthew 13:3-9) Once that seed is planted, it will be watered by either the revealed truth of God's Word or a lie from the testimony of your heart. The seed will survive the environments based on the ground it is sown into, and the balance of the water it is fed. Therefore, it will live or it will die. Ultimately the one who receives is the one who bears full accountability; however, it is written, *woe to the offender*. (Ref. Matthew 18:6-8) it would be better if a mill stone was hung around your neck, and you were cast into the abyss, than to offend one of His little ones. Great reminder to the man of the house as it was for Adam-male. If the seed lives, it will in its time produce fruit. It is written that not all fruit is good, and if it is good fruit, does it remain good? Some fruit has worms, is rotten, and is spoiled due to the enemies of the fruit. That is what happened in the life of King Solomon. There are trees that produce fruit in the time and order purposed for them, and then there are trees that refuse to do so. Those trees will be cut down and burned, for they are as those in Eternity Past, who fell into rebellion, and defied the Creator's perfect will, and plan. Their seed died and would be no more.

▶ God has no secrets from a humble, righteous man!

It is no wonder that the secrets of the LORD are hidden from the wise and the prudent. I am amazed at how few pastors and teachers are willing or able to actually teach the truth given us for our example, doctrine, correction, and instruction in righteousness laid out in God's Word. They choose rather to go to the Tree of the Knowledge of Good and Evil, which is a clear indication that they have no understanding of the fear of the LORD. In my humble understanding, the Bible clearly shows us over and over that pride is the first indication that the secrets of God have been hidden from the eyes of one who is lacking wisdom, understanding and knowledge. Therefore, we must look once again to the source. This means returning to the Tree of Life, (Olive Tree---Wisdom, Jesus Christ, and the Tree of Understanding, (Fig Tree—Holy Ghost) when what we are doing is not working, or we can clearly see our tree is not maturing in a manner pleasing to the origin and type we are created after The Tree of Knowledge, (Cedar Tree---The LORD/Father. For it is written that all creation is to reproduce after its own kind. Pride and humility do not go hand in hand with one another.

Here it might be wisdom to explain the Tree of Understanding. In the Book of Genesis God gave Adam-male and female trees that were good to eat. Now we have a clear picture of the Tree of Wisdom, the Christ who brought Olive oil light to the world and the Tree of Knowledge, the LORD who is all knowing however, let us remember God hid the fruit of the Tree of Understanding behind its leaves. When Adam sinned, he went directly to the fig tree and stole a leaf, not to eat but to hide behind. What was hidden behind that leaf was the fruit of Understanding, (lead me not into temptation, but deliver me from evil) the figs and who leads and guides us into all Truth, the Holy Ghost, had Adam-male and female been obedient to tend the Garden and to eat of **all** the fruit they would not have been tempted by the serpent. Now there is a lot that needs to be explained about the fig tree but this is not the place, time or order. I would suggest that you put this little seed in you seed sack and let God reveal it to you in His time and order.

The question is: When thoughts of pride and rebellion against God's perfect will for our lives come into our minds, why do we accept them and allow them to occupy that space in our minds? Why don't we abort that thought right there and then, instead of entertaining the words and voices of evil? The answer is: "We are babies. Our eyes, ears, noses, mouths, and hands are not spiritually mature." Jesus grew in stature for thirty years in all areas of His natural and spiritual life before He faced a head-on attack against His identity. His answer aborted the (virus) demonic voices by the words of His mouth: "Get behind me, Satan." Knowing that NO WEAPON formed against you can prosper is powerful however, the statement that no weapon formed against me will not prosper has been taken out of context by most of the Christian world, this is a single thread that stands alone, it has no beginning and no ending, it's one doctrine that can give the man or woman in trouble false hope. This is just one of the many scriptures that we as humans' mis-understand. You see, we think that it means what it says in doctrine, however that is not a principle of the Word. No weapon formed against me will not prosper when the righteousness of God within me is the one that the weapons are formed against. In Truth it is not about me at all. Without the Righteousness of Christ with-in me I lie desolate. (Ref. Isaiah 54:1-17)

We have heard the exiles summoned to leave Babylon, and have beheld the Savior becoming the sin-bearer. Here our attention is recalled to the still desolate condition of Jerusalem. (Ref. Nehemiah 1, 2, and 3.) Jehovah says, Sing, but Israel replies that she cannot sing so long as she lies desolate. In reply God declares His inalienable love: He is their husband still and has sworn that the waters of death and destruction shall never be able to separate them from Himself. The kindness of His mercy is everlasting, and His covenant of peace shall outlast the mountains and hills.
In the closing paragraph, we behold the chosen city emerging from her heap of ruins. Watched by the eye of the great Architect, wrought by unseen hands, tested by the line and plummet of righteousness, she arises to fulfill her mission to the world. To inspired hearts it seems as though her common stones are jewels. Her children are taught of the Lord. Every accusing voice is hushed. All weapons of destruction are impotent. The New Jerusalem seems to have come down from heaven. (F.B. Meyer)

Our identity in Christ enables us to understand how our spiritual makeup, body, soul, and spirit will empower us to overcome the lies and attack of the enemy, giving us the ability to get up quickly and with confidence, knowing that our God is a God of life, light and love for us.

You recognize the temptations that are placed in front of you that give you the opportunity to choose the tree of LIFE or DEATH. You are empowered to deal with the enemy as Jesus did during His time of testing. It places us in the position of wisdom to recognize the tactics of the enemy, and it gives us the MIGHT and POWER to stand, to acknowledge, take responsibility, and confess our sins without regret, shame or condemnation of our failures past and present.

Satan attacked the very identity of the Lord Jesus Christ in the wilderness. Satan's plan was to come unto the man Jesus and attack the divine Christ's origin and identity. He failed only because Jesus did not have to lower Himself to the level of man and become defensive. He did not have any interest in rebelling against the perfect will of His Father. After all, He knew Satan in Eternity Past and He saw what happened to him when he rebelled against the Originator. Therefore, because He knew. His response stopped the enemy in his tracks and he went away to wait another time.

Jesus was of the seed of the Father and the egg of the woman, Mary. By the time Jesus was led into the wilderness, He was mature in body, soul, and spirit. Jesus did not have to fight against self-righteousness, pride, selfishness, or self-centeredness. That had been settled before the foundation of the world. Jesus Christ knew the origin of the sins that were in man and they did not belong to His Father, Jehovah the LORD or His God. Yes, Jesus was tempted by all sin, yet He never allowed the thought to become a seed because He knew who He was. For it is written, "The Father is in me, and I am in The Father." (Ref. John 17:21)

When we know what we are to reproduce, and there is no question who is our Originator, it takes a very heavy load off us. When we do as Jesus did, we will get the results He got!

▶ **God will fill my treasure chest!**

In the book of Proverbs, we are told the course of our life is determined by our choices. Had I been spiritually mature enough to understand the difference between the fear of the LORD and fearing God I would not have given place to pondering wickedness throughout my life. I would have cherished a mindset of obedience. The key thought "abort" would have been the key antidote to the virus of rebellion that invaded my body, soul, and spirit before it entered. Had I used the Spirit of Christ that replaced my old dead spirit with my new spirit, and allowed it to be the Lord of my soul (mind, will, and emotions), then my body would have had absolutely no problem in rejecting all thoughts of wickedness! I also would have used my mouth (sense of reasoning) to speak a direct order to that virus of rebellion and anger that was attempting to enter into my body or vulnerable soul, commanding it to get out. I had a free will here, folks, as do you, and we can choose to allow the enemy in or abort it before it has a chance to get in. There is only one way abortion is legal, and that is before it becomes a fertilized seed. Once the seed is fertilized, it has life!

Let us revisit the last few lines in our introduction: "Know this, you who walk in the darkness of deception and think there is no secret hidden from you. Because you follow after your own wisdom, understanding and trickery, by peddling your counterfeit goods. You have gotten your riches and powers and have filled your treasure chests with jewels, gold and silver and your heart is proud and lifted up. Therefore, thus says the Lord God: Because you have imagined your mind as the mind of God, having My thoughts, which are always for your good, and My plans and purposes, which are only suitable for Myself, I am going to bring death and destruction upon your seed." Is your treasure chest full of seeds of Truth or fiction?

My treasure chest is filled with the jewels of Truth, not the darkness of deception of fiction. Many of us have allowed our treasure chests to be filled with carnal wisdom, knowledge, and the understanding of man, and worse yet, believed them to be genuine jewels. Working at a gift shop was a joy and so enlightening. We sold rocks of every color, shape, and size, which were our best sellers. Our second-best sellers were plastic diamond-cut-colored jewels in varied sizes and shape that adults and children loved.

Frequently, a child would pick one of them up and light up as she or he would ask, "Is this real?" "Yes," I would explain, "it is real. However, 'real what?' is the question."

Now is the time to take a hard, healthy look at spiritual truth. On the other hand, you can quit now and discard this book as pure fiction, yes, you can. You have a free will and you can choose to grow into the full mature stature of the Lord Jesus Christ, body, soul, and spirit or you can abort the fertilized seeds prematurely. After all, the organization, "Planned Parenthood," is noted for their belief in word and deed in principle, a fertilized seed is not alive until it comes through the soil. I do not believe this way. The fertilized seed has life in it from the moment of fertilization.

2. Pride is the root cause!

Looking back, I believe we might have uncovered the answer to the fourth question. Yep, you guessed it. The answer is pride. Pride is the reason why people are misled and misunderstand, speaking plainly, absolutely missing the mark of His high calling. The counterfeit here is in thinking that pride is a good thing. How could you have pride, and gratitude, and be well pleased at the same time? Pride has its roots in you being the god, -- yes, it does. Now, do not get all puffed up and think I am the one missing the mark here. Oh yes, pride is devilish, regardless of the form or package it comes wrapped in. I know you look at that baby girl, whirling and twirling, and you are just so pr -- Oops, almost thought it and said it. You might be happy, full of joy and thankful that God blessed you with such a beautiful little girl.

Right, now let us put it in the terms that are so very pleasing to God. We are so thankful for our baby girl and blessed by the ability given her by a loving Father to whirl and twirl. Isn't that a relief? You are no longer a little god and she is no longer an idol. We are getting this down, yeah. It will be so much easier to be the father, mother, sister, or brother, God meant for you to be when you are in your proper seat.

Pride is an accuser, as we see with the young man named David. David was sent to assist (serve) his brothers as they served in the Israelite army under King Saul. When the brothers saw the young David, they accused him of unrighteous motives.

The pride of your heart has deceived you, you who live in the clefts of the rock, whose dwelling is high places, who say in your heart, "Who will bring me down to the ground?" (Ref. Obadiah 3, Jeramiah 49:16)

The phrase here, "you who live in the clefts of the rock," is a very literal reference to the nation of Edom. When visiting the Holy Land, you may have gone down into the Negev area and visited the city of Petra, referred to as the rose-red city of the dead. This amazing city is approached through a tremendous fissure that runs for a mile or more right through the rock, a narrow path only a few yards wide that brings you at last into an open place where temples have been carved out of the rock -- giant temples with doorways in them some twenty-five to thirty feet high. It was the capital of Edom. The ancient city, whose people felt that because of these natural defenses they were impregnable, lifted up their hearts in pride. As the Lord speaking through the prophet Obadiah says, because of the pride of their hearts, they were deceived. They thought nothing could overthrow them, but God said it would be done. Just a few years after our Lord's Day, the Romans came in, destroyed the cities of Edom, and took this impregnable fortress captive. It has been in ruins ever since. However, the fertilized seeds of rebellion and defiance against God and Israel were sown and are evidenced today in the lives of many of those living in the Middle East.

This kind of self-sufficiency is evident in the man or woman who says, "I don't need God. I can run my own life without God, in my own wisdom, with my own strength, abilities, and talents -- that is enough. That is all I need to make me happy and successful in this life." Moreover, self-sufficiency is seen in the self-righteous Christian who says, "Well, I need God, yes, in times of danger, fear, and pressure, but I am quite able, thank you, to make my own decisions about the man or woman I am going to marry, or the career I am going to follow, or the friends I have, or the car I buy or anything else like that." That is the same spirit of self-sufficiency, isn't it?

The trouble with Esau was pride. Pride is the root of all human evil, and pride is the basic characteristic of what the Bible calls the flesh that lusts and wars against the Spirit of Truth.

The terrible thing about pride is that it's a trap. It tricks us and it trips us up. We don't recognize it until we have let it get us tangled in the web of deception, and then it is too late. We go stumbling along in our pride, arrogance, and vanity, thinking we are doing fine. Everyone else can see we are in trouble, but we go blissfully on, very unaware the limb we are sawing on is the limb we are sitting on, until it falls down and we are suddenly exposed.

In the beginning of Predestined Journey, I opened up a treasured seed sack of TRUTH that God has placed within me. He said, it is time to share my seed with those who have ears to hear and it is up to you the readers to go to God and your faith in who He is, before making a judgment as to the validity of the seeds in my sack. The question here, -- is what I am teaching you fiction, science fiction, truth, or a little of all three? How much pressure would be let off of this pressure cooker of guilt, shame, and the entitlement mentality we find ourselves in if every human-being took responsibility for the situations they find themselves in instead of blaming God, their parents, the government, the schools, or themselves, and just repented for their rebellious ways to a loving, forgiving Father and God who created them to live life according to His will, plan, and purpose for them.

Word of Wisdom -- Praise God for the Resurrected Blood of Jesus, repentance, forgiveness, and restoration. Never take them for granted, they are gold, silver and precious jewels.

3. Repentance, Forgiveness, and Restoration!

"Moreover, the LORD turned the captivity or *exile* (figuratively speaking a *former state* of prosperity) of Job and restored his fortunes when he prayed for his friends. Also, the LORD gave Job twice as much as he had before. (Ref. Job 42:10, 11) Then there came to him all his brothers, sisters, and all who had known him before, and they ate bread with him in his house, and they sympathized with him and comforted him over all the distressing calamities that the LORD had brought upon him. *Every man also gave him a piece of money and every man an earring of gold* -- keep this in mind, for it is a nugget of revelation as to why a man's testimony is so important." What a wonderful ending to an almost tragic story. For the LORD blessed the latter days of Job more than his beginning.

When we watch a movie or read a book, even though it may be a fictional event and does not involve us, we are more likely to allow ourselves to become drawn into the drama, even allowing the actions to play out in our lives. In today's world, the theater has a wide margin of what is real and what is imaginary or fictional. We are desensitized to the understanding that there is a fragment of reality and truth even in the most horrific story ever told. Do you ever set back and asked yourself, "What is in this for me?" Questioning what we hear and see will open up the door to God's throne room. God wants our story to end like Jobs; therefore, understanding that nothing written in the Word of God is fiction will help us divide theoretical truth from the world's perception of truth.

Far too often when we read a story, be it biblically or fictionally based, we are quick to judge the validity of the story and most often those named in the story based on our personal emotions revolving around the situations that make up the story. The story of David and Bathsheba fall into category.

The prophet came to a very rich man (David) and told him this story. There were two men in one city, the one rich, and the other poor. The rich man had many flocks and herds: But the poor man had nothing, save one little ewe lamb, which he had bought and nurtured and it grew up together with him, and with his children; it did eat of his own meat, and drank of his own cup, and lay in his bosom, and was unto him as a daughter. Then, there came a traveler unto the rich man, and he spared to take of his own flock and of his own herd, to dress for the wayfaring man that was come unto him; but took the poor man's lamb, and dressed it for the man that was come to him.

The rich man became very angry and he told the wise old prophet, "As the LORD lives, the man that hath done this thing should surely die: And he shall repay the lamb that he took with four more, because he did this thing, and because he had no pity."

It is easy to see and to judge the wrong of another. Here we see the rich man not only seeing and judging, but also pronouncing the sentence.

The prophet then spoke to this rich man; with the wisdom that only God can give, he told him that just as he had said, it would be done to him. You see, this rich man had stolen another man's wife, impregnated her with his seed, and killed her husband, and then he took the dead man's wife as his own wife. This is a very tragic story in itself. The rich man now had to face the real judge, God, and because God was a merciful God, he meted out to this counterfeit judge exactly as he had said should happen to a man who took what belonged to another, and gave him the sentence. We see this tragic story beginning with lust, deception, and murder has an ending of repentance, forgiveness, and restitution, for the rich man repented. However, his sentence was not stayed. The rich man lost his seed (child) to death, but because he repented -- not to the man whom he stole from, for he was dead, but to God, for it was God whom the rich man sinned against -- God forgave him and allowed him then to legally wed the wife of the man he had killed.

Did you see how we answered question number three, "How is God going to bring death and destruction upon your seed?" Clearly, we see that God allowed death and destruction to be brought upon the seed of the rich man. Here we see the Principle of God's Permissive Will. He permitted the choices and actions of the rich man to fulfill the law of an eye for an eye and a tooth for a tooth. That's right, the rich man brought death and destruction upon his own seed. Question number four went like this: "Why is God going to bring death and destruction upon your seed?" God is faithful to His Word. God told the rich man that He was not going require his life (because he had repented) for the life of the woman's husband; therefore, He would require "seed for seed." However, the seed of the rich man that was growing in the belly of the woman would die. And the curse of murder would never depart from the man's house, because he knew if he desired another wife, all he had to do was ask. God's perfect will is for us to ask. However, instead he became complacent and did not believe God's faithfulness to His Word, and he stole what belonged to another man. If for no other reason, I praise my Savior and Lord for His blood shed on Calvary's cross that covers the curse we bring upon our family and ourselves through our acts of pride. (Ref. 2Samuel 12:1-12)

When we pronounce a man and woman husband and wife, vows are taken, a covenant is made between them and God and are not to be broken. They are legally, morally and physically joined as one in the eyes of God until death do, they part! These vows are to be honored by man, and if they are not kept, it is said by God, "Because you despise Me." A vow is made, not unto man but unto God. (Ref. Ecclesiastes 5:2-5) "Be not rash with thy mouth, and let not thine heart be hasty to utter *anything* before God: for God is in heaven, and thou upon earth: therefore, let thy words be few. For a dream cometh through the multitude of business; and a fool's voice is *known* by multitude of words. When thou vows a vow unto God, defer not to pay it; for *he hath* no pleasure in fools: pay that which thou hast vowed. Better *is it* that thou shouldest not vow, than that thou shouldest vow and not pay."

When we lived in Africa, we were blessed to join men and women together in holy matrimony. There, the man has to pay the parents of the bride a hefty bride price. The couple present themselves at the house of the bride's legal parents or guardians, where the groom is inspected and either accepted or rejected, based on his status, name, and character. This is a custom or tradition, which is, according to them, absolutely biblical "in their perception." In the United States of America, the couple present themselves at the courthouse, which holds the legal ownership of the bride to whom the groom vows his headship. Americans are conditioned to believe the law in America and to obey, for it is their custom and tradition and is the right way, at least "in their perception."

When a child in America is born, unbeknownst to the awestruck parents, they sign over the ownership of their baby to the country and state he or she is born under. Oh, I realize this may take you back for just a moment. However, when you sign that birth certificate and get that social security card, know this, folks, you just registered your child as theirs. Why do you think the state has the right to regulate how you raise your child, what they are taught in school, whom they can worship (pray to), and who they can't? We are considered a country that offers freedom of speech, freedom to worship etc. today, however, that could change as we speak. The Constitution of the United States of America stands in question by the perception of the people in charge. Therefore, it should not surprise you at all, after reading this book, that when your female child reaches the age that the state says is legal; she can go to the courthouse and petition her "parent," the state, for a licensure of transfer, known to us as a "marriage license." The groom has now bought her and is responsible under state law to take care of her.

Moreover, if the groom is not happy with her, he can petition the one who was the source, "the state," for a writ of divorce. I know, ladies, you are not liking this "truth" at all, because the women in America have worked so hard for equal rights and independence. You think when you are not happy with that man who bought you for $35, you have a right to go to the courthouse and request a "writ of divorce," and reverse ownership back to WHOM? Right on, back to the state, of course, and it cost you a hefty fee to get them to take you back. Oh, you get your stuff and your name changed. However, ownership goes back to the state. And this is only the icing on the cake. In the Old and New Testaments, divorce was a big issue among both the believers and the unbelievers.

One question that has been raised frequently in regards to divorce came from a man who loved his wife and family and knew that the Word of God did not give place for a Christian couple to be divorced (at least in his perception). Therefore, because he did not want to violate his vows to God and his wife, he asked this question: Is there provision in the Word of God for two Christians to get a divorce? In the Old Testament, Moses' law dealt with this subject according to custom and tradition, all of which relates to the law of the flesh or the natural law. In the New Testament, Jesus dealt with the same concerns. However, He addressed them based on the spiritual realm and responsibility attached to a union of marriage, where a man and a woman are joined in wed*lock* before God and the witnesses of that union. In my search, I found only one provision for a man and woman who were joined in wed*lock* to legally get a divorce, and that was if one or both were *hard-hearted*, that is (specifically), *destitution of* (spiritual) *perception*: Destitute of spiritual perception, that person or persons was in total unbelief. Note I did not say that they were unbelievers. I said one or both were able to stand before God and the witnesses and enter into an unrighteous judgment based on the unbelief that was in their heart, and declare that the vows they made before God and man were made without honor. They were destitute of spiritual perception.

I am a woman who has been divorced more than once, and yet I could stand in any church and testify before God and man that I was a Christian. Did I love God? Yes, I loved God! What I had either never had or I lost was the fear of LORD. The lack of the fear of the consequences of being rebellious against the LORD and God had produced in me the hardness of heart. How can we stand before God and man, take vows of "til death do us part," and then stand before that same God -- forget the witnesses, because they forgot to hold you and me accountable for the vows we made -- and say we are Christians? It is a puzzle to me. I am so thankful that I found TRUTH and the ability to humble myself before God and man and repent for my double-minded, self-righteous, proud, and evil ways and turn from them.

Now that we have opened the subject of hardness of heart, let us go a bit further with the rearing of children. In God's Word, it tells us who is the source of our baby boy or girl. It tells us to train up our children in the way they are to go, so that when they are old, they will come back to the original source, being our Father God, completely matured, fully taught and trained. Your baby is on loan to you, and it is up to you to relinquish your right as the legal owner back to the Originator for the purpose of moral training, according to His perfect plan and will for your child, not only in Eternity Present but also in Eternity Future.

If we look past our noses, we can see the map is all drawn out for us, and all we have to do is follow it to the letter. However, pride tells us that heeding the map is excessively law-based, and we have rights and can always find fault with the ones who we chose to raise us. After all, the proof is in the pudding. Regardless of our age, we can look back and see the results of the demoralizing development of the generations behind us. It is at this point in our self-reasoning; we will use the counterfeit map of self-righteous pride, and do it the way of the world. Or even worse, we say as we most often do, "You got to raise your children the way you wanted to, and look how they turned out, so do not tell me how to raise mine." Society has shown that the result of raising children by the book of "I want my child to have more than I had," has reduced the level of respect and responsibility for God, the biological parents, and society in general, generation after generation.

Jesus, between the ages of seven to twelve years, reminded his biological mother that He had to be about His Father's business. Joseph was His mother's husband, but he was not Jesus' biological father. There is an order; however, since it is not written out word for word for us in the Word of God, we have to base our understanding off the natural order God has given us for the family unit. Joseph may not have been Jesus' biological father; however, because Mary, Jesus' mother chose him as her husband, (now because of cultural beliefs, it is thought that Mary did not have a choice as to who she would marry, because that choice was the responsibility of her parents, yet where is Mary, Joseph, and God in that kind of thinking? Truth is we all have been given a free will of choice.) and God chose Joseph as the man who would raise His Son to the age of accountability. Joseph carried the mantle of the father of his free will of choice. He was responsible for Jesus' physical and moral discipline, correction, and education until He reached the age of transition from an infant/child to a Son, at which time the priest took over to fulfill the legal law of moral development. Jesus was to be obedient to Joseph, the father God gave to oversee His upbringing. Joseph would be held accountable to God for the plans He had laid out for His Only Begotten Son.

Once a son is at the age of accountability, thought to be around the age of twelve years, the father and the mother must cut the second cord that binds them. Trusting they had been obedient to God for their part, letting the son follow the teachings and examples taught and yet to be taught. Hopefully, the son listened to the Word of God that proceeded out of the mouth of the father and mother, for if not, the Word will become like a hot branding iron on the back end of a calf, where its owner places his mark of ownership, ensuring him that the thief cannot come in and take what does not belong to him.

Sad but true, it takes time and energy to instill God's master plan in our children. Few parents are prepared to cut that second cord that binds at such a young age, however if we as parent have not instilled the fear of the LORD and the commands of Jesus to love the LORD and your neighbors as yourself by the age of twelve it might be too late. Wisdom reminds us not to delegate that blessing to others. However, obedience to the vow we make is a principle, or we might call it a law, making it a duty that will ensure blessings. Moreover, if we fail to be obedient as parents, the reward will not be a blessing. Instead, we will reap what we have sown and bring down a curse upon ourselves and the child entrusted to us to bring up. Man has his plans and ways that are the counterfeit plan of Planned Parenthood. We as humans are so accustomed to the ways of man that when we read the plans of God, they are foreign and hard to accept as fair or rational. Therefore, we bypass them as nonsense, old, and outdated ways. The Father taught us His way of doing and being, they are Kingdom Principles. After all, He is the Originator of parenting.

Contrary to our ancestors' ways, it is not common with our modern-day parents to tell their children <u>no</u>. And if they do tell them <u>no</u>, they really do not mean it, because they know the child will challenge them and they will give in out of guilt. After all, we live in the dispensation of grace; therefore, when they have been told <u>no</u>, <u>no</u> does not mean <u>no</u>. Parents do not tell their child no because they did not like being told <u>no</u>, and they do not want to be told <u>no</u> by those in authority. Yes, it is an authority issue, therefore the pattern of rebellion is established on the top of the hill, and you parents are at the top of that hill, not at the bottom. For you parents who are telling your child <u>no</u> and meaning what you say, praise God.

However, remember grace God's way comes prior to the first <u>no</u>. It is rebellion to go any further than the first no. Moreover, there are consequences for rebellion. I am not saying to send your child out into the street or to the next city, or to stone him or her, however, I am saying you, are in rebellion against the written Word of God, when you do not have rules for your children to follow, and those rules are to be obeyed. Dealing with a rebellious child is much like dealing with a small weed in your flower garden. Correction and instruction tell us that sin was already in the heart before it was placed inside the body being formed in the mother's womb, and the heart was desperately wicked. Who taught a child to get angry, to throw a fit when he or she does not get what they want, or defy you when you tell them not to touch the stove because it is hot, or when they run out into the street the moment their hand breaks free of your clutching grip? Oh, we make excuses for our sweet little child. We say he or she is just tired or hungry. The truth is that the weed of sin within our child might not look bad or ugly when it is small, when it comes through the soil. However, give it a little water and watch it grow into an ugly, poisonous weed with thorns that will in time not only rip your hand open, it will rip your heart out. The proverbs of Solomon. A wise son makes a glad father: but a foolish son is the heaviness of his mother (Ref. Proverbs 10:1)

Word of Wisdom -- pull that noxious weed the moment you see its ugly head. It is not cute or sweet. Regardless of how long it grows, it will never turn into a flower.

God is faithful. He sees there is an opportunity to disciple both the parent and the child through His loving hand of mercy. The Lord is faithful to Himself and He will not go against His Word. Correction comes, as does rebuke and reproof, from many individuals and in many different forms. It is written, spare the rod, and spoil the child. You do not spoil a child by giving them a truckload of gifts at Christmas. You spoil the child when you do not hold them accountable to the Word of God. God holds you parents accountable and responsible to Him when you are rebellious. He will not accept worldly justification from parents. Love comes in many forms, for God so loved the world that He gave us His only Begotten Son. That was a form of sacrificial love. God also gave His only Begotten Son up to the cross, that was another sacrificial love. I personally know about sacrificial love, and it is painful and pleasurable all at the same time.

Because, the next eight chapters contain subject matter, which may not be common doctrine in your churches, and around your dinner table, the author would like you to use the study guide provided in the back of **Predestined Journey**. This will help you in referencing scriptural addresses and explanations that needs more explaining, than has been offered here in the text.

CHAPTER 2

Eternity Past: Eternity Past is a time of existence before Genesis 1. It is a time before this earth was put into order and had no foundation. Before the world of man, animal, and plant life existed, as we know it. Eternity, is described as everlasting, evermore, old, perpetually, world without end. (Ref. Isaiah 57:15)

4. The First Garden of Eden

The LORD possessed me in the beginning of His way, before His works of old. I was set up from everlasting, from the beginning, or ever the earth was. When there were no depths, I was brought forth, when there were no fountains abounding with water. Before the mountains were settled, before the hills was, I brought forth: While as yet He had not made the earth, or the fields, or the highest part of the dust (mankind) of the world (being all His creation). When He prepared the heavens, I was there: when He set a compass upon the face of the depth: When He established the clouds above: when He strengthened the fountains of the deep: When He gave to the sea His decree, that the waters should not pass His commandment: when He appointed (predestined) the foundations of the earth: Then I was by Him, as one brought up with Him: and I was daily His delight, rejoicing always before Him; *Rejoicing in the habitable part of His earth—(not the earth); and my delights were with the sons of men* (souls of man). (Ref. Proverbs 8:22-31)

Predestination is for those who chose God as their Eternal Father against Lucifer in Eternity Past, it was there that God allowed the separation between the **Predestinated** and the **Foreordained**. For those, (the Stones of Fire) who chose to worship God, He put a hedge or a fence of protection around them and He Predestined them to Himself. Those who chose to follow Lucifer are Foreordained, they were given a free will to change their minded at any time in their Eternal Now existence here on earth. This separation was the result of each Stones of Fire choice while still in the womb of God.

Let us take a quick look into the first Garden of Eden where He possessed us. At that time, we were given a choice. We could choose for the LORD or for Lucifer. For those who chose the LORD they were predestined. Predestined means that they were sealed and a fence was put around them. We see this as Satan petitioned Heavenly Father for someone to bring evil upon. Satan told the LORD that he could not bring evil upon Job because He had a fence around him.

The LORD never foreordained anyone to be lost or to be sent to hell. The LORD and our God is not willing that anyone should perish but that all should come to repentance and be saved. (Ref. 2 Peter 3:9) The outcome of our eternal life now and in to Eternity Future is entirely up to each individual.

Let us remember that the Word of God tells us that God loved Jacob and hated Esau. They were brothers in the human womb of their mother but their eternal choices were what made the difference.

God's Sovereign Choice

I say the truth in Christ, I lie not, my conscience also bearing me witness in the Holy Ghost, That I have great heaviness and continual sorrow in my heart. For I could wish that myself were accursed from Christ for my brethren, my kinsmen according to the flesh: Who are Israelites; to whom pertaineth the adoption, and the glory, and the covenants, and the giving of the law, and the service of God, and the promises; Whose are the fathers, and of whom as concerning the flesh Christ came, who is over all, God blessed forever. Amen. Not as though the word of God hath taken none effect. For they are not all Israel, which are of Israel: Neither, because they are the seed of Abraham, are they all children: but, In Isaac shall thy seed be called. That is, They which are the children of the flesh, these are not the children of God: but the children of the promise are counted for the seed. For this is the word of promise, At this time will I come, and Sara shall have a son.

And not only this; but when Rebecca also had conceived by one, even by our father Isaac; (For the children being not yet born, neither having done any good or evil, that the purpose of God according to election might stand, not of works, but of him that calleth;)

(Ref. Romans 9:12, 13, 14) It was said unto her, The elder shall serve the younger. As it is written, Jacob have I loved, but Esau have I hated. What shall we say then? Is there unrighteousness with God? God forbid.

For he saith to Moses, I will have mercy on whom I will have mercy, and I will have compassion on whom I will have compassion. So then it is not of him that willeth, nor of him that runneth, but of God that sheweth mercy. For the scripture saith unto Pharaoh, Even for this same purpose have I raised thee up, that I might shew my power in thee, and that my name might be declared throughout all the earth. Therefore hath he mercy on whom he will have mercy, and whom he will he hardeneth.

Thou wilt say then unto me, Why doth he yet find fault? For who hath resisted his will? Nay but, O man, who art thou that repliest against God? Shall the thing formed say to him that formed it, Why hast thou made me thus? Hath not the potter power over the clay, of the same lump to make one vessel unto honour, and another unto dishonour? What if God, willing to shew his wrath, and to make his power known, endured with much longsuffering the vessels of wrath fitted to destruction: And that he might make known the riches of his glory on the vessels of mercy, which he had afore prepared unto glory, Even us, whom he hath called, not of the Jews only, but also of the Gentiles? As he saith also in Osee, I will call them my people, which were not my people; and her beloved, which was not beloved. And it shall come to pass, that in the place where it was said unto them, Ye are not my people; there shall they be called the children of the living God. (Ref. Romans 9:1-26)

Take time to meditate on these verses:

In Eternity Past we (the Stones of Fire) made their choice. It was there that God put a fence around us so that when we are born into the world we are protected. Now, know this, we are not protected from making wrong or bad choices. OH, we still have a free will to sin and do bad things, but it is like having a safety net under us when we are on that high wire. We still have to receive Jesus Christ as our Savior and Lord and we have to be obedient and live a godly life. The Holy Ghost is vital in our lives, for many reasons, but for our conscience's sake the Holy Ghost is our guide in our decision-making process. The Lord tells us to choose ye this day whom you will serve.

In Eternity Past those who chose to follow Lucifer, God's mercy abides. He gave them a free will so that when they are born as human's and see the difference between the Predestined and the Foreordained, they can repent and reverse their choice. As John Bullock says in his book, "Seeing with Fresh Eyes" We have to not only see God and His mercy we have to look inside of God for it. God is merciful and He is forgiving. The Esau tribe are those who are foreordained, they can become the children of God and choose to love Him and worship Him. They will have to make the right choice without the fence of God.

► **Time for School, Called the Master**
Doth not Wisdom cry? And Understanding put forth her voice?

Our Father in Heaven took the ashes and the dust that was on the outer face of the earth, and as He placed this mixture in His hand, He pondered just a moment because He knew the entire story. He knew that the choices this pile of dust and ashes had made in Eternity Past and the choices it would make in Eternity Present would result in great hardships. He knew that it would be a very long, and painful journey if they did not choose well and eat of all of the fruits and leaves on the tree of life and daily set under the Fig tree for understanding that He had so carefully placed in the middle of God's new Garden called Eden, in the very beginning on His newly ordered world. Right there and then, the Stones of Fire saw the first tear ever fall from our Father's eye. That tear was the salty fluid that landed in the middle of that pile of ash and dust, and out of it, Father, Holy Ghost, and the Son of

God formed a man who was created in their likeness and image. Father then took a seed (Stone of Fire); soul (conscience) assigned to live in that tent or body of dust and ash from out of His Holy Mountain within the Eden, the Garden of God, and placed it inside of this newly formed image that Father had created. Once this living soul was birthed from its biological mother's womb, Father would breathe into the nose of this very small image of the great big Father giving it a spirit (hope). For these two tools would help them in their decision-making process, getting them along on their journey called life. Then as the Father, Son, and Holy Ghost stood back and looked at their creation, they called them male and female. The Father gave His created male the name Adam, which means *ruddy*, that is, a *human being*, mankind, low, man (mean, of low degree), person, *show blood* (in the face), that is, *flush* or turn rosy, be (dyed, made) red (ruddy).

You see Name in Hebrew means nature and character. Often times we do not associate the name of a person or place with its character. We have been conditioned to just accept what we see without question what we are seeing. It is here that you may begin questioning Predestined Journey and the author. You will, of course, demand facts, proof, and my reputation if I cannot give you the exact book, chapter, and line for what I believe is TRUTH. As I said, it is good to question, it is good to require proof. Thomas did, when Jesus announced Himself to be alive after the crucifixion, after all, Thomas had witnessed with his own eyes what he believed to be the end of the man Jesus. How can we believe what we cannot see? The proof Thomas demanded, was provided, not by Mary, Peter, James, and John but by Jesus. In our labs today we are finding that DNA provides proof that cannot be detected any other way. Yet who is responsible for provide us with our DNA and who is responsible for proving DNA? DNA (Deoxyribonucleic Acid is what we mean when we talk about the term -- DNA.) If you want to keep things simple then think of DNA as a code. A code to the genetic makeup of a substance. Now this could get really technical and led us down a rabbit hole, so please forgive me when I tell you my readers, that to get the answers to many of the whys, you may have to go further in your research than I can take you.

▶ **DNA**

Recapping: the LORD God took the ash and the dust from off the highest part of the dust of the earth and from that He created the man, Adam. The Scriptures does not give us the exact spot or location on the earth's surface that this ash and dust was retrieved from, nor does the Word give us the exact location that the ash of Satan landed when he was cast to the earth (Ref. Ezekiel 28:18). However, the Scriptures does tell us that this body profits nothing, (Ref. John 6:63) and will in time go back to the earth it came from (Ref. Genesis 3:19). Then the LORD commanded all life that was created to reproduce after its own seed. Does it seem strange to you, or is this just my perception, that we are created in the likeness and image of the Godhead, Father, Son, and Holy Ghost, which were perfect, yet the flesh profits nothing? The flesh or body came out of the ash or seed which contained our caregiver's DNA…blood carries the DNA and the DNA carries the identity of the substance within the seed. Yep, I think this is one of those hidden secrets, which have been hidden from the wise and prudent… Maybe you are a geneticist, a medical professional or a minister of the gospel and understand all about what I am uncovering that has been hidden as one of those secrets. The truth is never given to just one person, and if it is truth, it will always have the witness of the Holy Ghost and the Spirit of Jesus Christ that dwells within the person God is entrusting His secrets too.

Therefore, you as a professional may be able to explain everything there is to know about our DNA on the natural side of the coin. However, spiritually speaking, the spiritual side of the DNA may be a mystery. I am certain that in the test tubes and diagnostic labs, blood, skin and cellular matter as such do not explain why that little baby you gave birth to acted like the devil shortly after it took its first breath, and that it only got worse by the day, month and year, until the day she or he found Jesus as their Savior. By all accounts please do not misunderstand me I did not say your baby is a devil. I simply said knowing the natural and spiritual side of DNA might explain the bad behaviors that come from a child that has not yet been exposed to fits of anger, stubbornness, rebellion, and even a little jealousy.

Now you might say, "I am really confused or I am one crazy woman." Either way, wisdom says it is wise to sit down, take off your know-it-all dunce hat, and go on this little journey with me. We are created in the image of the

LORD, yet we have the nature and character of Lucifer. Wow, how could that have happened? Well, just maybe since Lucifer was sent from Heaven to earth in a ball of fire and reduced to the ash that covered the earth, it might explain where the ash came from that the LORD used in the creation of man and why we have a double-sided nature and why we have to have a spiritual blood transfusion when we are saved. There are religions that forbid blood transfusions in the natural. Ever wondered why? I do know their explanation does not make sense to me, and this may not make sense to you. However, please do not be cheated out of the truth, if in fact this is the truth.

We are saved by the Crucified Blood of Jesus Christ, and we are redeemed by the Resurrected Blood of the Lamb which is not actual liquid blood but light. Animal blood in the Old Testament could not save the Children of Israel; it could only satisfy the Father's wrath over sin. When Jesus the man died on the cross at Calvary, His Crucified Blood spilled out on the ground. It only takes our faith to believe the Crucified Blood took our sins behind the back of God to the sea of forgetfulness to be changed and that His Resurrected Blood saves and redeems us, washing us white as snow and it only takes our faith to believe that since the ground that was infected by Lucifer's ash (DNA) in the beginning received that blood our Savior freely offered, the earth welcomes being cleansed by His blood because it has been Resurrected Blood bought. Jesus took His Resurrected Blood to Hell and took back the keys to the Kingdom. Lucifer has no power or hold over the earth any longer, nor does he have power over any of God's creation. Soon and very soon Jesus Christ and His Bride will take the Resurrected Blood and cleanse all of Eternity Past, Present and Future that was soiled by iniquity, so that when those who are predestined, called and chosen return to the Father with the only Begotten Son as His Bride, there will be no trace of sin and all will be forgiven, washed white as snow.

This is why Jesus said to Nicodemus that we have to be born again. We have to have a changing of our covering here. That old man (sin nature) has to give up his royal seat, for he is no longer king in the life of the born-again believer. We who are saved by the Resurrected Blood have had a spiritual blood transfusion.

Backtracking just a moment, I would like to share a nugget or jewel with you that absolutely has changed my entire life. I hope this does not throw a curve ball into the victim mentality that we all fall apart over. Now because I know we are all programmed to envision the fictional world of what is so far out there, called "sci-fi," it will not be difficult for most of you to get on board with this metaphor. Be advised that what I am going to share with you is not hyperbole.

Who chose the mother (Mary) of Jesus? If you say the Father, you are absolutely correct. (Ref. Isaiah 7:14) Therefore *the Lord himself* shall give you a sign; Behold, a virgin shall conceive, and bear a son, and shall call His name Immanuel.

In our study guide, I give you the addresses in the New Testament where Jesus declares that He and the Father, (Adonai, Elohim, Jehovah) and God are one, and that if you have seen Him (Jesus) you have seen the Father. Jesus and the Father are one. Jesus Christ the Son, the Father, God and the Holy Ghost are one, the Christian body of believers call this oneness of relationship "The Trinity." This is truth and not exaggeration. Therefore, who chose the mother of Jesus? Right, Jesus chose His own mother. I cannot imagine the Trinity choosing Mary to be the mother of His Only Begotten Son and not giving her a chance to choose to be His mother. After all, God did give us all a free will before we were formed in our mothers' wombs. Now because I know that the Word of God created us equal, male and female, bond and free, black and white, rich and poor, I also know that if you live in Africa, it is because you chose to be born to a woman who lives in Africa. "Where does the Bible say children choose their parents? It sounds like science fiction to say parents have control over their chromosomes, determining which characteristics the baby would inherit from each parent. Where is the biblical foundation for this teaching?" Great questions. I told you that we had to be careful not to go down into a rabbit hole. Yet here we are.

Our first block in the foundation is RESPECT. Jesus chose Mary to be His mother. Now I know Jesus is Jesus the Only Begotten Son of the Father, and you are only one of His created sons or daughters, so is the Word lying when it assures us that God is NO RESPECT OF PERSONS? (Ref. Romans 2:11, Colossians 3:25 NKJV) Respect is a word that denotes a biased judgment, which gives respect to rank, position or circumstances instead of considering the intrinsic conditions, judgment, or favorable treatment when dealing with people, and He expects us to follow His example. Respect, equality, favoritism, partiality, distinction, conditional preference. (Strong's Exhaustive Concordance of the Bible #4382 and Spirit Filled Life Bible NKJV)

Second block in the foundation HONOR. "Howbeit in vain do they worship Me, teaching for doctrines the commandments of men. For laying aside the commandment of God, ye hold the tradition of men, as the washing of pots and cups: and many other such like things ye do. And He said unto them, Full well ye reject the commandment of God, that ye may keep your own tradition. For Moses said, honour thy father and thy mother; and, whoso curseth father or mother, let him die the death: But ye say, if a man shall say to his father or mother, it is Corban, that is to say, a gift, by whatsoever thou mightest be profited by me; he shall be free. And ye suffer him no more to do ought for his father or his mother; Making the Word of God of none effect through your tradition, which ye have delivered: and many such like things do ye." (Ref. Mark 7:7-13) (vs7:9) "The purpose clause indicates that their tradition is more important than God's Commandment to Honoring. They reject what is primary, in order to keep, that which is secondary.") Spirit Filled Life Bible NKJV pg. 1361

God commanded that we honor our father and mother. This command if broken was punishable by death. I believe that we cannot bear the thought that we could be responsible for the outcome of our existence here on this earth. Eve blamed the serpent, Adam blame God for giving him Eve and who was to blame for Cain murdering Abel? -- No one, or only one (and I am speaking to every reader of this book) has to take the responsibility for the messes that evolve in their lives. Cain chose and Abel chose. We are humans with five fingers and one is always pointing toward someone else. How could you think that our Just, Righteous, Good, Faithful, Merciful, Heavenly Father could or should take the blame for all the good and bad situations you incur in your life time. Was it the mothers or fathers' fault or sin that the man was born blind? No, it was neither, so whose fault, was it? God's fault? -- No, it was not God's fault or choosing, and it was not the result of sin or fault of the mother or father. KEY--- The blind man chose it, in order to bring glory to God and fulfill the prophecy spoken that the

Messiah would give sight to the blind. (Ref. John 9:2, 3, Luke 4:18, (Ref. Isaiah 42:5-8)

We will go into this level of choice a little further in the book however, for now, I want to clarify that there are no victims of child abuse, sexual abuse, violence, poverty, etc. regardless of how horrific it may be. I am aware of the injustice of any type of abuse, and will fight against it as long as I have breath. I am not talking about abuse; I am talking about behaving as a victim or claiming to be a victim and blaming someone else, even though another may be the one holding the gun, stick or words that kill, steal or destroy. Too many people have portrayed Cain as a victim, Esau as a victim, Saul as a victim, the children of the Egyptians as victims. Keeping in mind, God is Sovereign; He is head over all things. As we will see, God would be to blame if all the horrific events and circumstances were the fault of God. I am not trying to confuse anyone here, as simple as it is, God is not at fault and He is not to blame for the outcome of our choices. Someone somewhere made a choice that brought about an event or circumstance. If we did not make the choices in Eternity Past as to what was to transpire in our lives now in Eternity Present, then how could God have predestined us to conform to His Son the Lord Jesus Christ whose purpose for coming to this earth was to bring us back to the KINGOM of our Father who art in Heaven? (Ephesians 1 and 2)

For it is written – we know that all things work together for good to them that love God (how could we know if we had not been told), to them who are the called according to His purpose (Ref. Romans 8:28). For whom He did foreknow (yep, He knew us in Eternity Past and better yet, we knew Him), He also did predestinate us to be conformed to the image of His Son, that He might be the firstborn among many brethren. Moreover, whom He did predestinate, them He also called: and whom He called, them He also justified: and whom He justified, them He also glorified (Ref. Romans 8:29, 30). According as He has chosen us in Him before the foundation of the world, that we should be holy and without blame before Him in love: Having predestinated us, unto the adoption of children by Jesus Christ to Himself, according to the good pleasure of His will (Ref. Ephesians 1:4-11). Truth and fact, we are not the Father's first choice -- the Children of Israel were – however, they rejected and crucified His Son, therefore, the Gentiles were and are adopted into the family of God.

Whose fault is it that the prisons are full? Whose fault that the road to hell is wide and many are on it? Whose fault that the road to heaven is narrow and few are on it? God sends no man to hell; man's choices send man to hell.

Speaking personally here, in Eternity Past I was set up (predestined) from everlasting to everlasting by Heavenly Father! This principle is given a broader explanation in Chapter 3. (For those, the Stones of Fire) who chose to worship God, He put a hedge or a fence of protection around them and He Predestined them to Himself.) Now, we are in the dispensation of the Son, or as many refer to it as the dispensation of grace. Here His chosen is having a prophetic encounter with the Son of God: We too are to be sons and daughters of God. The son or *bane* is defined as a *builder* of the family name, in the widest sense (of literal and figurative relationship, including *grandson, subject, nation, quality* or *condition*.) Choosing Jesus Christ as my Lord and Savior was the first wisest choice I have ever made. Choosing is a daily commandment given us by our Heavenly Father. It is not an option it is a commandment. Choose ye this day whom you will serve.

The voice of Wisdom cries, because she understands the entire situation, with great passion from the top of her lung capacity. She begs with every sense of reasoning for those who are subjects to partake of the consequences of the situation in the Garden of God's Eden. Does not Wisdom call? Does not Understanding raise her voice? Wisdom begs "On the heights beside the way, at the crossroads she takes her stand; beside the gates in front of the town, at the entrance of the portals she cries aloud: 'To you, O men, I call, and my cry is to the children of man. O simple ones, learn prudence; O fools, learn sense. Hear, for I will speak noble things, and from my lips will come what is right, for my mouth will utter truth; wickedness is an abomination to my lips. All the words of my mouth are righteous; there is nothing twisted or crooked in them. They are all straight to him who understands, and right to those who find knowledge.'" Only the truth can straighten the twisted and crooked path (mindset). (Ref. Proverbs 8:1-8)

Notice here that Wisdom is begging you. Prudence is your actions, your walk, your way of doing and being. Understanding must come with her raised voice so that you can find and receive, Knowledge.

▶ LUCIFER'S FIRST MISTAKE

You became proud because of your beauty. You wasted your wisdom because of your greatness. (Ref. Ezekiel 28:11-19) Gods Word

When I was but a seed I lived on and in the holy mountain of my Father, with my brothers, and sisters. My Father and God provided us with everything we needed out of Eden, which was His garden, for He was of great wealth and power.

▶ Shepherd of the flock

We had a caregiver whose name was Lucifer. Lucifer was created by our Father and was the seal of perfection; he was our Father's most loved cherub.

He had been given almost everything my Father possessed, therefore he was placed in a very high position over the Stones of Fire to protect them, for we were many, as we worked in our Father's Garden. As our caregiver walked up and down, back and forth in the middle of the Father's seeds, which were known as **"the Stones of Fire,"** (Ref. Ezekiel 28:14)

Lucifer became angry with us because we did not worship, praise and adore him. After all, was it not he who did everything good for us, and was he not our constant provider? Yes, this was all true; however, our worship was to go to our Father and God from whom all blessings flowed. Our God had many breasts with plenty of food to go around. "El Shaddai" The God of many breasts. Thus, God is the All-Sufficient, All-Bountiful El. (Ref. Genesis 42:24-25);

The Hebrew word "shad" or "shadayim" (meaning "breast" or "breasts") El of your Father who helps you and the Almighty Shaddai who blesses you with blessings of the heavens above. (Ref. Genesis 49:25) El Shaddai a compound name meaning "the All Sufficient One." The exact derivation of the word "Shaddai" has a wide range of definitions.

Provision, substance, blessing, one who nourishes, supplies, and satisfies (Ref. Isaiah 60:16, 66:10-13.) The name Shaddai occurs 41 times in the Old

Testament. 29 times in the book of Job alone. I have found that Shaddai is written on the Mezuzah Scroll and can be researched in detail on the internet.

▶ Lucifer, the accuser

Our caregiver then became infected with a terrible virus called "iniquity." This virus had never been seen by the seeds (Stones of Fire) in God's Garden of Edom before it manifested as (moral) *evil*: perverseness, unjust behavior, unrighteousness, wickedness and anger toward our Father. He demanded his rightful portion according to his perception. He wanted all of the praise and worship from the Stones of Fire and all of Father's holy angels that were also our family. This made our Father very angry to the point of wrath; therefore, He cast His appointed caregiver to the earth, which was in total darkness, moreover, since our caregiver was in such a state of rebellion and anger, he became a ball of flames, and as he descended into the darkness, we <u>the Stones of Fire</u> watched him disintegrate and fall to the earth as ash.

▶ All that was left was the ashes

We all thought he was gone forever (forever was just that, because in our Father's Garden there was no sense of time), therefore when that ball of flames lit upon the angry winds from Fathers breath, they became scattered ashes upon the surface of earth beyond. It would have been thought that our existence in the Garden of God would have gone back to the harmonious life we lived before iniquity entered into our space of knowing; however, that was not what happened.

▶ When the caregiver is away, the Stones of Fire become unruly

After the caregiver was gone, it became evident that the thoughts of iniquity had infected many of our brothers and sisters. Even one-third of the host of angels followed our caregiver to the earth, bearing witness to the fact that even the angels had been given a free will. Disobedience began to be seen in little patches among the Stones of Fire, and the praise and worship to our Father was not powerful or in unity. Father knew that to restore harmony and peace among His Stones of Fire, He would have to give them the opportunity to see the iniquity manifest as evil -- misery, woe, affliction, and pain, so that there could be repentance and restoration. It was time to repair the former, and the only way they could do that was through relationship. The scriptures clearly show us that it was a setup. The Father,

God and His Son planned it in Eternity Past. They set it up, and they set us, the Stones of Fire up, to bring us back to the time and order of peace and harmony with the Father in His Holy Mountain.

▶ The Little Red School House

Therefore, He took the earth that was in total darkness and in a very short time he had it ready to make a new home for His seeds (Stones of Fire or as we know them today as the souls of man) that were in and on His Holy Mountain in Eden, His first Garden.

The word Stone here means to build, building material, or to obtain children.

He looked over all that He had done in dressing and establishing the new earth, and since He saw it was good, and He was well pleased He began His task of filling it with all the forms of creation that were in His mind.

We are told often of the prophets' visits to the chosen of God in the Old Testament. Stories of David and Goliath, Daniel and the lion's den, Samson and Delilah, and then we move into the New Testament where we see Peter and the three cocks. The little red school house is a place where we all have gone at one time or another or are guaranteed to go for education and training purposes if our plan is to be called, chosen, sanctified, and identified among the overcomers when we stand before our Creator on Judgment Day. Oh, wait maybe you have been taught that those who have accepted Jesus Christ as their Lord and Savior are not going to be amongst that group, you do not believe that you will have to stand before God on Judgment Day. Right, I know the main grace-based denominations have taught that there is no judgment for the believer. However, that is not what the Word of God teaches us. It tells us that we will answer for every idle word and deed. There will be for all believers, the separation of wood, hay, stubble, gold, and silver. Please do not be deceived and find yourselves unprepared to give cause for why you chose to rebel against your Creator for any reason on Judgment Day, just in case there is a Judgment Day, for all us saved-by-grace believers. For certain, you will stand before a great cloud of witnesses who will testify against you.

"Now therefore hearken unto me, O ye children: for blessed are they that keep my ways. Hear instruction, be wise, and refuse it not. Blessed is the man that heareth me, watching daily at my gates, waiting at the posts of my doors. For whoso findeth me findeth life, and shall obtain favor of the LORD. But he that sinneth against me wrongeth his own soul: all they that hate me love death." (Ref. Proverbs 8:32-36) Not one of the Stones of Fire that was offered a first, second and seven times seventy opportunity to repent and turn to the Lord for forgiveness and restoration, can or will stand before the Father, and plea the case of ignorance on Judgment Day; No, Wisdom will be there to testify that she instructed, and warned all who, back in Eternity Past and here in Eternity Present were given their opportunity. The Messenger of Wisdom says, "We were all there."

It is at this point that my arrogant young grandson would say, "Is that a threat, Grandma?" No baby, it is a promise, not by me but by your Creator. God is faithful to His Word; He keeps all His promises.

Let us keep in mind as we go further that when the Father looked over all His creation, He ordered them to reproduce after their own seed or kind. It is here I would like to say that in our day and time there are people who are calling themselves "heshes." These people are born a man but have declared themselves to be a woman, or born a woman but declare themselves to be a man. This completely goes against God's plan for man-kind be you a man or a woman. What you are born with you are. Your decision to be something else it an Abomination and God will send you straight to hell unless you repent of your choice to call God a liar and disobey His command to reproduce after your own kind. I must say there are people, dogs and cows that never reproduce, this is not a sin or the fault of God's Commandment, sometimes it is a choice and sometimes the body is not able, none of which is an abomination or sin against you, God, or kind. Therefore, let's continue our story just a little bit.

CHAPTER 3

5. Eternity Present: Eternity Present is what we know now, as occurring at this time.

In Chapter 2 we briefly visited Eternity Present. However, because it stretches over such a lengthy time, thousands and thousands of years, we need to camp here for a little while so that we can get what I would like to call "revelation knowledge and understanding." Eternity is a very long time, or is it? I have heard it is the blink of the eye. My mother used to tell us that if we did not mind her, she might just knock us into eternity. So, my perception of eternity might be blurred by a lack of understanding, or the failure to receive the knowledge I needed to understand what I had not been taught in the form of truth.

It was an eye-opening awakening when I learned the truth about margarine, being one molecule away from plastic. It looked like, and smelled like and it even tasted like butter. However, it was not butter. It was the counterfeit. I had not been raised in a so-called church-going family; therefore, I knew very little about God. And even after I was grown, what I received from the pulpits did not answer my many questions. Therefore, I would go on many journeys into the Word of God in the quietness of my room, searching for the answers to the problems of the day, the newest fad, the economic crisis, or a question that had arisen during one of my frequent dreams or conversations with friends or family members.

The Second Garden of Eden

God did have a reason for taking a mass of soil he called land, water, and sky, and in three days He completely changed the order of what had been laid waste, for no telling how long, into a world, which was to be the home of all that he created in six days. Remember that in the beginning there was no day or night, it was void, useless, and dark.

In the last three days of creation, God brought life in the form of plants, mammals, fowl, fish, and then they created humanity, which He said was created in Their likeness and image.

Knowing— means I have an understanding of, I have a relationship with. **Webster's Dictionary** explains knowing -- as affecting or revealing shrewd knowledge of secret private information. Therefore, given that each thimble-full of knowledge represents only one special little jewel of information, my treasure hunt became much more intense and filled with questions that only God Himself could bring to light. He holds the keys to all the mysteries of the Kingdom He had created. The fourth jewel was that of the Principle of the Seed.

The Word of God tells us that the LORD walked and talked with Adam-male and female, in the Garden of Eden. However, the LORD did not walk long with man in the place He reserved for them called the Garden of Eden before they disobeyed Him and He had to send them out of the garden He had created for them. Now they are getting to see the other side of the earth, not because God was upset or angry with them but after all, they disobeyed Him, and had He allowed them to stay in the Garden of Eden they might have eaten of the Tree of Life and remained forever in the state of evil consumed with wickedness (sin). Remember I told you that love comes in many forms and once again it is sacrificial love, actually it is the beginning of sacrificial love in Eternity Present. The Word reassures us, that God wanted only the best for all His creation. Remember, it is not God's fault. We chose bad behavior and because He is faithful to His Word, He must do what His Word commands Him to do out of His great love for His creation.

God's first plan was that man and woman would live happily ever after in the beautiful Garden of Eden that He had created for them, but since we know God is all-knowing, He knew His original plan would not last long, because where there is a will and a way, man will foul up the plan. Therefore, before Father, Son, Holy Ghost, known as the Trinity or three in one, redesigned the earth and created the world, they came to a mutual agreement that the Son would give up His place on the Throne beside the Father and come to earth as a human baby, to a man and a woman who were not married. Sound familiar? The difference here is the biological Father was the LORD, so He sent His seed by way of the Holy Ghost to a young woman who was pure and clean. God sent His personal angel to Mary and the man who would raise His Only Begotten Son, to inform them of God's predestined purpose and plan for His Son's life in Eternity Present, which explains the role of real planned parenthood. God laid out the entire world in the form and order of the cross His Son would have to one day bear. Let me clarify the word he, in Eternity there is only one pronoun in the language of the LORD God and that is "he or his". In our English language we have lots of pronouns and we us them as we see fitting.

The Trinity knew that after they created man and gave him life, he would fall short of their expectations of the perfect man and woman and fall prey to the nature and character of the original son of the morning star, Lucifer, who had been one of God's most treasured created beings. They were not surprised, or taken aback, they just patiently waited for mankind to acknowledge their rebellion and repent. However, when that did not happen, they had no choice but to put plan B into action. I once heard a pastor tell the congregation that with God, there was no plan B. Today I can tell you for a fact, God does have a plan B. However, it comes with a very costly price tag. You think Macy's department store is expensive. It is nothing compared to the price tag attached to plan B.

God's Creation:
A. God created the Heavens and the Earth
B. God created the fowl of the air and the fish of the sea

C. God made the beasts of the field

D. God created man male and female

✓ 1. Time

The Master determines our time and the reward we will be gifted when we stand before Him to account for the time we were given here on this earth. The master of the vineyard writes it as a question! "Is it not lawful for me to do what I will with mine own? Is thine eye evil, because I am good? Therefore, the last shall be first, and the first last: for many are called, but few are chosen." It is written that the Master will not require anything from us that He was not willing to do or to give. Time is an idol if it is not used according to the plan and purpose of the Master. (Ref. Matthew 20:1-16)

The word *time* is used 617 times in the Old and New Testaments, according to the **Strong's New Exhaustive Concordance**.

When old age befell King Solomon and the end of his mortal life drew near, he found the one person who would never leave nor forsake him, to be all that he had left in this world that really mattered, and had value to his eternal being. He then began the search back, and through his writing he made peace with that one person (his Creator). King Solomon is credited as the one who wrote the book of Ecclesiastes (everything outside of God is vanity and vexation of the soul). Based on the time of the writing and the literary content, it is believed that Solomon redeemed the time and repented of his self-will. Realizing he had lost the fear of the LORD, he turned his heart back in the right direction.

Word of Wisdom -- The scriptures tell us not to take time for granted, as we are not given the very next minute.

✓ 2. Order

I learned that in the beginning, God created the Heaven and the earth, which was in chaos. It was in darkness and had no order. The entire earth was a formless mass that did not have a day or a night. The water and the land had no boundaries and time was nonexistent. I soon had my treasure chest where I could put the jewels I would find, pearls of wisdom, rubies of knowledge, and diamond seeds of understanding. My first jewel was the Principle of Time, my second jewel was the Principle of Order, and my third jewel was the Principle of Obedience, which would take me far and fast into areas beyond my greatest dreams or imagination. Discovering the importance of being obedient to and following His perfect will and His plan for all of humankind changed my entire point of view about the LORD God. Remember, I just told you that my fourth jewel was the Principle of the Seed, which could be according to Jesus the most important of all.

I know that most pastors and church goers/bible readers think that God created the heavens in the beginning however, that is not a truth. This is one of the first of many mis-informed lies fed to God's Children through human reasoning. Let us go back to Genesis 1:1 KJV In the beginning God created the heaven and the earth. Heaven is singular here not plural.

Genesis 1:31 KLV And God saw everything that he had made, and, behold, *it was* very good. And the evening and the morning were the sixth day God made the animals and again He saw that it was good, this is the beginning of the sixth day, then in verse 26 we see that God said let us make man in our image, after our likeness and He blessed them. Here we see God is finished with His sixth day and then things begin to change. Genesis 2:1-2 KJV Thus the heavens and the earth were finished, and all the host of them.

Genesis 2:2 KJV And on the seventh day God ended his work which he had made; and he rested on the seventh day from all his work which he had made.

Here we see that from day one through the first half of the sixth day God looked at the Creation and replied, it was very good, however after they, the LORD God created man and blessed him, He did not say "what He saw was good," but the seventh day the LORD God ended His work and He rested. What happened on the sixth day that prevented the LORD God from seeing that the man they made in their image was not good? And when did He create the Heavens and why were heavens needed. These are just a couple of the questions that I struggled with for years. I knew that in the Lord's prayer He began with, Our Father which art in heaven, Hallowed by thy name. Thy kingdom come, Thy will be done <u>in earth as it is in heaven</u>. (Ref.

Matthew 69-10) (Ref. 2Corinthians 5:1-2) For we know that if our earthly house of *this* tabernacle were dissolved, we have a building of God, a house not made with hands, eternal in the **heavens**. For in this we groan, earnestly desiring to be clothed upon with our house which is **from heaven**:

God knew that there would be what we call "death" in the future of man-kind and He knew that there would be a time of resurrection of that body, but where would the resurrected ones live out eternity in Eternity Future??? The church has taught that all believing Christians go to heaven, we the believers are all put into one large group, However, even if that was true, not all Christians will go to the same heaven. For there are many eternal heavens.

Jesus told us that when we pray, we need to speak to our Father who is in Heaven, yet after our Father God created the heavens, the earth, all creation and man, we will speak to that as we travel through our predestined journey.

It is really rude to treat God's creation differently than He treats it. Recently, I heard people yelling, "Black lives matter." I also heard that an organized body of Americans is actually selling parts of unborn babies that had been murdered in the wombs of women who had no clue about God's time and His order. Is not our seed (babies) our fruits? After hearing many who are racist yelling that only the black's life mattered, I went to God with the question. Is it only my perception or does no one understand what and who really matters? (Ref. Genesis 4:4,5) Realizing that the LORD did not show partiality between the two brothers, Cain and Abel, brought words like prejudice and fair into the light of my understanding. What applied to one applied to them both, however, Cain chose to defy the method and the order of bringing the first fruit offering back to the LORD while Abel was obedient and respectful. It is written, the LORD did not respect Cain's offering, because Cain did not respect the LORD'S order. Moreover, we have no right to question the LORD God's order or His time, that can be seen as blaspheme. Where was or where is the fear of the LORD? Who is to blame, and who is at fault? My spirit was grieved to think there is such a lack of respect in our world today for human life, simply because it is God's creation. We are seeing a world that has no respect, and no fear of the

LORD. Cain blamed Abel and killed him. Regardless of our race, color, or creed, unrighteous judgment is pointing the finger at God.

All lives matter. It is not God who comes to kill, steal, and destroy your body, soul, and spirit, it is Lucifer! And as we have seen, he has no power unless we give it to him. Life and death have their time and order, both belong solely to our Creator, God. Man has had his (soul) mind scrambled like a bunch of eggs to the point in time that it is almost impossible to identify the white because the yolk is so very overpowering in color and taste. However, the texture of the white is unlike the yolk in every aspect of its consistency. Yet both matter and have their individual properties and functions. The mind of man will (re)member the original order of the egg and seeks to recapture what it was before it became scrambled after we who have been predestined in Eternity Past stands up and yell with our entire being that Jesus Christ and Him Resurrected Blood (life) is all that matters.

Recently, there was a documentary on television about the "Church of Scientology." During the many interviews, my mind was drawn back to my example above. It amazed me that so many well-educated, successful people in our government, entertainment world, and general population could have allowed themselves to fall into the mixture of egg-white and egg-yolk. I do understand the hunger for knowledge, however, they are leaving out wisdom and understanding (these two are not learned they are gifted to us when we ask for them from our Creator God) of who you are and what you have to do to obtain success, recognition, and status in the natural and spiritual world, as we know it. Therefore, based on the contents of ***"Predestined Journey"*** and my continual hunger and search for the truth, I could feel compassion for those who woke up from the world of delusion and chose to (re)member what they knew and had been taught by the LORD God in Eternity Past as truth about life then and now, and began to separate that truth from the fiction that had been spoon fed them. I hope they are following the example of King Solomon when he was old and returned to the plans and purposes of his Creator's perfect will and plans, He has for them. I pray for all who are called, for the scripture tells us that many are called but few are chosen. For there is an appointed time when we all must choose whom we will follow, God, or man.

Word of Wisdom -- It is written, the last shall be first, and the first last: for many are called, but few are chosen. (Ref. Matthew 20:16, 22:14)

6. Body, Soul, and Spirit

Now we know God created man from the dust or ashes of the earth, at least his shell, but we also know that humankind or mankind, as we refer to man, is not only a body. He or she also has within the body, a spirit, because the Word of God tells us God blessed them with life when He breathed upon (or into) them. He then gave them the ability to reproduce after their own kind. Humankind was made different from the cattle or the beasts, the fish, and the fowl in that mankind were all given their own purpose on this new hunk of dirt. This purpose was to achieve wisdom, knowledge, and understanding of the Creator and to develop a personal relationship with Him. This required an intellect far above the rest of life. Humankind not only required a spirit life; they required a soul life.

That is where my search for truth became almost allegorical. The spirit life of man was being explained and taught in the modern-day church; however, it was not explained so that we could see the whole of man. What I saw in my spirit, was God breathing the breath of life into nostrils of the man, and man's spirit and body, becoming a living breathing soul creature. The body was alive but the spirit was a dead dark hole and the soul was full of sickness, death, and evil after the sin of disobedience in the Garden of Edan. Most Christians have been taught the reason God made mankind with a higher level of intelligence was so He could have a relationship with them here on earth in the spiritual sense which is true and wonderful. However, Him having a relationship with man serves only man and God's Eternal purpose was to bring man back into a healthy relationship with Him here now and in Eternity Future. Since the natural is a type and shadow of the spiritual, we have to have understanding in the natural sense first. That is why Jesus taught His disciples and the multitude in parables, until they grew in faith, wisdom, knowledge, and understanding they had to be fed milk and baby food. Therefore, understanding how our spiritual make-up is put together according to God's order will revolutionize your relationship with God and man.

▶ Five Senses of the Body, Soul, and Spirit

Let me just give you a quick overview. We have five natural senses; they are the make-up of the body, soul, and spirit. You guessed it; we have the eye, the ear, the mouth, the nose and the hand, which give us sight, hearing, taste, smell, and touch….and since the natural is a type and shadow of the spiritual [you are getting this, right on], we will now review our fifteen spiritual senses.

Beginning -- the **Spirit** of the [*eye*], which is said to be the window to the soul, is the pathway of our faith, the [*ear*] is reverence, the [*mouth*] is prayer, the [*nose*] is hope, and the [*hand*] is worship.

Second -- the pathway of senses is the **Soul** of the [*eye*] which is the imagination, the [*ear*] is memory, the [*mouth*] is reason, the [*nose*] is the conscience, and the [*hand*] is the affection.

Third – the pathway of the **Body** is the eye, the ear, the mouth, the nose and the hand.

1Corinthians 12:13-27 For by one Spirit are we all baptized into one body (Jesus Christ), whether *we be* Jews or Gentiles, whether we be bond or free; and have been all made to drink into one Spirit. For the body is not one member, but many. If the foot shall say, Because I am not the hand, I am not of the body; is it therefore not of the body? And if the ear shall say, Because I am not the eye, I am not of the body; is it therefore not of the body? If the whole body *were* an eye, where were the hearing? If the whole *were* hearing, where *were* the smelling? But now hath God set the members every one of them in the body, as it hath pleased him. And if they were all one member, where *were* the body? But now *are they* many members, yet but one body. And the eye cannot say unto the hand, I have no need of thee: nor again the head to the feet, I have no need of you. Nay, much more those members of the body, which seem to be more feeble, are necessary: And those *members* of the body, which we think to be less honorable, upon these we bestow more abundant honour; and our uncomely *parts* have more abundant comeliness. For our comely *parts* have no need: but God hath tempered the body together, having given more abundant honour to that *part* which lacked: That there should be no schism in the body; but *that* the members should have the same care one for another. And whether one member suffer, all the members suffer with it; or one member be honored, all the members rejoice with it. Now ye are the body of Christ, and members in particular.

The lights in your tunnel of understanding will come on when you realize you are a new creation; you walk in super-spiritual abilities, favor, and the super-spiritual call of God on your life. You begin to understand the grace upon your life, knowing, and understanding that God looks at you based upon who you are in the Spirit, and not after the flesh or the soul (mind, will and emotions) until you are free from the soulish issues so that the enemy has nothing to attack you with. Once again, we see the value of receiving Christ as our Savior and the benefits that will indeed free us.

God, the Father, Jesus Christ the Son and the Holy Ghost cannot have a oneness relationship with a dead spirit that is a dark hole, and the soul that is full of evil, sickness, death, and wickedness. This is why we are told to die daily. Your spirit may be saved, made alive, when you accept Jesus as your Lord and Savior but your soul is still full of wickedness.

I am most sure this is a foreign teaching or doctrine as you might say, because it is not what most pastors or theologians teach when it comes to body, soul, and spirit, at least not in my world of Bible teachings. However, this principle is scriptural and foundationally based. The body, soul, and spirit are complete books in themselves; therefore, please refer to the study guide for scriptural references. I will refer back to the five senses from time to time throughout this book and other books to come, God Willing. So, I ask you to keep an open mind. When I touch on a mystery in the Word of God that you do not have the same revelation of, please do not trash what might be a jewel. Experience has caught me groveling in the pig pen, hunting for what I thought was nothing more than coal, only to find down the road it was a diamond, or a pearl. I realized what was thrown away had value and now I had need of it, yet out of a spirit of confusion I threw it away. This can be a costly lesson. It is much easier to put the uncut, unpolished word into a jar and set it on the back burner, as my grandma use to tell me to do with some item of food I wanted to save for later. If what I tell you is not a truth, God will allow it to spoil in the jar. Never fear being poisoned, for it is written that nothing deadly will harm you if you handle it with wisdom.

CHAPTER 4

7. Rod of Correction
The rod and reproof give wisdom: but a child left to himself bringeth his mother to shame.

Word of Wisdom -- He is in the way of life that keepeth instruction: but he that refuseth reproof erreth.

▶ A Relationship with Requirements

Therefore, this relationship between God and man now had requirements. Frequently as I search the scriptures, so I know in what my salvation lies, I come across the word "IF." "If" is only two letters; however, it carries the weight of Heaven and hell. Therefore, we see that to have a relationship with the Father, God and the Holy Ghost now we have to go through His Only Begotten Son, and to reunite the spirit and soul with God once the body was dead it is completely dependent upon the Father's Only Begotten Son, Jesus Christ for life and understanding.

It was at this time that the Principle of the Seed came to life in mankind, and much like our little couple in the introduction, I am 100 percent sure they had no idea what procreation required. When did planned parenthood begin? Wow, the order just changed direction. Now the man and woman are outside of the garden, and God is no longer walking with them in the cool of the evening. They have to prepare their own breakfast, lunch and dinner, and the man is in charge of bringing home the bacon.

All seemed so farfetched to me at first because I knew nothing about this soul business. Remember, I had learned about the spirit in church, but nothing was taught about our relationship with God and there was never mention of the Holy Ghost or what role the soul played in the saga of Eternity Past, Eternity Present and Eternity Future, therefore I was confused and thought that the spirit and soul were one and the same and the Holy Spirit was the Holy Ghost. I often wonder if the Pastors and Teachers in the Church actually read the Word of God and study what they are feeding the body of believers. Soon to come we will only get messages called the Sermon of the day coming out of the Artificial Intelligence mouth. Stay tuned because we are going to look closer yet at this powerful and very important subject.

Years ago, I had a wonderful little dog I was sure knew God much better than most humans, and he surely did behave better. We had such a loving, trusting relationship, yet that bond could not compare to human with human. I knew the natural typed and shadowed the spiritual, and both animal and man had the ability to love, trust, be loyal and faithful. However, my little dog did not seem to struggle in the emotional areas like humans. I knew that to have a relationship with my Father, God and the Lord Jesus Christ, I had to understand the Principles of Separation and Attachment. The second commandment Jesus gave the disciple is to love your neighbor as yourself. Once again, my little dog did not struggle in loving me based on my actions or his, therefore he exhibited what I had heard the grace-based teaching describe as unconditional love. I knew I was commanded to love the LORD my God with all my heart, mind, will, and emotions. I remember looking for the seed within humankind that was to be reunited back to the Creator God, and asking this question: Where and what is the soul?

How many of us really know God loves us, let alone with the word "unconditional" attached to love. He tells us He loves us; He shows us that He loves us; we say He loves us, and we say we are blessed, chosen, and highly favored. But do we believe without any doubts that He loves us unconditionally? I was sure my little dog loved me unconditionally, and I knew without a doubt that from time to time, I questioned how conditional my love was for him, based on his behavior. I have to go back frequently in my relationship with my little dog to remember why he loved me unconditionally. *He was a dog and I was the master.* When I get the role here in its proper place, I understand the process of the master/servant or father/son role. How frequently I hear God is an unconditional God, and I wonder where in the world this doctrine evolved. It is almost as ludicrous as the tadpole theory of evolution. Old and New Testaments are full of "if's" and "when's," and every "if" and "when" which means there are requirements.

Love and hate are soulish words. Jesus saw the motive of the crowd and spoke to their soulish realm. The disciples saw the crowd, and they recognized their needs, yet the disciples were the first to judge the need based on motive. Not based on the love and compassion of Jesus, but based on their own soulish needs and issues. Compare not, and judge not lest ye be judged. Jesus then turned to the disciples, and in a confrontational manner to get them to see their motives, said, "So then, every one of you who does not forsake all his possessions, he cannot be My disciple." What kind of God is this who requires us to give not only ourselves, but also all we have, in order to have that personal disciple relationship? Personally, I want to be wanted for who I am, not for what I can do or give. How about you? I believe, Jesus knew that people who are not willing to give their all would never be loyal to the cause at hand.

The multitudes followed Jesus and cried after Him to meet all their needs; they capitalized on His love and compassion for all humankind, which finally pushed Him to the point of reality orientation. What is true love?

Great crowds went with Him. And He turned and said to them, "If anyone comes to Me and does not hate his father and mother and wife and children and brothers and sisters, yes, and his own life also, he cannot be My disciple." (Ref. Luke 14:26, 27) So then, every one of you who does not forsake all his possessions, he cannot be My disciple.

Speaking of ownership: Let us hit this ball in your court of thought. Plagiarism: One morning I went to my church book store to find the door was no longer open to me. I was shocked and confused, as we were studying to show ourselves approved unto God as leaders, teachers, and pastors. I had been sending out teachings by the senior pastor in that church, who has great revelation. God reminded me to make sure to give credit to whom credit is due, so I included in one of the teachings who the senior pastor was and how to get more of the books and teachings, which would truly bless them. After being unable to buy any more of the books at their bookstore, I was notified that I was a copycat and a plagiarist. I wonder if the Apostle Paul ever rebuked any of the followers of Jesus Christ for using the revelations, he sent them in his letters? If he did, I am sure he did it in the correct way in the order described in his teachings. I reminded our church pastors that the instructions in the Word of God were not followed; moreover, they definitely were not done with love toward a brother or sister in Christ. It is written, though their pastor speaks with the tongues of men and angels but have not love, it is nothing more than a sounding brass or a clanging cymbal. Though their pastor has the gift of prophecy and understands all mysteries and has all knowledge, and though she or he has all faith so that mountains could be removed but has not love, all these things are nothing. I doubt very much that our pastors took this Word back to the leadership. After this attack, we had two choices according to the Word of God, and that was to bow to the authority in that church or remove our light, shake the dust off our feet, and leave in peace. God led us to leave in peace with forgiveness in our hearts.

This is a great time to give you permission to copy, repeat, and use any or all of this book for the Glory of God. If I do not have to have the Apostle Paul's permission to use the Book of Romans, Galatians, Ephesians or Corinthians etc. you do not need mine. However, because even the Church and its leader follow man's laws you have mine.

We as Christian believers need to realize in these circumstances that these are tests, and if we pass them God will springboard us to another level. Otherwise, we will get to go around that mountain again, and the next time might not end well for either party.

Once again, I see how a lack of natural and spiritual wisdom, understanding and knowledge can cause disruption and havoc in our lives. Then if we had an overdose of perception, we most likely would find navigating through an awkward situation difficult. ***Perception*** is defined as, "A single unified awareness derived from sensory processes while a <u>stimulus</u> is present." (**Webster's College Dictionary**) We live in a world where alcohol, marijuana, cocaine and other stimulus are completely legal, it is no wonder that we are in bondage to everyone's perceptions.

In 1972, during my morning prayer time with the Lord, He said, "Fly no man's banner." At the time I lived in Germany, as I was a military wife and it only made sense to me at that time that I might be a woman without a country. It took me many hours in prayer before being comforted by the Holy Ghost. I was blessed to understand that the word "banner" did not mean the flag of the United States; it meant the Lord did not want me to fly man's standards, or take his mark (identity). (Ref. Isaiah 11:10 Psalms 74:4) After that, when we would go into a church, the first thing we were asked to do was sign a membership role. Taking membership classes were the rite of passage, or else we were not considered part of the body of Christ and we could not teach a class, work as an usher, or take part in church business. For many churches they required we be a member of that church in order to partake of the Lords Supper, or as many of us call it Communion. Needless to say, we were not asked to do much in the way of ministry in the churches we attended.

Relationships among the disciples were identified by their relationship with the Lord Jesus Christ, not their occupation, location, membership or status, and certainly not based on the home congregation they fellowshipped with. The Word of God is specific and I cannot find the Lord giving the disciples specific rules for church membership. There were those who argued the laws or rules based on culture, customs, and traditions, and Paul allowed them to go their own way.

The Christian world has gone its own way, and our natural government, and religious government are in chaos. Can we possibly find the way out of the mess we have made by our rebellion attitude toward the

LORD, not until the men a women of God find the grace to walk into the offices they are called in to.

► Man's Responsibility in God's Plan

In the Book of Ephesians, the Apostle Paul lays it out clearly our responsibility in our divine calling. Ephesians 4:7-8 & 11-21 (Passion translation) And he (Jesus) has generously given each one of us supernatural grace, according to the size of the gift of Christ. This is why he says; "He ascends into the heavenly heights taking his many captured ones with him, and gifts were given to men." And he has appointed some with grace to be apostles, and some with grace to be prophets, and some with the grace to be evangelists, and some with the grace to be pastors, and some with the grace to be teachers. And their calling is to nurture and prepare all the holy believers to do their own works of ministry, and as they do this they will enlarge and build up the body of Christ. These grace ministries will function until we all attain oneness into the faith, until we all experience the fullness of what it means to know the Son of God, and finally we become one into a perfect man with the full dimensions of spiritual maturity and fully developed into the abundance of Christ. And then our immaturity will end! And we will not be easily shaken by trouble, nor led astray by novel teachings or by the false doctrines of deceivers who teach clever lies. But instead, we will remain strong and always sincere in our love as we express the truth. All our direction and ministries will flow from Christ and lead us deeper into him, the anointed Head of His body, the church. For His "body" has been formed in His image and is closely joined together and constantly connected as one. And every member has been given divine gifts to contribute to the growth of all; and as these gifts operate effectively throughout the whole body, we are built up and made perfect in love.

► Immortality

Because the spirit and soul of man are immortal, meaning they existed in Eternity Past, Eternity Present, and Eternity Future, they have always been and will always be. The soul being part of the mind, thoughts, will, and the emotions takes us to the soul's origin, which is divine. Since the Old Testament was transcribed from Hebrew into English the true and complete understanding of the word soul or souls are not well explained in the English Translations, and since we are not going that direction, I simply want to say that there is a lot to the issue of the soul. It lived as a Stone of Fire in the loins of the Father in Eternity Past. The soul was in the image of God before the LORD, God made the body, which He also made in His image to house the soul. It would behoove the Christian believer to understand that every-body has a soul and is responsible for what the will of that body does. The body does what the will dictates it to do. The spirit of man is the breath of God, breathed into him at the time of birth. A baby is alive in the natural body and <u>soul</u> (**H5315 Strong's Exhaustive Concordance**) in utero; however, the body and soul does not <u>have its spirit (breath of life) (H5397)</u>, for that comes when it takes its first breath then it becomes a living soul (a soul that is alive in the natural). (Ref. Genesis 2:7) The LORD God is the giver of breath and no one but the LORD God can take that breath away. Do not self-reason this scripture. There is natural life in the body and soul in utero, however, the spirit is given at birth when God the LORD breaths the breath of life into the body. The spirit and soul wait as prisoners within this body made of dust and ash, which is mortal, decaying material. The body knows it will not live forever, for the day will come when the body will die and return to the dust and ash to await the resurrection of the overcomers in Christ Jesus. At that time, the body will be changed from mortal to immortal. The spirit and soul, which were set free at the time the LORD reclaimed the breath, will be reunited with the immortal body and return to the parent of its origin, the Father, where they will live forever in Eternity Future.

When Jesus Christ lived on earth and was a man, He could not dwell within man; He could only dwell with man. However, once He died, was buried, and then after three days He was resurrected, He could return in Spirit form and dwell in all men. Scriptures show that the Spirit of the Father dwells in the Son and the Holy Spirit of the Son dwells in the Father, and together They dwell in Spirit in the believer. What a wonderful revelation. It was now up to man to believe in Him as the Son of God, the Messiah and to receive His living Spirit in exchange for the dead spirit of man, which was placed within him at birth. It is written "son of man" and the spirit in that man is forever doomed unless it is replaced by the Spirit of the Only Begotten Son of God, who is alive and well in Spirit form.

The soul of the born-again man or woman must be changed also because it has been corrupted by the sins of self-righteous pride, selfishness, self-centeredness, greed, lust, covetousness, etc. It can only do that as we confess them and allow the Crucified and Resurrected Blood of Jesus to be our covering. We must also renew our minds by the Word of God, which is Jesus. He is now our eternal caretaker and is continually interceding for us. He said He had to go back to the Father when He died, so He could send us the Holy Ghost to lead, guide, and comfort us during our time of dying to ourselves.

The soul has all our memories of Eternity Past locked up inside it, and from time to time we will have flashes of truth slide through the crack and into the light of our conscious awareness, people call it many different things. I call it deja-vu. The Word of God tells us He knew us before we were born, and if He knew us, then it is for sure we knew Him and many other souls as Stones of Fire. From time to time, I will meet someone I am sure I have met before, yet try, as we will, I cannot put place or time with this feeling of familiarity. I have had dreams of people and places I am sure I should know or had a relationship with, yet once I wake up, I am saddened that the memory is not strong enough to bring the faces and places into reality.

▶ God the Provider

Dreams are funny. They can seem like they take all night, yet they really only take a few minutes and they are not always complete. Now it was time for me to go to my little treasure box and find my jewel "Time," for I knew in time I would find my answer to all the questions I had locked in my mind. Then I wondered: Where do all these questions come from? Knowing that our spirit was in the mind of the Father is my assurance that the answer to all my questions have always and will always be there for me. This helps me not to get discouraged when it seems I am not moving fast enough into revelation knowledge and understanding. I think about the scripture that tells us of a time when Jesus asked His disciples a question, "Who do men say I am?" Only Peter could answer Him correctly and Jesus replied back to Peter that he was correct. However, he did not know the answer to the question by human knowledge but by revelation from the mind of God. Peter knew in consciousness, memory, reason, imagination, and affection in his soul who

Jesus was, however now Jesus told Peter to tell no one, for it was not time. Once again, we see there is a time and an order for all things.

Noting here: there is a difference between the Holy Spirit, which is the Spirit of the Lord, and the Holy Ghost, which Jesus told the disciples, in the book of Acts just prior to His ascension, they would be baptized with not many days hence. I realize the majority of churches teach they are one and the same. However, those same churches also teach the Trinity. Which is it, pastors? Two or three? The Father is a Spirit, the Son is a Spirit, and the Holy Ghost is a Spirit. How about honoring them by name? Yes, I do realize and acknowledge that all of the creation must come in the name of Lord Jesus Christ. Most Christian churches teach that they honor the name of Jesus Christ and believe we are in the New Testament Dispensation, which began after the death, burial, and resurrection/ascension of the Lord Jesus Christ. However, most Christian church doctrines use the Gospels (Matthew, Mark, Luke and John), which are still in the Old Testament Dispensation of Faith, for Jesus had not yet fulfilled the covenant of grace therefore completing the requirements of baptism. Furthermore, in the book of Acts, after the fulfillment of the covenant of grace was completed by Christ, the body of believes went to Peter and asked him what they must do to be saved. Peter addressed them through a reminder of who they were, and who they were in debt to. "Therefore, let all the house of Israel know assuredly that God made this same Jesus, whom you crucified, both Lord and Christ. Now hearing this, they were stabbed in the heart and said to Peter, and to the other apostles, men, and brothers what shall we do? Then Peter said to them, Repent and be baptized, every one of you, in the Name of Jesus Christ to remission of sins, and you shall receive the gift of the Holy Ghost. For the promise is to you and to your children, and to all those afar off, as many as the Lord our God shall call." (Ref. Acts 2:36-39 KJV)

Word of Wisdom -- OBEDIENCE to the Word of God is the key to blessings.

Salvation is through the blood, fire, and water. The Blood of Jesus Christ was shed as a sacrificial offering of love for us on the cross at Calvary. We will never need the shedding of animal or man's blood again to satisfy our Heavenly Father. However, there is the issue of the water. Jesus did not shed only His Blood, from His side flowed blood and water. Throughout the Word of God, the water parted, it flowed, was used to drink, bath in, water the entire face of the earth, and it was used to destroy and to save. The Word of God is referred to as the water of life. Salvation does not come from saying a few words at an altar. Through faith, we must take the cup and eat the flesh or we cannot be His disciples. Salvation is a process of laying down our lives daily as our love offering, in faith and sincerity, to Him at the brazen altar or foot of the cross, which frees us, thereby saving us from the sins of the soul that so easily beset us. Then we must come to the laver (the water or Word) to be cleansed daily of the ash left behind from the fire of the Holy Ghost as it cut away and burned up our fleshly nature.

We find this principle laid out for us in the form of a cross when we look at the Old Testament tabernacle made with man's hands. (Ref. Exodus 37&38) The third stage of our walk is as Peter said: the receiving of the Holy Ghost. Once we leave the sacrificial blood and fire at the brazen altar, we ascend up to the bronze laver, made of bronze mirrors, full of water for cleansing, where the sins of man were revealed and the water washes off the ash left from the purifying fire. Our third stage is found as we rest at the altar of incense, which is at the heart of the Holy Ghost. There we received new Light of Cheerfulness and Gratitude and are fed fresh manna every day. The Father did not let the children of Israel starve to death in the wilderness experience of their journey just because they were still whining crybabies who had not matured enough to trust Him as their natural and spiritual provider. He sent them manna. Moreover, He will not let us starve now in our wilderness journey, just because the churches of the twentieth and the twenty first centuries are full of idolatry and idol worship. And sins of all types are swept under the carpet at the altar and the Watchmen on the Walls are asleep in the pulpit. The manna is still there for the faithful man and woman of God who will ask, seek, and knock. The manna/Word of God comes by the grace of God today to the righteous. What do you suppose He has up in Heaven prepared for His ungrateful church of today?

Word of Wisdom -- Listen, things can change directions very quickly when man is not in charge of the program.

CHAPTER 5

8. The Counterfeit

Abraham, father of the bastard son Ishmael…Ishmael being the first-born son…sent away, became twelve princes according to their nations in the area of Arabia.

This book is being written to introduce us to the misconceptions, and even more boldly put lies that have manifested because of a counterfeit mindset, which has been passed down from generation to generation. Right now, our politicians are in a battle over what an organization called Planned Parenthood stands for, and what they are practicing daily right under the nose of the church. I say the church but actually I am addressing the entire body that claims to be believers in God the Father, the Lord Jesus Christ, and the Holy Ghost. It is not fair to attack the prophets, apostles, pastors, teachers and evangelists for their lack of interest in finding out the root causes for the problems they witness in the body, when the body themselves sit back and wait on someone else to do all the hard labor.

Abraham must have repented of his sin of adultery and he had to cut ties with the bastard son Ishmael because God blessed him with the promises of Israel. The problem here is that Israel lived their lives under the misconception of what the LORD God required of them. Self-righteousness, and pride prevented them from humbling themselves to the promised son, Jesus Christ the Messiah. Jesus told me that when I commit a sin be it in omission, or commission and I repent and turn from that sin, that sin is taken behind the back of God and never remembered by God anymore. However, I have to turn from my wicked ways and live according to Kingdom Principles. Kingdom Principles are the LORD God's way of doing and being.

The counterfeit is the substitution of the truth for a lie, opinion or a perception. The counterfeit is taking an original and reproducing it. We refer to this as a knock-off. The counterfeit is taking a principle, be it of God, the Holy Ghost or of man, and reinventing the identity of that principle to look like, smell like, and even taste like the real butter or olive oil, when in fact it is only a look alike; it is not the real thing. The counterfeit is substitution.

Early in the life and marriage of Abraham and Sarah, God spoke to them, giving them the promise of a son. Abraham concerned, because he did not have an heir in his household. Years passed and Sarah did not conceive and bring forth a son. So, Abraham went to the LORD and the LORD reminded him of His promise. Now they were both old, yet the LORD is faithful to His Word. He was to name his son Isaac. (Ref. Genesis 17&18) However, impatience plagued Abraham's household and Sarah offered her maidservant to Abraham because she could not conceive. Abraham readily accepted and the handmaid, Hagar, conceived and bore a son he named Ishmael. (Ref. Genesis 16:1-16) Ishmael was the counterfeit or bastard son not the promised heir the LORD spoke to Abraham about.

I have tried very hard to explain the counterfeit, therefore to make it very clear, I offer you the plain Word of God. There is only one original. Written by the Apostle Paul, "For I am not ashamed of the gospel of Christ, for it is the power of God unto salvation to everyone who believes, to the Jew first and also to the Greek. For in it the righteousness of God is revealed from faith to faith, as it is written, "The just shall live by faith." I encourage the readers to read Romans 1:16-32. Living by faith and trusting in the entire Word of God will prevents us from falling into the traps Saten sets for us which leads us into thinking it is ok for the Christian man or woman to live in a counterfeit life style that the world has through their democratic vote said is ok and acceptable for all to live in today and if we do not agree with and refuse to go along with the counterfeit ways we are racist, bigots, religious, or non-conformists hoping to cause us to become discouraged based on rejection and forced separation from many friends, family and other parts of the body that we have valued and have a relationship with..

▶ The Antidote to the Counterfeit

Truth most often is not tasty to man's pallet, as we said in our introduction, yet the Word of God tells us that the truth will set us free. The truth in any situation is the antidote for the counterfeit. Had Abraham and Sarah lived out God's plan in His time and His order there would not have been a counterfeit (bastard) son.

▶ Knowing your true identity

Once God took me back in to Eternity Past and I saw my book, He had written lining out my predestined journey I learned the TRUTH about the Fig Tree of Understanding. Since this was not Truths that were being taught in the church it explained why so many did not have revelation knowledge and understanding about their true identity and were not able to walk in wisdom and prudence, after all if you knew who God created you to be there would not be those who are "today" questioning whether they are male or female.

1. Knowing and understanding that we are a new creation after we accept Jesus Christ as our Lord and Savior, and that we walk in super-spiritual abilities, favor, with a super-spiritual call of God on our life helps us to accept who and what God meant for us to achieve while we are in Eternity Present. We begin to understand the mercy and grace upon our life, knowing, and understanding that God looks at us based upon who we are in the spirit and soul, and not after the flesh. He accepts us based on our choices every day that is why the Apostle Paul tells us to CHOOSE whom you will serve and to die daily. We are set free so that the enemy has nothing to attack us with.

2. Knowing and understanding that NO WEAPON formed against the righteousness in us can prosper is powerful. That is why we are told we have to put on the full armor of God. We must do our part. His righteousness

is a onetime covering, we receive the garment/robe of righteousness when we are baptized in His name, death, burial and are raised up in Him, a new man.

3. Understanding how our spiritual makeup will empower us to overcome the lies and attack of the enemy will enable us to recognize the temptations that are placed in front of us. This gives us the opportunity to choose which tree we will serve, the tree of LIFE or DEATH. We are empowered to deal with the enemy as Jesus did after His time of testing. It is written, "Away with you, Satan." (Ref. Matthew 4:10 SFLB) You shall not worship or serve any other God. It places us in the position of wisdom to recognize the tactics of the enemy and it gives us the MIGHT and POWER to stand, to acknowledge, take responsibility, and confess our sins without regret, shame or condemnation of our failures past and present. It gives us the ability to get up quickly and with the confidence that our God is a God of life, light and love for all who believe and trust in Him.

Back in my early days of searching to find out why life was so hard for me and others around me, I was asked to attend a seminar in Denver, called "Making things Happen." One of the first lessons we learned was about pain. The instructor told us "No pain, no gain." The next lesson was how to get from the pain to the gain.

Only as we mature in Jesus Christ can we be like Stephen, who felt only joy as he was being stoned. Andrew Wommack once said, "when a man is on the slab (dead), you can kick him and he will just lie there, if in fact he is dead." However, if he is still alive, he will get up off the table. The Apostle Paul said to die is gain. The scriptures tell us that we must die daily. Yet if we have no sin, what do we die of? If you say you have no sin, you are a liar and the Lord is not in you. Wisdom is to not only check your heart daily, but to ask God to send the Holy Ghost with the search light deep into the recesses of your fleshly mind, will and emotions (soul), and search your heart for any seed of self-righteous pride, selfishness, and self-centeredness, all of which are sin and are evil. Evil is pain, misery, woe, and affliction. One of God's many gifts of grace to us is repentance, and He is so loving, faithful, kind, and merciful that He is just waiting with open arms to forgive us of the acknowledged and confessed iniquities, transgressions, and sins so, that He can fill up the lake of forgiven sins that have been washed away by the Resurrected Blood of Jesus forever. Praise His Holy Name

The imagination has drawn many immature Christians deep into deception, yet I wonder where did that all come from? Today I believe I have found several new jewels that will go into my treasure chest and hopefully yours. Therefore, since you have allowed me, to open up possibilities that might answer many of the questions that we all have had about so many subjects in science, the supernatural, science fiction, and even issues on evolution I invite you to look deep in to the recesses of your imagination and allow the Holy Ghost to bring up out of Eternity Past your choices so that you can lay them out before our God for inspection.

▶ Who is your master?

Honestly, by observation of the Christian world, it is evident that few actually believe in the Sovereignty of God. Even fewer understand who the LORD of the Harvest is. I say that because I have been a born-again believer for forty-five years, I have been involved in the organized church world most of those forty-five years, and it is seldom that I see or hear Psalm 23 spoken as a promise -- The LORD is my Shepherd (The LORD is the one who views and stands us up as a seed, He inspects that seed, He calls, anoints and appoints that seed to be what it is called and chosen to be), *I shall not want.* The apostles in the New Testament Dispensation were never in want, or at least that is their testimony. I do not hear the pastors or congregation of the churches today testifying that they operate out of the spirit of unbelief; yet what they demonstrate to the world is lack and want. I attended a Bible College that taught healing was God's perfect will, and by all means it is His perfect will that there be none sick amongst the believers. However, I saw very few who understood how to operate in the gift of healing and that stood regardless of the situation that day in their healing. It is easy to claim to have the understanding of healings and deliverances but to actually walk your healing out every day is another story. You can attend a healing school and witness healings, yet after leaving the school, I would have to ask you, "How is that working for you?" In school there were others who were there to support your faith and to coach and encourage you, but when you are on your own, is your faith enough to heal the sick or raise the dead? I would have to say the proof is in the pudding. We need to follow the Apostle Peter around after his experience with the Lord Jesus Christ and the Holy Ghost. (Acts 1&2 KJV)

If you do not have the Holy Ghost with the evidence of speaking in tongues you cannot operate in the gifts by faith given by the Holy Ghost. Most all translations of the Bible other than the King James Version has changed the name of the Holy Ghost to the Holy Spirit.

Let me just explain that if you look up the Holy Spirit in Strongs' you will find it there only one time. Jesus Christ comes to us as the Holy Spirit, He dwells within us and it is through Him that we receive the fruits of the Spirit. **Galatians 5:22-24** "But the fruit of the Spirit is love, joy, peace, longsuffering, gentleness, goodness, faith, meekness, temperance: against such there is no law. And they that are Christ's have crucified the flesh with the affections and lusts. If we live in the Spirit, let us also walk in the Spirit."

The little congregation I fellowship with has more sick people in the pews than healthy people. Illness is not just in the body, it can also be in the mind, which is the seat of the emotions. There is no understanding of the authority and power of the will to choose, they have no understanding of the Principles of Binding and Loosening, and they use the name of Jesus and His life giving, cleansing Blood with such disrespect. Now let me tell you how frustrating it is when the leaders in the church are closed-minded. There is absolutely nothing any other part of the spiritual body can do to wake up the heads, Apostles, Prophets, Pastors, Teachers and Evangelists.

I spoke with a young woman just recently who had an occasion to be in the emergency room late one Sunday evening. She said the waiting room was full; they arrived at 8pm and did not leave until 3am. Now I have no idea how many born again believers were there that night; however, I have not lived to see the hospitals cleared out by the power of God. I am speaking here to myself as well as to all who are believers. We as believers have been given the power and authority over all evil, all disease, all sicknesses, all infirmities, all ailments and whatever else I have not covered. Jesus said if you do not believe My words look at My works. No wonder the world has such a difficult time believing and following those of us who call ourselves Christians. Our works are no better than our words.

I often wonder, "In whom do the believers sow their seeds of faith?" Can you say, "I sow my seeds of faith in Jesus Christ"? Or would you have to say, "you sow your seeds of faith for your healing in your church attendance, prayers, faithfulness to resisting or quoting the Word, the doctor, medical professionals, good diet, etc."? Do not misquote or misunderstand me; I am not against church, prayer, reading, or speaking the Word of God, doctors, medical treatment, or a good diet. My question is, "*Are you sowing your seeds of faith for your healing, deliverance, financial well-being, ministry etc., in Jesus Christ?*" All the good works in the world will not heal your spirit, soul, or body. If you are a man reading this book and you have a wife who wants a baby, you will have to sow your seed into your wife and trust that she has the seed of life within her—not spill it out on the ground; or into a test tube, or into the belly of a whore.

One of the first revelations God gave me was called "**the fear of the LORD.**" I quickly understood that without that, I would have no wisdom, understanding or knowledge. Frequently I would sit in a congregation of Christians who, by their actions and words demonstrated a total disrespect for the word "reverence." The sanctuary was filled with the clutter of chatter and few if any were on their knees, honoring the one they claimed they were there to worship. The dress of many was, to say the least, right off the street; there was nothing modest about the length of the skirt, which by the way most women seldom wear to church. Tee shirts in the pulpit have become normal, and very few men wear dress pants, and shoes with socks, let alone a tie and jacket. I often wonder if a dignitary, such as a president or the Queen of England, were to be honored that day in that church building, if the dress would be so informal and the attitude of the guests would be so lax.

When I lived in Africa, the Christian world was intent on teaching the natives of that country that we do not need to fear God because He is not really an austere God, when in fact the word austere means severe in manner or appearance, strict, rigorously self-disciplined, and severely moral. According to the entirety of the Old and New Testaments, it is evident that the LORD Jehovah, Adoni, Elohim, God, is and will always be an austere God. It is written that He is a God who never changes. Now let me speak to the Christian Church; you have heard it said, "When in Rome do as the Romans." The scriptures tell us, "Be in the world but not of it." Therefore, to the Churches of the Lord Jesus Christ, remembering whom you represent and that you are in Christ, body, soul, and spirit, and they are in you and this will help you in your choices of behavior, as well as your dress so that when your motive is centered on drawing in the presence of the LORD during your time of praise and worship. I honestly believe it is wisdom to come before Him in a form of dress and attitude expecting Him to meet us there. In addition, when there is an atmosphere of respect and reverence, He will show up to meet us. Moreover, we will be open and prepared to receive His love, mercy, and grace. When we draw near to Him with reverence and respect, He will draw near to us.

My question to all believers is: How often have you actually felt and experienced the presence of the LORD God Jehovah, Christ Jesus in your fellowship at church? If you have, it is only because you are amongst the few who actually fear the LORD and believe He is a God who keeps all His Words. Again, let me say, you are among the chosen few. Please forgive my presumptive attitude, however, when the presence of the LORD graces your prayer closet, your eyes will not be dry, and when He graces your congregation, not only will the eyes be wet, there will be few if any standing on their feet, chatting with their neighbor, or playing on their phone, or iPad, but the floor will be laden with the bodies of men, women and children who have felt His glory and His presence.

Now that we have an understanding of who we are in Christ, who Christ is in us, and who our Master is, we will move on to how to find the gold the Master has hidden for us.

▶ Digging for Gold

With pick and shovel in hand, we began our adventure of mining for gold. We first had to search the land for signs of the ore. We had been told it was hidden deep in the earth, however as the crust of the soil was eroded by wind and water, the gold nuggets and dust would wash down into the shallow pools of water in the streams that would seek to make their way to the large rivers below.

Learning not to lean to my own understanding meant that I had to get what the old miners called "gold fever." I had to want the gain more than I felt the pain. Desire is the absolute most important tool when digging for gold or finding any other precious metal or stone. Actually, I would list desire as a major key to opening our treasure chest. Without desire you might as well stay home.

It took me the full three days to uncover the gold nuggets. Some were hidden in the soil, under rocks covered with moss, and some were in the water, hidden in pools of black dirt. However, since I had the desire and I had gone to the best to learn the art of mining and I had taken all the right pans, picks, and shovels, my labors paid off. I left the seminar a wealthy woman. My instructor told us right before we left that it is not the spoon or the hand holding the spoon that is a cure for a cold, it is the medicine on the spoon. It may taste nasty; however, it will cure what ails you. Acknowledging Truth and Repentance is the antidote for the counterfeit. No, of course, I never took a class on mining gold; Acknowledging the truth and repenting of the misconception with is a lie will change the entirety of the story, which will change the outcome of our predestined journey. The seminar I attended was on making things happen. Isn't it wonderful all the directions we can go to accomplish a single goal if we have the desire and know the one in charge -- or in this case the master of the ceremony?

Chapter 6

9. You Knew or You Should have Known

I have always believed that actions speak louder than words, however, in God's case His Word is what got things done. Understanding that actions and words are both in the same category of the phrase, "faith without works is dead," faith is both an action and a word. Knowing this principle has helped me when I read through the Bible about the importance of working out our salvation. Planned parenthood is a term that is so loosely used and has a multitude of meanings, words and actions. Before we left home this morning to go shopping, I had spent time with the Lord, and during that time I was thinking about my own three children. They are all grown, married, and have children and grandchildren of their own.

As I thought about them, my mind was drawn back to the time that I had my first baby. I had just seen him on a Facebook post honoring his grandma, whom he called Nanny. This is the seventeenth anniversary of her passing on from this life into Eternity Future. He really did love her, and it was so good to see how his memories of her had not faded. I am so very thankful that my son respected her memory. He could not have done that if he had not respected her when he was but a youth. The more I thought about my children and my mother, the more I was drawn back in time.

As I went down the stairs, I heard the Holy Ghost speak to me concerning my children, and I said aloud, "Lord, if I knew then what I know today, I would not have birthed any children." Now, do not misunderstand what I just said. I love my children; all three of them have had a huge impact upon my life. However, before and during those early days, I did not have a clue about being a true parent, parents like Abraham and Sarah with Ishmael and Isaac. Isaac who was planned and purposed by God to be a blessing to his parents and who was planned and purposed to fulfill God's perfect will for His chosen people. Then there is Ishmael who was conceived in sin and who has been a thorn in the side of all Israel. God has always been the head over all things, even sin. Yes, God is head over sin but He did not create sin yet he is head over it. I was completely unaware that parenthood was a gift, which was to be met with diligence and out of obedience, not obligation or human desire. Oh, how the word "respect" plays such a vital role in parenthood.

You knew, or you should have known! How is that possible? In the book of Job, Chapter 1 you read about a man named Job, who must have heard the words spoken over him by his Father God in Eternity Past much like this. The LORD God knew Job, it is then in the knowing of who we are that we enter our predestined journey. I believe that this is sort of what was said to Job as he made his choices and began his journey; "Job, when you become successful, and pride and self-righteousness enter your heart, remember today. Remember your choices and the calling I gave you here before you were formed in your mother's womb. Job, you chose your path to be a righteous and upright man but now because of your flesh and the free will I give you, you are going to play God, therefore I must remove the hedge of protection I placed around you to protect you from the enemy, Satan." Remembering the plight of Job from start to finish reinforces the fact that our (re) memory can be a powerful blessing or a horrible curse.

Had Job allowed his spiritual ears to store the memories of God's goodness and faithfulness during his life in Eternity Past, he would have retrieved the Truth, the fact memories and he would have responded in a manner pleasing to God, with reverence and respect for the decisions that were made by him and God when he was a Stone of Fire.

Many of Job's choices did reflect God's plans and purposes for Job life in Eternity Present; however, Job got lost in his fleshly desire to be successful, loved, respected and worshiped by others even to the destroying of his family and taking of all his possessions and earthly wealth. Much like Lucifer, <u>Job was given much and he saw it all to his own glory</u>. God does not forget our choices in Eternity Past nor does He forget the plans He has for us <u>regardless of our choices</u>.

It was a blessing that Job did not follow the advice of his wife who told him to curse God and die, instead he beat himself up by bemoaning the day he was born, questioned with a hundred whys and how comes.

Memory is one of those things we all pray we do not lose on one hand and on the other hand wishing to forget. Yet, if respect is not the membrane that encases our memory, then our memory will be stained red with pain, which will force us to resent and have regrets, and the past will be sickening to every fiber within our minds. Many of us hunger to forget. We take pills, drink alcohol, and inject heroin and other sedatives into our veins, we bow our heads and turn our lives over to the effects of forgetting, -- which causes us to live out our lives under a curse instead of the blessings offered us as we look down at the Words from the finger of God written in the sand. As I said a little earlier, I went to a seminar called "Making Things Happen" with the desire and intent of recalling what had been buried, yet not totally forgotten in my past. I had hoped to forget all the bad and negative issues that had caused me pain so that I could move on. However, through dreams and those little flashbacks that would sneak up on me when I least expected, forgetting was not the end of the story.

Remember, without clarity and truth we walk around in the dark with our heads in the sand, so when the picture presents during a dream or during those little flashbacks that are prompted by the flesh, instead of remembering the truth, what is remembered is just a lie I conjured up, or made up to protect my image. It was just my perception or something someone told me that seemed to fit what I thought I remembered. Motive is a wonderful yet powerful ingredient in our memory. Getting to the motives for my actions helped the memory take responsibility through truth, which opened the way to repentance, forgiveness, and restoration. Truth is the KEY in keeping the memory sharp, alive, and well. Faith comes by hearing and hearing by the Word of God.

I have spent several chapters addressing and hopefully explaining Eternity Past, Eternity Present and Eternity Future. But just in case I was not clear, or you still might have questions let me very quickly go over it one more time.

Eternity Present is the earth we live on, and the world we live in, right now. Eternity Present, began the very moment God, "thought" this world into existence. Every man, animal, and plant existed in the mind of God before creation as we know it, and none of this will end until the last word in the Book of Revelation is fulfilled. As I said, "Eternity is a very long time." Then, there are two more eternities: Eternity Past is where all that we know today was alive and well in the mind of God, as the Stones of Fire which consisted of your mind, will, and emotions. They are known as your soul and were tucked away in God's Holy Mountain, the first Garden of Eden. Eternity Future is what we commonly refer to as Heaven, hell, or the great beyond; that time begins the moment we make our last free will choice here on earth and take our last breath of earthly air.

I hope that by now you have some of your own questions answered. Or maybe you have some seeds of truth sprouting, about to poke their hungry little heads through the surface of the hardened crust you have covering that area of soil you are so very protective of. With regard to your heart, which is that spot or area you think belongs to you and probably because of your perception it does, at least for the moment. I love her with all my heart, type of belonging. However, I would like to use the mind in conjunction with the heart. As a man thinks in his heart or as the mind thinks in its heart, therefore we know the mind has the ability to give life to thought. Thought comes before actions can occur.

Now back to Job: Why would the LORD point his finger at Job when Satan presented himself before the LORD? the LORD asked Satan a question, to draw out the motive for his visit to the Throne of the LORD. Satan was looking for someone who was favored by the LORD, to harm. And because it is God's responsibility to grow us up and to protect us from ourselves and others, the LORD remembered Job, a man who was upright, and loved God but, who was needing to be fertilized. Therefore, He took down the hedge of protection and gave Satan permission to act as the fertilizer spreader. If you put too much fertilizer on whatever type of plant you are feeding for growth, you will burn it up and it will die. Therefore, the LORD used the scoop Himself to measure out the dose. The LORD knew exactly what Satan's methods was, for they never change, he is the enemy that comes to kill, steal and destroy. Therefore, he began with Job's children and possessions, but that was not enough fertilizer to bring the expected internal change the LORD was hoping for. When the eyes see and the ears hear but the heart remains unchanged the LORD'S job is not finished. Job refused to curse the God who had given him the choices to always make God his God and allow God to be the God of his entire household or to be the God of his family and his possessions. Job's memory knew, or should have known, that what had happened to him was a result of his pride and self-righteousness. After all, Job not only had the memory of the LORD'S goodness, etc., he had the memory of the LORD's righteous judgment. Job was one of the millions of Stones of Fire that witnessed Lucifer's demise.

Second go around—if you don't succeed with one scoop try two.

Satan presented himself back before the Throne of the LORD with the request for another scoop of fertilizer, which was granted. The LORD is faithful to His Word -- all things work together for good to those who love the LORD, and are called according to His purpose. Let me make it very clear here that many are called but few are chosen, Job was not only called he was also chosen. It is a funny thing about our memory. It usually only takes a little pain to get it started going back to where it got off track. However, for Job, it took him a lengthy journey with lots of evil (misery, woe, affliction and pain) along the way before he remembered his original choices and got back onto the right track. As stated earlier, Job saw the error of his ways, he listened to the LORD, he repented of self-righteous pride, and unrighteous judgment of his friends, and he forgave them as is required to be forgiven.

10. Will it be Heaven or Hell?

As a born-again believer I do not have to question will it be heaven or hell my question lies in the question the Corinthians posed to the Apostle Paul in 1 Corinthians 15. Paul told the Corinthians that **if** they believed and received the Gospel, he taught them then the salvation of their spirit was sealed and they would for sure go to heaven. And **if** they were dying daily of the body, and soul (mind, will, and emotions) then since we have been born the image of the earthly, we shall also bear the image of the heavenly. The question was which heaven would be their heavenly home. For we were told that the LORD God created heavens. You see most religions believe we are all going to go to the same heaven or hell, however, Paul explains that because there are celestial bodies and bodies terrestrial that they are different. For there is one glory of the sun (bride) and another glory of the moon (bride maids) and another glory of the stars (the guests of the groom and bride). I explain this a little deeper in a further chapter. But since I believe we can choose our destination and if we are obedient to His perfect plan and purpose for us, and if we have a firm foundation of the Blood, Fire, and Water, we will walk in His light, eat of His body and transcend into His glories.

Word of Wisdom -- Hell and destruction are before the LORD: how much more then, the hearts of the children of men?

The brother just younger than me is an opinionated man who seldom will ever admit that he could possibly be wrong. During one of the frequent visits, I made to his home, and according to our tradition and for the convenience of all, we would get into our cars and go to our favorite local restaurant for Sunday morning breakfast before I returned to my home, wherever that might be at the time. One such morning, I put myself in the position that would give me cause to once again be challenged with questions that would give way to hours of study and pondering before my Lord. At that time, I was attending a Bible college, which was, according to my sister, "my latest fad," therefore the main thing I wanted to talk to my brother about was, "Are you going to heaven or hell?" Tact and beating around the bush were never two of my strong points, and since I knew I only had his attention for a few minutes, I cut right to the chase.

After we ordered our breakfast and everyone began to eat, I looked at him very intently and said, with as much courage as I could muster, "You know we are not getting any younger and you know that God loves you and wants you to know that if you died today that you could go to heaven to live with Him." Without putting his fork down or stopping chewing his food, he informed me that he did not know that God loves him because He is a no-good son-of a-bitch and he had no use for a God who would let little children suffer, go hungry, or die during hurricanes, tornadoes, etc. And if He is so great and loved the world and me so much, He had a heck of a way of showing it. My brother said, "Age has little to nothing to do with when you die, because I have lost lots of friends that were not old and I do not care where I am going, and the only thing I am concerned with now is getting through my breakfast." From that day to this, I have not brought up his choices or the choices of others to him, and other than a prayer of grace at a meal, subjects that have anything to do with God are not discussed. I know that God sent His Only Begotten Son because He loved the world, to save my brother, and He wants a personal relationship with him. However, I also know God will not force anyone to do anything in this world which is contrary to his or her will. He will however, allow the forces of evil to be their constant companion.

Please do not misunderstand what I am saying. I love my brother in the flesh; however, I must live according to the Word of God, and I must believe that what Jesus said He was to do is what I am to do also. Again, I must say, "Father, forgive him, he does not know the consequences of his decisions." The LORD is a big God, when our prayers, actions, and words fail us; we always have time -- until time is no more.

Word of Wisdom -- You are God, and I am not.

Recently my husband brought home a book by Billy Graham entitled, "Where I Am." The inscription on the front reads, Heaven, Eternity, and our life beyond. I think that really sums up my hope for where I am and where I intend to live out the rest of my heavenly life. Heaven and hell are spoken of frequently in the Old and New Testament. In the King James Version of the Bible, I could find the word heaven listed 582 times, heavens 134 times, and the word hell is listed 54 times. (Please forgive me if my numbers are not as you count them.) Hell is referred to as a subterranean retreat, the world of the dead, hades, grave, and a pit. Which would you suppose is the most important to the Originator of the Word of God, heaven, or hell?

Not knowing Billy Graham personally, I really cannot speak this as truth. However, in my perception and according to his lifestyle, nature, and character known to the public, this is a man whom God favors and has placed in him Godly wisdom, understanding, knowledge, and prudence. He is among those who are referred to as "Watchmen on the Wall." Billy Graham believes all the Word of God and he quoted Luke 12:48, "To whom much is given, much is required."

My brother is not on the same road as Billy Graham and may never be. However, the Word of God is impartial: "to whom much is given, much is required."

▶ **Who is your father?**

Being raised by a man who was keen on respect, I was taught to call men Mr., Sir, or Uncle and women Ms., Ma'am, or Aunt. In the upper class, the children only called their father, Daddy when they were very young. However, when they were in the mid-teens, they changed Daddy and Mama to Father and Mother. This was done out of respect for their parents as well as an indication of maturity. I personally do not refer to my Heavenly Father as Abba or Daddy even in our prayer time. I have need of a deeper relationship from my Father. I cannot see a child being given responsibilities of depth, width, breadth, and height by their father when they are not mature enough to understand the concepts. Jesus gave His disciples their lessons in the form of parables because they were spiritually immature and needed to be able to see the Word in a natural form first before He could reveal the spiritual application of that parable. Since I was brought up in the country, that might explain why I did not have a difficult time growing up or maturing in the natural, because I have always referred to my mother as Mama and my father as Daddy, and Heavenly Father as LORD, God or Father.

Word of Wisdom -- The thermometer of obedience to authority registers your degree of respect.

The scribes and Pharisees questioned Jesus, made fun of Him, reviled and crucified Him based on the truth of this issue, "Who is your father?" I can see this being the question that will divide the sheep and the goats in the last days. It will be a fence or a wall between families. When the time to take that stand presents itself, my prayer is that you will have settled the issue in your heart and mind and matured to the place that the disciples of Jesus found themselves during their time of moral growth and development.

Jesus asked the disciples this question: Who does the world say I am? The answer He received from His followers told Him and them that not only did they not know who He was by revelation, the scribes and Pharisees and those who followed Him out of curiosity did not know who He was either. Therefore, Jesus told the scribes, Pharisees, and those who followed Him – "If God were your Father, you would love me: for I proceeded forth and came from God; I did not come into this world of myself, but He sent me. Why can't you understand what I am telling you? Is it because you cannot hear my word? You are of your father the devil, and the lusts of your father you will do. He was a murderer from the beginning, and lived not in the truth, because there is no truth in him. When he speaks a lie, he speaks out of his own mouth: for he is a liar, and the father of it. Moreover, because I tell you the truth, yet you do not believe me. I am the way, the truth, and the life: no man can come to the Father, but by me. If you had known me, you should have known my Father also." (John 8:42-45 Paraphrased) (Reference study guide)

Throughout the ministry of Jesus, the subject of His relationship with Father God was asked by the "spiritual" world repeatedly. Because they were as Jesus said, the children of the devil (Satan), they were in darkness and could not understand what Jesus was saying, nor could they see the light that radiated off Him or His disciples.

Today, the world revolves around fatherless homes. The children of those homes do not know the love of a father be it biologic, foster or adopted, and the relationship they have with the male world is generally less than favorable. I personally am not surprised at all by the violence demonstrated in the Middle East or even on our streets in the inner cities of America. God gave humankind a father and a mother because that is the structural foundation of the family unit, and is the type and shadow of Eternity Past, Present and Future. Satan's job is to destroy the foundations God put in place for our blueprint; he is corrupting the testimony of the Church, our ancestors, and those who have been assigned the responsibility of fathering the souls of man. Our Heavenly Father set the example, not only for His Only Begotten Son, but also for His entire created family. Jesus was never a natural husband or father; however, He knew by example how to lead His disciples. Christ is the head of the natural father who is the leader or head of his home; he is the head of the family unit just as Christ is head of the spiritual unit. It is Christ's example that those who are in servitude under Him are to follow out of respect for who He is and what He represents.

Today, I would have to ask the church and all those who claim to be followers of Jesus Christ, "Who is your Father?" Can you say as Jesus said; do you believe that I am in the Father, and the Father in me? If for one moment you had to ponder that question, you might have a problem with who your father is. For Jesus said, believe me that I am in the Father, and the Father in me, therefore if Jesus is in me then the Father is also in me. "On that day you shall know that I am in my Father, and you are in me, and I am in you." (Ref. John 8:42-45, John 14:6-31)

Periodically I watch and listen to church on one of the television channels. Generally, the topic is "for God so loved the world that He gave." Yes, God loved the world and He gave -- Now listen to this, my dear ones, as Paul Harvey would say, to the rest of the story: IF, yes IF and for those who believe and receive His Only Begotten Son whom He gave, they would have eternal everlasting life. Jesus did not come to condemn the world, for if you live under the leadership of your father the devil, you are already condemned by your own choices. Jesus could not change the minds of those whose father was the devil. Why do you think you can change their minds by offering all the programs that tickle their flesh? Wake up, Church, your job is to be an example of holiness, and without holiness you cannot see God. Moreover, if you refuse to be holy as He was holy, you will persecute those who are holy. Jesus came to bring the Kingdom of God, to bring understanding to a dead and dying world. He had to bring life to dead spirits, and once there were born-again live spirits, he had to send them the Holy Ghost and fire. Maturing the body (heart) required the cutting away the ites. The Old Testament refer to them as the squatter in the promised land, Amorites, Hittites, Jebusites, Canon-ites etc. The ites that live in our fleshly heart (soul) today which we have to get rid of and kill right down to the baby seeds (die to daily) are found in Galatians 5:19-21. Now, the works of the flesh are manifest, which are these; Adultery, fornication, uncleanness, (homosexualality) lasciviousness, Idolatry, witchcraft, hatred, variance, emulations, wrath, strife, seditions, heresies, envyings, murders (thought of abortion), drunkenness (over eating), revellings, and such like: of the which I tell you before, as I have also told you in time past, that they which do such things shall not inherit the kingdom of God.

The Church cannot live on love alone. It does not work in the natural and it will not work in the spiritual. Yes we must love others, and we must love the LORD, God and Jesus Christ but we must be like them, one with them in word and in deed. The Church is works related and driven, and believe me I am not against working but it is working out the salvation of our soul. More programs and bigger buildings is not working. Doing the same thing over and over and expecting a different outcome is the definition of insanity.

Word of Wisdom -- I, *John, saw the holy city, New Jerusalem, coming down from God out of heaven, prepared as a bride adorned for her husband.* What Jesus became comes from the example of His Father. (Reference study guide)

▶ **Persecution from a Judas**

Who are the Judas's of our day? This is a question I hope you will ponder and watch for; they are out there just waiting for the weak to fall behind.

Who are the persecutors of the Truth? **Modern-day Scribes and Pharisees are definitely out there**. To expect otherwise would be a setup, and as I have said, wisdom is to guard your heart.

The Lord said that persecution of the Messenger of Wisdom/the Watchman on the Wall has always been and will be until the very last day, known to come as the Battle of Armageddon. Jesus, the twelve disciples, Paul, all the Messianic and Gentile believers who followed the teachings of Jesus were persecuted by the Jewish high priests, leaders of the different sects or tribes of Israel, plus the nations such as the Romans, Greeks, Syrians and the other nations and surrounding countries who, according to the Word of God, murdered them by beheading, stoning and by hanging them on the cross. Judas Iscariot was one of the twelve disciples whom Jesus loved. He was counted as one who walked, ate, and even slept in the same lodging with Jesus, yet he turned Him over to the scribes and Pharisees as a devil in the fulfillment of the Scriptures. It should not be a surprise when the Word of God calls the City of Jerusalem the whore, and a city of evil.

***Word of Wisdom*--** Asks the question, Was Satan not referred to as—the father of the scribes and Pharisees? Who are the scribes and Pharisees today?

"Remember the word that I said to you, the servant is not greater than his master. If they have persecuted Me, they will also persecute you. If they have kept My saying, they will also keep yours. Nevertheless, all these things they will do to you for My name's sake, because they do not know Him who sent Me." (Ref. John 15:20, 21)

▶ **God possessed me**

"The LORD possessed me in the beginning of His way, before His works of old. I was set up from everlasting, from the beginning, or ever the earth was." Is this not an amazing thought? Before anything was, the LORD possessed me. Remembering back to Chapter 2 we saw that in Eternity Past we were Stones of Fire or souls in the Holy Mountain of God, known as the Eden of God. Now we see that according to Jeremiah, God informs him that before he was formed in the belly of his mother, God knew him; and before he was born out of the womb, God sanctified him. Therefore, we know that not only does God know us, He possessed us and He is the one who sanctifies us. (Ref. Jeremiah 1:4, Proverbs 8:22-24)

We have shown the importance of knowing who your biological and spiritual father is. I realize that many churches call the man who stands in the pulpit, father. (Ref. Matthew 23:8-11) There are those who call him bishop, reverend, pastor, deacon, or brethren, all this has to do with cultural taste, and by all means, I have no qualms with your taste. However, no one can take the place of a biological father and mother in the home. We live in a world that has no clue the damage that is being done for all eternity, due to the failure of the family structure. Strangulation of the family unit seems to be an okay thought among the media and the world's viewpoint. Even the churches have a deaf ear and a blind eye to the growing number of single mothers with boys and girls growing up not having or knowing who their biological father might be.

Jesus instructed the disciple to place no man in a titled position that was in superiority to the least of Gods servants. Since there was such an issue amongst humans of power and status based on one's title, their garments, the seat they chose to set in and the food they chose to eat. It is a godly man or woman who will take the back seat, live humbly before those who look up to them, and serve, as they would like to be served. (Ref. Romans 12:16)

Word of Wisdom -- Be of the same mind one toward another. Mind not the high things, but condescend to men of low estate. Be not wise in your own conceits. (Ref. Romans 12:16)

When God spoke to me early one morning and said, "I am sending you to Africa to train pastors to be pastors," I never stopped to consider the fact that I had never been a pastor, I had never been to Africa, and I was single woman who lived from paycheck to paycheck. However, I knew I had heard God and I knew that as a nurse, when I went to work my employer was there with all the instruments, tools, and equipment I needed to do the job I was given to do. Therefore, I knew that God was my employer and He would take care of me. I would not have to go door to door and beg others to pay my way. I went and He provided. When promoters spoke to me about schemes to raise funds, I would ask my employer (God) if that was His best, and for the last eleven years He has continued to tell me No. "I have called you; I have ordained you; I have set you apart, and I will promote you and provide for you, you are My possession."

The LORD is an eternal God; He has no beginning and no ending. He is everlasting, eternal, forever, and evermore. The scripture refers to Him as being the source of all existence, past, present and future. The Hebrew word for eternal is Keh-dem, which means in front, aforetime, ancient time eternal, and everlasting.

In Eternity Past God formed His master plan and purpose in His own mind. Then He begot His Wisdom-Word, His Son, and just as God fed the Stones of Fire from His many breasts His perfect will and plan, He fed His Son. We have been told that we are His workmanship, created in Christ Jesus unto good works which God predestined or foreordained so that we would be able to walk in them. The Word tells us that Jesus did nothing that He was not instructed by His Father to do. He knew what to do because He had been taught in Eternity Past. It is written, "You can do all things which I did – and even more."

11. Family reunion

Oh my, is procreation a setup, and how in this world could all of this be for our good?

With all of the technology we have today, it is really difficult not to find your way from point A to point B. It is as simple as plugging your GPS into the satellite system and you are on your way. Unless you are of a genetic disposition that cannot, or simply does not want to follow the directions given you by someone else, it is extremely difficult not to arrive at the destination you have planned. Many of us stand guilty of that charge, while there are others who make sure they look, listen and obey every single clue given. Those individual personalities are the ones I want to humble my proud self to follow in the natural and the spiritual. Pride is generally the reason we fall short of the destination that is predestined for us by God.

Speaking of journeys and destinations that had a bucket load of holes in the road and lots of wrong turns, let me share with you my latest adventure of jewel hunting, filling my treasure chests with jewels, gold and silver.

Word of Wisdom -- There is a generation that curses their father, and does not bless their mother. There is a generation that is pure in their own eyes, and yet is not washed from their filthiness.

When my mother was alive, she was our origin of communication. Mama kept track of all of her five children, their spouses, and their children. She knew where they all were and what they were doing most of the time, up to the day and hour. After her death, the entire communication system went silent. As I read the encounter of Jesus' death, and the fears that the eleven disciples experienced, I can relate how difficult it was to accept His leaving them behind. Each of Mama's five children was feeling their age and their children were grown and scattered all over the United States. Back then there was no Internet or Skype; we had pen, paper, and the telephone; however, each call was very expensive. For the disciples, they were even at a greater disadvantage. Communication was difficult and costly regardless of the generational dispensation. As time went on, our family communication all but ceased because it was thought of as a means for gossip or receiving information that was none-of-your-business. Our family get-togethers stretched further and further apart, due to inconvenience and a spirit of indifference. By the year 2000, all communication became almost nonexistent. Only a select few even spoke, therefore getting together was a thing of the past. For us, our source of origin was gone in body, soul, and spirit; therefore, since the relationship we had built was only fleshly, there was nothing but blood and memories holding us together and with time memories fade and our blood ties no longer has purpose. For the disciples, they had the Spirit of the Son and the Father within them and they had the baptism of the Holy Ghost, which was their link to communication. Yet with all of that Jesus told His followers to take communion often and when they did that, they would renew the purpose. Therefore, the more tests, trials, and persecutions they faced, the stronger their relationship became and their communication became easier and continual. It is very important we continue in having family meals be it in the natural or the spiritual so as to renew the purpose given us by our Lord.

It is important to remember that just because you are a blood family in the natural or the spiritual Jesus ate and drank with His disciples right up to his time of departure after His resurrection. Breaking bread and drinking wine are not a small act that hold us together and it is not a once a month or year ritual. Jesus went from house to house daily, OH, how we have fallen short and it is no wonder we have little to no relationship or communication.

Our father and mother are our examples of what is okay and what is not okay, when one or both are predisposed to anger, we will most likely be angry. If they are happy, we will be happy, if they are murmurers, we will most like murmur and complain. I can go on and on with the behaviors of those I watched as I sat back, drew in a deep breath, and gave the Heavenly Father thanks. I wonder when we all get to heaven if it will be a joyous family reunion. Again, I thought about Billy's Graham's message as a Watchman on the Wall, "To whom much is given, much is required."

As the eldest of the five, I always felt a sense of responsibility and yes entitlement. I wonder if that was how the Apostle Peter felt. I should be told, I should know, even when Mama was alive, I tried to mother my siblings even when my own life was a total mess. This is a breeding ground for offence, resentment and unforgiveness to grow and mature until it is to big to destroy. This is where I believe the disciples might have been who now were apostles. At this point in the comparison, I began to see that they were not only bonded in the spirit and soul realm, they were bonded by the Redemptive Blood of Jesus Christ. I have been told, "They know I love them," when there were problems in a relationship. That is a wonderful thought, my friend, brother, and sister; however, natural love is not the glue that binds. The love that binds come from the Redemptive Blood of Jesus Christ which is light, and without His blood there is no assurance of a natural or spiritual family reunion. The Blood of Jesus came from sacrifice, His sacrifice of love. We fail because we are not willing to sacrifice our time, energy, resources, and our rights. The example Jesus left us with was that of sacrifice. He expects us to do as He did.

It is very common in my family to be selfish, self-centered, self-righteous and have no respect for others. I believe the root of pride must have wormed its way into the apple seed way down the line. My only hope is not changing anyone else; I must allow the Spirit of God to look deep down in the recesses of my own soul (mind, will, and emotions), and find all those little demonic wormy behaviors. I must fill my own ruts in with the words and principles from the Word of God as I journey back to the first Garden of Eden of my God, and I must respect the choices that others are making before my choices are going to be respected; therefore, I must prepare in dress and weaponry for warfare. I have to have the garment of His righteousness on therefore, as the Levites went to the Laver every day I to must go to look into the mirror of my life and wash out the filth from foot to head.

You are so right. I have no right to compare -- for I dare not compare myself to others. And I have no right to judge the person, yet I do have a right to judge the behavior, be it godly or ungodly amongst other believers but never amongst sinner, because sinners do what sinners do. I better be careful not to judge if I don't want to be judged for that is thought of as, karma. It is generally easy to see predisposed behaviors, for they stick out like a sore thumb and demand their own way, just like the ruts in the road, especially when they are big enough to engulf the car. (Ref. Obadiah 1:15, 1 Corinthians 5:3, Matthew 7:1)

Noting all of this was helping me to see all the ruts in the road I had been encountering as just that -- "ruts," placed in the road for me to only observe, not to fix. Due to my years of rut fixing, I had watched the ruts being dug out, filled in and dug out again, making them bigger and more dangerous as the generations hit them at the speed of lightning. You know we are all in such a hurry to get where we are going that we hit those ruts with a blind force, giving no thought to the damage it is going to do to us and to others. This day was a reinforcing of the truth that had been gleaned out of my many years of parenting in the natural and spiritual. The only role I could play in either family was as an observer. The blood that runs through our veins only keeps us alive physically, not spiritually, and without that spiritual Redemptive Blood of Jesus, we are like Esau and Jacob. I thought about my Savior and Lord as He watched His beloved disciples scurry up the hill when the religious ones of the day nailed His body to a hard, heavy cross, and all He could do for them then was observe -- and pray, "Father, forgive them, for they have no idea what they are doing or the consequence that will follow their words and actions." He knew even then that they were family, and He told them He would never leave them nor forsake them.

Do not misunderstand me; I understand these behaviors all too well. I frequently find myself operating in those spirits of evil, as I said, "Who is driving my car" as often as I was allowing them. Therefore, now I must ask myself the question: Are my observations totally my perception, or could I have been influenced by my personal persuasion? Many people ask me what the things of the spirit are. They ask me to give them some examples. So let me give you thirteen fruits of grace, thirteen being the number of the bride, out of my spirit, all listed throughout the Word of God: sincerity, surrender, humility, and mercy which accompany the nine fruits of the Spirit listed in Galatians 5:22, 23 "Love, joy, peace, patience, kindness, goodness, faithfulness, gentleness, and self-control. Therefore, they that are all after the Spirit which desires the things of the Spirit: prayer, worship, faith, and hope." The Word of God is so wonderful and balanced, it not only gives us the fruit of the good seeds (Spirit), it tells us that adultery, fornication, uncleanness, lustfulness, idolatry, sorcery, hatred, fighting, jealousies, angers, rivalries, divisions, heresies, envying, murders, drunkenness, raveling, and all things like these bad behaviors, are bad seeds after the flesh and do reproduce the things of the flesh. (Ref. Galatians 5: 16-21)

Given the right conditions, a seed will grow. If it begins it will not change. I have yet to see a thistle turn into a lily just because it got past its terrible twos.

Word of Wisdom -- Nip it in the bud!

We long to hear our Father say, "Well done, my good and faithful son," when we walk through the door after a long journey. I long to hear the voice of my Mama again in Heaven, as she is heard in praise and worship to our Savior. No, I did not mention that repentance of my evil ways had to come after I saw and acknowledged that I had fallen short of the fruits of the Spirit.

Only repentance will bring me to the jewels I put into my treasure chest yesterday which are respect, reverence (the fear of the LORD), and forgiveness.

KEY---For we through the Spirit wait for the hope of righteousness out of faith. Job reverenced God in all things because he remembered God's faithfulness to Himself, yet that did not stop Job from murmuring and complaining.

Patience produced all that Job had lost, even though they were not the ones he lost. I remembered time and order will work in my favor when

I am repentant and when I can be a blessing to others. If I choose, I can do that by waiting my turn, not being selfish and greedy, knowing that all things do and will work for my good, because what I want more than anything is to have the disposition of the LORD, God and the Lord Jesus Christ as my example of who and what I am predestined to be. Motive is the key in finding truth here, and the naked, honest truth will always set you or me free.

▶ Curses: (The Curse)

What in the world is a curse? In Chapter 5 I taught on the counterfeit, what is the counterfeit in our world and Church today?

The Church has plainly declared that we born-again believers are free from the curse of the law. We are justified by faith and are redeemed from the curse of the law. (Ref. Galatians 3:5-14) Yet in the very last chapter of Revelation, it tells us that in the end when everyone has made their choices, the final judgments are all said and done, and that every curse, meaning more than one or two, will no longer be, for they are all washed away by the Blood of the Lamb, the water of life, and the fruit and leaves from the Tree of Life. (Ref. Revelation 22:3) Therefore, today we are still fighting the curses of our generations.

In the book of Deuteronomy, we find God giving His servant, Moses His perfect will and plan for those whom He calls, His special people. (Ref. Deuteronomy 7:6) He commands them to be careful to observe (be obedient to) His statues and judgments with all their heart and soul. God does not mince words or play around with His perfect will and plan for His chosen people. So why would He allow us as His called and chosen to play around with what is so very important to Him? We as the church ride on the hope that God's permissive will protects us because we are under His Resurrected Blood. I am going to give you one example: Ananias and Sapphira's, testimony of the price they paid for not walking by faith. (Ref. Acts 5:1-11) They knew what God required, they had the knowledge of God's perfect will, His plan and His purpose for them and for the body of believers who were there at the time. We will soon see there is only one law that we must be obedient to in order to avoid falling into the trap of deception and death. The scriptures (Word, Jesus) tell us exactly what we must do to avoid having the curses of deception and death come upon us. We are living in a world that thinks nothing of a lifestyle where their women change the natural use of their bodies into that which is against nature: And likewise, also the men, leaving the natural use of the woman, burned in their lust one toward another; men with men working that which is unseemly, and receiving in themselves that recompense of their error which was the consequences of immorality. And even though they did not likely to retain God in their knowledge, God gave them over to a reprobate mind, to do those things which are not convenient; Being filled with all unrighteousness, fornication, wickedness, covetousness, maliciousness; full of envy, murder, debate, deceit, malignity; whisperers, backbiters, haters of God, despiteful, proud, boasters, inventors of evil things, disobedient to parents, without understanding, covenant breakers, without natural affection, implacable, unmerciful: God gave them over -- God is sovereign, God is the head over all things, even the mind. (Ref. Romans 1:17-32)

Lying to the Holy Ghost might not seem like such a huge offense against God; however, in the eyes of God it was, therefore, wisdom tells us to be mindful of the methods we use in opposition to God's perfect plan. Pride comes in so many ways. For Job it was self-righteousness, for Saul it was disobedience, for David and Solomon it was the lust of the flesh and the pride of life, for Ananias and Sapphira it was greed, jealousy, and envy. For the Apostle Peter it had been the fear of man. Offense against the Lord is a major problem in our church world today. John Bevere has a wonderful book called, "The Bait of Satan." Please, if you have not read it, do so; it will change your life.

Personally, I believe self-righteousness to be the curses the world in general face daily to be the biggest problem the Christian world has, and yet because it is so big it is the least addressed, and if it is addressed it is only dealt with by covering it over with a band-aid. The world wonders what to do with ISIS or the Islamic State because of the deadly attacks they bring upon the unseen number of individuals through the population we call civilization. They have been a curse upon the Children of Israel, the Jewish nation since Abraham chose to willfully go against God's perfect will and plan for him and Sarah. They did not walk in faith, believing that the LORD God Almighty was then and is today true and faithful to His Word.

You are absolutely free to believe as you wish on the subject of curses, however, as for me, I will believe that *anyone who* **willfully chooses to be in opposition** *to the perfect plan, purpose and will of the Father walks not in or by faith and is therefore placed under the law of the curse.*

In the book of Revelation, it is written, "Every curse will no longer be"; therefore, we will not enter into our eternal state of being under any curse < HOORAY> and we do not have to wait until after the rapture, the tribulations and all the other horrible events that the creation (humankind) is bringing upon themselves and the world, because humankind as a people are willfully disobedient, rebellious, and defiant toward and against the commands of our Creator, Father, Husband and LORD. Eternity Future began for the Christian the moment they accepted the Lord Jesus Christ. "Christ redeemed us from the curse of the Law, being made a curse for us (for it is written, "Cursed is everyone having been hanged on a tree") (Ref. Galatians 3:5-14 KJV)

For just a moment I would like you (the readers) to give the Holy Ghost your imagination, now your imagination dwells in the soul realm of your eye. That means you cannot see what I am going to share with you in the natural realm of your sight. In the Gospels there is a portion of Scripture where Jesus is seen walking toward John the Baptist who is in the water baptizing those who had come to him by faith for the cleansing of their sins. We know that Jesus had no sin to be cleansed of by the waters so why did he need John to baptize him. I prayed about that question for years and had many try to explain it however, none of there explanations bore witness in my spirit. One day when I was in prayer, I had the Lord speak to me concerning His baptism, He told me that He was not born in sin as is all of mankind, because He was conceived with the robe of righteousness and that that robe of righteousness protected Him from being attacked by Satan and his army of demons.

John could not understand why Jesus who had no sins had to be baptized. It was not about who was baptizing Jesus, it was about why Jesus had to be taken down into the waters of death, burial and resurrection. Because Jesus was born with the garment, or the robe of righteousness from the Father no weapon formed against Him could prosper. Nothing Satan had planned for Gods people could tempt Him. The Lords prayer tells us to pray "lead me not into temptation, but deliver me from evil." Jesus as a young man had lived his life as the Father directed, He was clean, perfect and pure. Satan could not lead Him into temptation therefore, no evil could come upon Him. Now here is where I was blown away. As Jesus went down into the water, He gave up His robe of righteousness. He did it willingly knowing what the price was. The Word of God tells us to count the cost. Jesus counted the cost that day. He knew that when He came up out of that watery grave, He would be naked. He left the robe of righteousness there for you and for me. That is why it is so important we be obedient to Act 2:37-40 Now when they heard this, they were pricked in their heart, and said unto Peter and to the rest of the apostles, Men and brethren, what shall we do? Then Peter said unto them, Repent, and be baptized every one of you in the name of Jesus Christ for the remission of sins, and ye shall receive the gift of the Holy Ghost. For the promise is unto you, and to your children, and to all that are afar off, even as many as the Lord our God shall call. And with many other words did he testify and exhort, saying, Save yourselves from this untoward generation.

Jesus came up out of His baptism spiritually naked and expose to demonic world of evil. He could no longer stand on the promises that was given to Him when He was covered with the robe of righteousness, now the Word tells us that Jesus being lead by the Spirit into the wilderness faced the beasts, those beasts were not lions and bears, they were the beasts of evil, He had no defense against the sins of the world that so easily beset us. Jesus left His garment of protection in the water so that when we go down in baptism in His name we receive our garment or robe of righteousness and are resurrected clean of the sins and protected by faith and grace . Peter knew what faced the generation to come, that is why he boldly said " Save yourselves from this untoward generation."

The Scripture (Word, Jesus), foreseeing that God would justify the nations through faith, preached the gospel before to Abraham, *saying*, "In you shall all nations be blessed." So, then those of faith are blessed with faithful Abraham. Therefore, know this, my dear ones, that if you want to do all that you do out of obligations to the world and its demands, then you surely find yourselves doing what you do out of the works of the law and will, most surely as I am sitting in this chair typing these words on this white screen, fall under one or more of the many curses that are listed throughout the scriptures. He left none of the curses to our imagination. He was faithful to list for us all curses, all blessings, and how to obtain them all, for it is written, "Cursed is everyone who does not continue in all things which are written in the book of the law, to do them." (Ref. Galatians 3:10-13) The Word tells us that no one is justified by the law in the sight of God is perfectly clear, for, "The just shall live by faith, and the law is not of faith; but "The man who does these things shall live in them." It seems very clear to this writer, that it does not only take faith to live by the law. It takes obedience to use the gift of faith and grace which is why so many leave off the second half of salvation (Ref. Philippians 2:12) We have been led down a bad path of deception, all of which will prevent the babes in Christ from recognizing a curse, which was brought upon them or that they brought upon themselves, due to an offense taken. Any offense is against God regardless of who He uses as the fertilizer spreader.

Word of Wisdom--The labour of the righteous tendeth to life: the fruit of the wicked to sin. (Ref. Proverbs 10:16)

CHAPTER 7

12. The Web of Deception

Word of Wisdom— it is not wisdom to take what we are given for granted. Many times, we are given a one time only opportunity. That opportunity will never come around again, when it is finished it will dry up at the root.

As my husband, Patrick, and I stood in line at Costco's food bar, I noticed a woman who was approximately forty years old, with a couple of very small children. The little girl, about eighteen months old, had blonde hair and looked cold, tired and cranky, so I said, "You are going to freeze those sweet little legs off. Where are your pants?" The woman, who I thought was her mama, said, "If you think that is bad, a few moments ago I turned around to find she had taken off her diaper. She did not get her nap and she is hungry."

I said, "Are you hungry?" and she stood up in the food cart and pointed to the counter where food was being served to the gentleman just ahead of us. Her little brother, who was in the infant carrier in the food cart, began to whine. He was also blonde and was about seven or eight months old. The woman reached down and got his bottle that was empty and put the nipple to his mouth, which quickly disappeared. I looked at the lady and said, "Are you, their mama?"

"No," she replied, "I am their grandmother." At first, I was surprised, however it is not uncommon for the grandmother to baby-sit the children and watch the cart. I just figured mama was still shopping or maybe she had gone to the restroom, so I said, "What are they going to call you, Grandma, or Granny or Grammy?" I thought since that was common in most families, it might be something we had in common.

She said, "Well, right now she calls me Mama. Her mama is in rehab."

So, without thinking I said, "Rehab, was she in an accident?" No, she said she was in drug rehab. I really felt bad for her, as I had opened the door to a very difficult subject for so many. And here it was, almost Thanksgiving. I said, "I do understand. My grandson who turned thirty-two yesterday is in jail for theft. However, he is a heroin addict and I pray he stays in jail until he is dried out, because he also has a little boy that my daughter is raising and I hope and pray he will get his life together and be a responsible daddy to his little boy."

She smiled at me and said, "I hope so, this is my daughter's third time in rehab and she is only nineteen. Never married, with two baby's ten-and-a-half months apart."

I looked over to see that Patrick had our hotdogs, cups for soda, and was heading to a table, so I reached over and hugged her, telling her to enjoy her chicken wrap, then I joined Patrick for our lunch. I looked around the room for her as I sat on the bench to eat my hotdog, but I never saw her again. My eyes lost track of this little family, but my mind thought about her the remainder of that afternoon and even into the night. I am 100 percent positive that the young lady who gave birth to those two little children did not understand, nor had she even given a first thought about what was going to happen to her during those few moments of pleasure that she and her partner were experiencing. Yet now three years later, her mother was raising her seed and his sperm. Where was Planned Parenthood? Is Planned Parenthood just an organization, or is it the choices that are made by a man and a woman to procreate according to what God created in the beginning?

Let us go back to chapter 2 for a moment and recall when and why God founded Planned Parenthood. In Eternity Past we (the Stones of Fire) made our choice. We were given a free will and could use our will to go our own way or His way. We seldom consider the consequences of our choices, because when our choice brings on pain instead of pleasure, we blame God or even worse the devil.

What I witness every day in the lives of those my Heavenly Father created with such tender hands and loving care is that they have absolutely no fear of the LORD. Not only do they not fear the LORD they do not reverence Him as their LORD.

Since I live in the world of the flesh and I experienced the pains of not having the fear of the LORD one of my greatest pains came from the sin of fornication.

What are the consequences of having sex outside of marriage or sex in marriage without the mindset of planned parenthood?

I was visiting with a young woman a short time ago. Her sister, who we are going to call "Lisa," is raising her grandson because his biological mother and father are in prison for stealing from one of their parents. Such a sad sick story, both parents are heroin addicts and to support their habit they resorted to stealing. The report was that they had stolen new goods from department stores, however, that did not generate enough income, so they had to look for quicker and easier ways to get money into their pockets.

At one time the young man we are going to call "Tom" had been in prison for theft to support his growing habit of methamphetamines. Tom served his time in prison and was released on probation. He tried going back to school; however, that only lasted a short time. He worked here and there but could not make enough to live off, so he resorted to living with and working for his mother, which was not conducive to his "free spirit" lifestyle until he met and married "Mary," who already had multiple children by multiple fathers, and they soon had Lisa's grandson. See the patterns here; bad after bad cannot bring good, not that Tom and Mary were bad. After all, they could have gotten their lives on the right track and turned a very difficult situation into a storybook Cinderella tale. How hard would it have been for them to get married, rent a little three-bedroom house with a white picket fence, which was Tom's dream, get pregnant, and live happily ever after? This sounds like the perfect lifestyle for Tom, Mary, Lisa and the new grandson.

Oh wait, that would have been way too simple, they had to have the icing on the cake first. I always believed, but did not live, first comes love, then comes marriage, and then comes Tom pushing the baby carriage. The sad ingredient missing in both of the above stories is truth. Truth is what we are not seeing as the outcome to this perfect white picket fence story. No one talks about the commitment of the covenant. Dating is nothing more than the Web of Deception. We can date, live as a couple and when things are not coming up roses, we can part our ways as if nothing had happened. Marriage without a commitment of the covenant between man/woman and God means that again when we are not happy with the situation, conditions or vows we can go to mans judge and get a divorce, yet we said in our vows to each other and to God let no man put asunder what God has joined together. These young people are no different than I was at their age, which is no excuse and will not stand up in a court of man's law or God's court, because they got our time and order out of His time and order.

The scriptures tell us to seek first God's way of doing and being. However, that is not what we see happening in the life of the individuals we are writing about. Tom and Mary chose to bring a child into an atmosphere filled with violence, anger, and hatred for everything and everyone that stands for good, therefore they cannot expect their lives and the lives of the ones we say we love to end in success, happiness, peace, and harmony.

▶ The Spirit of Ingratitude

You say you love me, yet what is going to happen when the spirit of rebellion drives your car right into the very pit of hell?

Job took the role of God upon his own shoulders, because his fear was that the God, he remembered was not big enough to be a fair and just

God for his children. (Ref. Job 1:4, 5) We read that his children were doing ungodly acts in their houses, and since Job had lost his fear of the LORD, his children did not fear, reverence, or respect Job's beliefs or God's way of being and doing. Children will follow the behaviors and attitudes that the parents set. Sin begins small and behind closed doors, yet there is no sin too small or too big for our God to obliterate or to cover if we are willing to admit that sin and iniquities are wrongs committed against God, and allow Him to deal with it or them according to His scales of judgment.

A virus of ingratitude in the memory will cloud one's judgment, causing an individual to forget all the really great things our parents have done for us, the sacrifices they have made so that we might have a nice home to protect us, good food to take away hunger pains, and stylish clothes to cover our nakedness. Then that spirit of ingratitude lurches its ugly head out of that sweet little boy or girl we wooed and awed over, cursing the day they chose you to be their mother because their memory has a virus and the only shot available to cure them is Jesus. Yes Jesus, He is the antidote for that ugly spirit of ingratitude. I know this is just too wild to believe, right?

Word of Wisdom—it is wisdom to guard your heart from becoming attached or established to the ways of the world.

▶ Who is at fault?

Now before you read the remainder of this book, I will confess, many people have told me that the principles in this book called Predestined Journey is just too farfetched and they have had difficulty in following the concepts taught. So let me think positive here because you are just about halfway through this book, which I believe, means you are open and seeking more insight into the hidden mysteries that are spiritual truths the Father is excited to reveal to you. It is still likely you will find it hard to believe the upcoming principles. It could be an allegory, fiction or it could be truth, the fact lies in how much you believe the whole Word of God. Will you ask God for His revelation, understanding, and knowledge, or is your belief system based only on your own perception of truth? Will you exercise your free will and search the scriptures so that you will know beyond a shadow of a doubt that the Word, principles and metaphors give here are TRUTH? We have just left the spirit of ingratitude, and now we are going to look the spirit of unbelief smack dab in the face.

I have shown in the preceding chapters the Principle of choice, is based on the free will Principle God gave every man and woman. The free will of choice for humans is limited to what is in keeping with human nature. Humans cannot will to fly, live under water and all the other things that are not part of their God given nature. I have given Scriptures on Eternity Past, Present and Future, where we came from, who the originator was, and the plans and purpose He had for choosing to bring us to earth to the best of my knowing. God gives humans the opportunity to make choices that genuinely affect their destiny. Therefore, if this Principle of free will of choice applied to Adam and Eve, Abraham, Moses, Job, Jeremiah, King David, the twelve disciples, Judas Iscariot, and everyone else, it also applies to you, concerning all the choices that have been made throughout their/your lives. The question remains, who gets to pick which choices are free will choices and belong to you and which choices was not of your free will and belongs to God or someone else for their choosing of your destiny? Recommended reading on the free will— "Chosen but Free" written by Norman Geisler

Great, take a few moments to ponder and think about this question. After all we are talking about your entire life here. Jesus told us to count the cost, He knew what was planned for Him as did the Father and God therefore, they did not leave or forsake Him in the wilderness. The dove came down upon Him as He came up out of the baptismal waters and the Father spoke to Him, Matthew 3:17 And lo a voice from heaven, saying, "This is my beloved Son, in whom I am well pleased." The dove represents the Holy Ghost. I think of the Holy Ghost as our spiritual mother, our comforter, the one who will never leave us unprotected. Jesus walked into the wilderness with faith knowing who was leading Him would never leave Him and He knew that by being obedient to the Word and His memories of His past would give Him the faith and grace He needed to fight the enemies of sin.

Do you believe that everything that has happens to you throughout your entire life happened because of a choice? Or do you simply believe in luck, accidents, circumstances, or life just happened? Let me ask you this last question. Do you believe the choice of your destiny, (from where ever you consider your beginning began), was just put into a hat and accidentally happened? Because I do not believe that, and I surely hope you do not either. I believe you need answers to this great big contra-versal issue called "CHOICE." Therefore, I believe you chose your mother before you were formed in her womb. I do not believe someone else had that power to choose for you, putting whoever that individual was in charge of your predestined or foreordained journey.

Oh, and if you say it was God, you are calling God a liar, because the Word of God says, "For I know the thoughts that I think toward you, saith the LORD, thoughts of peace, and not of evil, to give you an expected end." (Ref. Jeremiah 29:11) In addition, since you chose your mother, she must have chosen your father, because she had to have allowed his seed to be planted within her. Yes, even in the case of rape. That rape was part of your predestined or foreordained journey; you must have chosen to be in the wrong place, at the wrong time. Please understand I know how difficult this is to comprehend and believe. You may want to consider counseling if this is a subject that has caused you pain. They had the freedom of choosing where you were born, your skin color, and even your hair and eye color. Your biological father chose your sex. Bummer, right? That's right, there was no mistake. You have the male hormones or the female hormones by order and guess what, you chose them and you ordered them, it is much like ordering a pizza. Most of us will order pepperoni and sausage with one being the predominant meat.

The catch here is you chose them, them being every aspect of your being, before you were formed as a body and placed in your chosen mama's womb. God was and is so merciful to you; He never took the free will He gave you, away from you, after your natural birth. The choice to change continues with us throughout our predestined journey. Better be checking for that little spirit of rebellion, because the very second your baby is born it is there! Oh my, another question; or is that an explanation? Who is responsible for these outbursts of pride, self-centeredness, self-righteousness, rebellion, bitterness, resentment, hatred, un-forgiveness, anger, etc. seen in your baby? On the other hand, maybe I should pose the question: Who opened the gate that let the dogs get out, rather than who let them get in?

No one wants to step up to the plate and take the responsibility, which would mean taking accountability. We could just say as I so often hear, "Oh, it's just your perception," or better yet "It is just because they are tired," "They need a nap or they are hungry." Bad behavior does not have to be explained, it speaks for itself. Someone is responsible for it being allowed and someone is accountable for its outcome. Think pastors, parents, and teachers about the school shootings. The Christian world has let down the ball, thrown in the towel, justified, and excused the devil and all he is doing to kill, steal, and destroy our young people.

As we continue reading, we will need to put on our whole spiritual armor, and that robe of righteousness. Satan really does not like those whom he has a right to. After all, he absolutely intends for you to accompany him into the lake of fire, for it was created only for him and his possessions. Moreover, since you are ash and your nature and character before you accepted Jesus Christ as your Savior and Lord was just like his, it makes perfect sense to me that he would want to keep you stupid, ignorant, and blind.

Number 1: Therefore, the first thing you will have to do to take back your whole body, soul, and spirit is to know that you know, that you know, that you belong to Jesus Christ. Because just as the man Nicodemus had to be born again, you must be born again also.

Number 2: You will have to be willing to take the responsibility for whom and what you are right now. That means you let God off the hook for everything that did not seem 100 percent great in your past life, like where you lived, who your parents were, or were not, your disabilities, etc. I was born to a family that was completely dysfunctional and so were we all.

Number 3: Now that number 1 and number 2 are out of the way, we will work on repentance. Repentance is not a one-time event; it is a continual event. It is written, "I die daily." (Ref. 1Corinthians 15:31) There are religious organizations that believe in the process of confession, and restitution or absolution. However, it is only to man i.e., human. It is written that confession is to be offered to man when you have a wrong that man can absolve you of, however, repentance is to be done before God, for if you have sinned it is only against God.

Number 4: Forgiveness is one of those acts of mercy we all want and need if we hope to live in peace with all men and God. It is written, forgive us this day, (forgiveness is a daily need) Lord, as we forgive those whom have trespassed against us (which is also a daily need). (Ref. Matthew 6:12) OFFENSE is a subject that I will leave to John Bevere in his book "The Bait of Satan." Unforgiveness is the cause of wars, rumors of wars, and all manner of evil (misery, pain, and sufferings).

You cannot walk in peace, and be totally out of bondage if you are not walking in line with numbers 1-4. Plain and simple, this is the truth and fact.

It's just your perception

▶ **Who has believed our report?**

Who hath believed our report? And to whom is the arm of the LORD revealed? (Ref. Isaiah 53:1)

The word "perception" is a very important word and its application in our lives determines whether our lives are bland or flavorful, believed, or doubted. Frequently when I share my life and beliefs with family and friends, the reply I generally get is, "That is just your perception." Therefore, I have spent many hours searching my perception.

Perception means the act or faculty of apprehending by means of the senses or the mind, cognition. A single unified awareness derived from sensory processes while a stimulus is present. (Webster's College Dictionary) As I understand this definition; it is a fancy way of saying that the one or ones whom are relying on their perception as their understanding of a fact/truth might be under the influence of a drug, alcohol, anger, bitterness, unforgiveness, self-righteousness, self-centeredness, pride, lust or an overabundance of sugar filled love teachings from pastors that have never bothered to ask God for revelation understanding for them or their flock and have most likely never read the Book of Leviticus. All of which impair (dull, sedate, or enlarge through fabrication) their senses, mind and cognitive ability to navigate through the Tree of the knowledge of good and evil. Those who can justify the factual truths in the Word of God, by saying, "that is just your perception," most likely have never been to the Tree of Life or the Tree of Understanding.

Even though the mind of man has been reprogrammed to "act" first and "think" later does not mean that is the best order or even the right order. However, because we enter this world to live with and be trained up by men and woman who are narcissistic, sociopathic and are functionally dysfunctional, we are expected to believe all of their crazy perceptions of who they are and who we should be are in His perfect will and His plan for every human being procreated on this earth. Today we are homophobic, raciest freaks if we believe a girl is a girl and a boy is a boy and that a man is to marry a woman and that the color of your skin has nothing to do with your perception. Here we see the seasonings (flavorings) being the primary ingredient in our chicken casserole. Is this just my perception or do I have the order out of order?

It is very difficult to refute what you believe has happened, or what did happen when another person has a different picture, a different perception, a different mindset. The scriptures tell us that if you have a cause against a brother, you must bring two or more witnesses to testify on your behalf. I have to go back to the Word of God. Where does TRUTH actually come from? We know it does not come from man's fleshly, dead, dark, and corrupted heart. Therefore, let us take a look at motive (pride, self-righteousness, and self-centeredness) which drives us to defend our point of view, perception, or opinion. Jesus tells us that *if* we are in Him and He is in us, then we have the Spirit of the Father and the Son. *If* we have the Holy Ghost dwelling within us, then we have the full Trinity living within us, and *if* we live according to the scriptures, which teach us all judgments, covenants, statues, commandments, precepts, testimony, and laws, we are no longer compelled to justify our behaviors, be they good or bad. The difficulty here is that few individuals can be withstood by another individual and not defend or justifies their belief or perception. Jesus expects us to do as He did, not as we do. You, my brothers and sisters, expect your children to do as you tell them to do. I hope they never withstand you because they were expected to do as you said to do, not as you did do.

As you continue to read, I have given you two very common personality traits that I see and experience frequently, which play a big role in the inability to make healthy choices. Please note, I am not pointing my finger at anyone in particular. However, if you see your way of doing or being described here, praise the Lord, we are on the right track.

A sociopath is an individual who exhibit an antisocial personality disorder, also known as psychopathy or sociopathy. Individuals with this disorder have little regard for the feelings and welfare of others, especially when they are not evaluating their personal motives. They are selfish and self-centered and find it hard to submit or humble themselves to the needs of others. Anti-social behavior describes personality traits involving carelessness toward others' safety and frequent conflict with authority. Sociopathic behavior also involves an inaccurate and excessive appraisal of self-worth contributing to an extreme sense of entitlement. Those who work with sociopathic people have reported that their behavior can be manipulative, cunning, and even dangerous. They are alluring and can turn on the charm to get things to go their way. They generally are not good employees, and frequently have differences of opinion with those who are in authority. In so many words, "they are the boss."

A narcissistic person feels grandiose and self-important, exaggerates accomplishments, talents, skills, contacts, and personality traits to the point of lying, and demands to be recognized as superior without commensurate achievements. They are obsessed with fantasies of unlimited success, fame, fearsome power or omnipotence, unequalled brilliance (the cerebral narcissist), bodily beauty or sexual performance (the somatic narcissist), or ideal, everlasting, all-conquering love or passion. They are firmly convinced that they are unique and, being special, can only be understood by, should only be treated by, or associate with, other special or unique, or high-status people (or institutions). They require excessive admiration, adulation, attention and affirmation – or, failing that, wish to be feared and to be notorious. They feel entitled and demand automatic and full compliance with their unreasonable expectations for special and favorable priority treatment.

They are "interpersonally exploitative," i.e., use others to achieve their own ends. They are devoid of empathy, and unable or unwilling to identify with, acknowledge, or accept the feelings, needs, preferences, priorities, and choices of others. They are constantly envious of others and seek to hurt or destroy the objects of their frustration. They suffer from persecutory (paranoid) delusions, as they believe others feel the same about them and are likely to act similarly. They behave arrogantly and haughtily; they feel superior, omnipotent, omniscient, invincible, immune, "above the law," and omnipresent (magical thinking). They rage when frustrated, contradicted, or confronted by people they consider inferior to them and unworthy.

Oh, and let us not forget that big five-letter word CURSE, which is brought on when someone is in opposition to God's will, plan and purpose. Now most churches today do not believe we have any past generational curses, such as the bastards curse (not having a legal biological father), or the curse of Cain (being disrespectful toward God's order), to name only two of the hundreds that need to be dealt with, in the pulling down, rooting up, and tearing out. Yes, I am fully aware that Jesus Christ took on the curse of the law so that, becoming a born-again believer, which is referred to as a Christian, according to those who practice the Christian faith, is all that is needed to free us from any and all curses. However, being a professing Christian, I am of the mindset that all the genetic diseases, disorders, and discomforts we are told to list on our family history form before a doctor will even lay his stethoscope to our chest to listen for what he calls the heart of man, fall under the category of generational or hereditary curses, regardless of the source of the problem are all from the root of evil. Now I am not making an accusation, I am simply explaining to the Christian world that thinks they have no need of deliverance and repentance in the event your mama and daddy were not legally married at the time of your conception. You might want to visit the Word of God, which will explain to you why life is not a bed of roses for you or your parents. For those who profess to be a Christian, you probably do not care about curses because they are like roaches on a hot humid day in the ghetto.

I will show in this book that teaching complacency, tolerance, and works related ministries by our Christian churches is another lie conjured up by Satan to confuse us into believing we have no need of a downright war against the prince of the underworld and all his little weeds/seeds/roaches who are the enemies of all of God's seeds. His intent is to bring only death, and destruction, to kill, steal and destroy the truth about the I AM, Almighty LORD, God, the Holy Ghost and the Lord of lords, King of kings, the Alpha and Omega.

God is not to blame

Since you took time to work through numbers 1-4 of who's at fault, you already know that it is not God, who is to blame, for the type of life dealt you and you are now living. God predestined the life that you chose to live based on your choice in Eternity Past to either live for Him or for Satan, yet He made provision for you to change the course or direction you are on, at any time through His gift of repentance. Taking responsibility for our part in the decision-making process of our predestined journey here on earth is vital in determining the outcome of every situation we find ourselves in. It puts the fault of all situations good or bad; be it the pregnancy of a child, marriage, ministry, school, or even buying a car, where they belong.

Word of Wisdom--Taking credit [or blame] and giving credit [or blame] to whom it is due.

God gave all mankind a free will of choice. A sure sign that you don't believe this is if you instantly pity the good people for whom bad things happen to (Those who think of themselves as victims, widows, orphans, homeless, etc.). If you truly believed God gave us all free choice, wisdom is to consider all things which includes 'bad things' nothing more than outcomes of the choices they have made.

God's plan for us is always good and never for evil. God is impartial; He does not see us based on our economic status, mental capacity, gender, or ethnic orientation. Evil is generally perceived as a bad thing or person; however, the word evil, in its original text, actually means misery, pain, suffering, and affliction. Moreover, because of the nature and character of God, our Heavenly Father, who created us and loves us, evil would have never been God's perfect plan for us. His plan and will is that we live according to

His plan and will, and not ours. God's ultimate purpose is that we know Him and His Son and that we want to have a personal and intimate relationship with Them on a daily basis, and because in Eternity Past God gave us a free will, meaning we have the right to choose the paths we are going to take, remembering that man has his will and God has His will. He is not to blame when man's path turns onto a road laden with sadness, misery, pain, suffering and affliction. Now when we are ignorant of, or simply refuse God's perfect will and His plans for others, or us, all we have to do is stop the car where it is and go no further. Take time to focus on the pain, pain be it physical, mental, or spiritual is an indicator light (conscience) on our dash board that tells us something is wrong. God is the fixer of all pain, if we can stop, and pray for His grace and mercy. Acknowledgement that there is a problem has to take precedence over our need for fulfillment, time, and pride. Repentance is easy once we have gotten past the acknowledgement stage, because seeing the problem is 90 percent of the problem. Fixing the problem only takes the mechanic a second. However, ignorance of one of Gods gifts will not stand up as a valid excuse for why we did not do what was morally right. We all know we are given so many opportunities, billboards, flashing lights, and other warning tools to redirect our live, and as we have already seen, God is always faithful and absolutely good. God gave us ears to hear and eyes to see, naturally and spiritually, which are our GPS showing us the path we are on is safe and healthy, leading us, as the Psalmist says in (Ref. Psalms 23:2, 3) "He leadeth me beside the still waters. He restoreth my soul: he leadeth me in the paths of righteousness for his name's sake." Or one that will lead us over those bad hump days that inevitably present themselves. Note here I said, -- help. Please, for your sake and the sake of others, define the word "enabler." Helping a person in their time of need is a God thing, enabling a person who is in need is not a God thing. Remember that we do have that free will to choose to continue down the road of destruction, or we can exit that road, turn around, and get back on the road that will take us to the destination that was planned for us before we were formed in our birth mother's womb. God might protect you when you are ignorant, however it is written, "Tempt not the Lord thy God." (Ref. Matthew 4:7) Stupidity is tempting the Lord.

Jeremiah was told that God knew him before he was formed in the womb of his mother, so does it not make sense since we know God is no respect of person, that God knew you also. The Heavenly Father has the road back to Him paved with ruts and holes or as you might prefer, tests and trials; Remember, God is not to blame, He is not the one that has chosen this road we are on. However, because He predestined our journey, as well as the outcome of this journey, and because, God is a sovereign God, He is head over all things. (Ref. Ephesians 1:22) We can be sure that His hand of mercy and grace was what allowed every test and every trial. It is up to us to choose to be on a road that is ordered by God's plans for us, and we should be mindful and obedient to follow others of like mind. Then our road will be smooth as glass and laden with jewels of blessings.

I am aware there are many individuals, such as young children, and those with mental disabilities, who do not have the mental ability to choose right from wrong, or good from bad in Eternity Present. We can be grateful to a God of eternal mercy, for in Eternity Past all people not only knew the beginning and the end, they were perfect in mind, emotions, and they had a free will. In other word dear ones, we all knew what we were doing as Stones of Fire. Therefore, it behooves us today as Christians to keep in mind the elderly, the orphan, the young, the poor, the disabled mentally, physically and spiritually that we encounter every day, in our homes, families and amongst those we see on the streets, in the stores and in our churches that in Eternity Future (Heaven) the Word tells us there will be no sin, therefore there will be no sickness, no one will be old and dying, everyone will be in full knowing body, soul and spirit, so not only was God a God of mercy in Eternity Past where every Stone of Fire chose the life he or she would live out here on earth, which is what I have referred to as Eternity Present, Gods mercy extended right on into Eternity Future. God is merciful to all of His creation now, and He expects us to be also. Just a reminder that just as God judged the world prior to Noah because of sin, and again against Sodom and Gomorrah for the choices they had made, God's hand of mercy will only be stayed a short time before He brings judgment against every nation, every tribe, and every individual in this "the dispensation of grace."

Word of Wisdom -- Your spirit maybe saved and sealed by grace; however, your soul is a work in progress. We are assured, "We are saved by grace, yet we must work out the salvation of our body and soul [mind, will, and emotions]."

We have already discussed what took place in Eternity Past, so just remember that to have a casserole that is full of flavors, we have to put in all the ingredients in the proper time and the proper order. Now if we are rebellious, stubborn, and impatient and choose not to listen to directions and continue on the way of our fleshly desires, it is likely that the end results will not be happy ones. The world is full of unhappy people. Who is assigned to make you happy? Let me see here just a moment. When you are a baby, your happiness comes from your parents. As you grow up, it comes from others around you, brothers, sisters, teachers, etc. Then you get married and it comes from your spouse. Wow, how seldom do we think it is time to let all those around us off the hook and take responsibility for our own state of happiness, joy, and peace? Get off the bottle, be it pills or liquid, and put that joint in the garbage. All the excuses you have will not give you a peaceful night's rest. All the laws passed legalizing your sedative will not still the hand of judgment against you for not living out your life according to God's perfect will and plan for you. God's moral laws have never and will never pass away or are fulfilled. The Father, the Son, and the Holy Ghost put all moral laws in place for our moral development. Therefore, until we are morally developed which is to be completely furnished unto all good works, that we may be presented to the God of peace Himself, for it is He who sanctifies us complete, until then it will stand. Only when we have eaten from the Tree of Life, which is Jesus Christ, and the Fig Tree of Understanding, which is the Holy Ghost can we lawfully eat of the Tree of the Knowledge of Good and Evil, which is Jehovah Father. Then and only then, will we who believe have fulfilled the purpose for all the trees is the Garden. (Ref. 1 Thessalonians 5:15-24) Then there will be complete fulfillment of all God's laws, testimony, precepts, statues, commandments, covenants, and judgments. Amen

Not taking responsibility for the choices we have made, as well as not being thankful for the ability to make choices, is a sin against God. Oh my, this is a huge problem and the only one who can fix it is YOU, my dear friend. It is totally a single walk with God. No one is going to go with you to the cross, no one went with Jesus, He had to walk that walk alone. Yes, it is true Jesus promised He would never leave us or forsake us. Let us make sure not to leave or forsake Him.

CHAPTER 8

13. Multiplication Principle

He that is wounded in the stones (seed sack or testicles), or hath his privy member (penis) cut off, shall not enter into the congregation of the LORD. (Ref. Deuteronomy 23:1, Ref. Leviticus 21:17, Paraphrased) If you cannot procreate you will not multiply, and in God's perfect plan and purpose for humankind, that gives cause to be excommunicated, disowned, or disbarred from fellowship.

We read encounters of God's chosen disciples being persecuted, stoned, thrown into dirty sewage-filled prisons that were overrun by rats and infestations of disease, Paul was shipwrecked, bit by a poisonous serpent, mocked and ridiculed by his fellow believers, yet they grew in maturity and number. Yes, because of persecution they scattered, far and wide, resulting in the seeds of the Gospel being scattered like dandelion fluff on a windy day. Only the LORD God Almighty is the God of the wind, rain, and all such weather-related issues (news flash it is not global warming in charge of our ice, hail, snow, tornadoes, hurricanes, volcanoes and all water-related events around our world), God is sovereign, God is in charge of all creative events. As we will read in the principle of the seed, there cannot be a multiplication of anything until there is growth. Nothing can remain fixed or the same and stay alive. There must be growth for there to be life naturally and spiritually. Throughout the Old and New Testament God required a perfect offering. It is written "Now may the God of peace Himself sanctify you completely, and may your whole spirit and soul and body be kept blameless at the coming of our Lord Jesus Christ." (Ref. 1 Thessalonians 5:23) "And may the Lord make you increase and abound in love for one another and for all, as we do for you, so that He may establish your hearts blameless in holiness before our God and Father, *at the coming of our Lord Jesus* **with all His saints**." (Ref. 1 Thessalonians 3:11-13) Ever wondered about this scripture?

I have attended churches, as already stated, since 1971, and I heard the same prayers, same pleas for help, the same message from the pastor repeated over and over from one year to the next. If there was any new revelation brought forth, it almost always gave way for a church split. It would be one of those sought-after miracles, if pastors practiced line upon line, precept upon precept. Churches could grow in God's time and order. It is written—let us leave the milk of elementary doctrines of salvation behind and grow up. (Ref. Hebrews 6:1-4 Paraphrased)

I read the entire Bible from Genesis through Revelation on a yearly basis. I generally try to get a new Bible so that I can make notations as I travel from book to book, searching for new revelation. I know I can build on old (word pictures) revelation word or receive a completely new revelation that I had never seen in my previous years as a believer. I love new (seed) revelation wisdom, understanding, and knowledge. However, what I have learned is that it takes the breath of God to breathe on the Word for it to multiply as new life within me and I have to be asking for more. Open my eyes, nose and ears so that I can see, smell, and hear the Truth being spoken. Enlarge my heart, LORD, as You did in King David and King Solomon, and give me diamond seeds and golden wisdom from Your Throne of grace. I never tire of reading my Bible. I wake up with a longing in my soul for new fresh manna every morning. We need the written (logos) Word as our foundation, but we also need the spoken Word for direction. We have the written Word, to stand on. We have to allow the Holy Ghost to bring us *rhema* Word to mature us. Breath on me the spoken (*rhema*)Word, so I know what to do and where to go. I was years into my Christian walk when I discovered the principle of multiplication. Naturally and spiritually, line upon line, precept upon precept sounded great however, since I had not been taught about growth and maturity in Christ, I did not understand how that worked or what a miracle that was. I have to say here that going to church never helped me grow-up in my relationship with Jesus Christ, or the Holy Ghost and I never understood the importance of who the LORD is. The majority of the denominations I attended was interested in the number of seats filled each Sunday and how much money was put into the offering bucket. (Ref. Isaiah 28:13) (Remembering God's balance, equality, time, and order) I had to be in a foreign country and watch bricklayers building a house for it to make sense to me. *It was there that I not only found the principle of God's hot breath of judgment, I also found the principle of His icy (humility) breath of mercy.*

That day I prayed He would not let the hot (breath) winds of judgment and persecution blow through the windows in my life as I hunted for the seeds of new manna. I prayed also that His cold breath would not freeze up what I would uncover, waiting for me to gobble up, that He might store His seeds of truth deep in my treasure chest, which was not too cold or too hot but was dark and safe. There my newly found seeds could await their season for planting. I look for peace in this time of humility, and if I cannot find peace then I contend in that humble place of repentance with my LORD during that time of impotency.

Word of Wisdom -- Cast not your diamonds, and pearls (seeds) before the swine—give only in due season.

Throughout the Word of God, we see *the Principles of our growth and moral development* which comes by way of chastening (to instruct), scourges (to physically punish, disciple), pruning, trimming, or cutting away the old and the dead vines. Moreover, it is also instructed if chastening or scourging is needed as a result of willful disobedience and rebellion, and the individual does not accept the correction, with a spirit of humility, that is sent from the Lord, by way of a parent or responsible individual, that person who is in need of correction will be referred to as a bastard, not a son. (Ref. Deuteronomy 23:2, Hebrews 12:8) Wow, sounds serious to me...

I go back to the Children of Israel when they reached the Red Sea. The Red Sea was not, as some scholar's project, knee-high with water. (Ref. Exodus 14:21) The Word tells us that when Moses reached the edge of the water, it was high enough that the Children of Israel feared drowning more than they feared the bondage and pain of the Egyptians who were in hot pursuit of them. (Ref. Psalms 106:9) "He rebuked the Red Sea also, and it was dried up: so, he led them through the depths, as through the wilderness." Here we see that the Word distinguishes between the Red Sea and the depths. When dealing with the Word of God we must not do so as man is so prone to do. Here we see God dealing with the Red Sea and depths differently. God in His mercy told Moses to stretch out his rod, and when he did the cold breath of God parted the water and froze up the sides of the water, opening a path through the middle of the depths of the Red Sea (Ref. Exodus 15:8) then the hot breath of God blew from the east to dry up its surface, so, the Children of Israel could walk across on dry ground. (Ref. Exodus 10:13) (Notice; God's methods of blessings, curses, mercy, and judgments does not change.) When the enemy tried to cross on the same ground the Israelites had just walked across, God's hot breath of judgment blew across the icy waters of mercy that were congealed, thawing them so the words Moses spoke came to pass, "for the Egyptians whom you have seen today, you shall see them again no more forever. The LORD shall fight for you, and you shall hold your peace." (Ref. Exodus 14:13-16) I praise God for His judgment and for His mercy. To have one without the other would not be balanced, as we see in the case of the Israelites' moral development. We know God is a not a partial God and the Word of God was written for the purpose of helping us to live our lives as was foreordained. God is our protection, He is our provision, He is our judge, and our mercy.

As I pondered this Principle of Multiplication, I turned to my old friend, the Word of God, and found a young man and his seed, which to this very day refuses to pursue peace with all people. This young man, Esau, was born a twin and he began his battle with his brother before they were formed in the womb of their mother. It was said that the twins were so very violent that their mother, Rebekah, went to the LORD [back then they believed that He (the LORD) had the answer to all their problems], and it is written that the LORD said, "You have two nations in your womb and two people will be separated from your body." The LORD told her that one people would be stronger than the other and the first-born would serve the second-born. (Ref. Genesis 35:21-34)

Jewish history says that according to the customs of the time, the first-born would receive the birthright, carry on the inheritance from the father, and be the head of the family. Yet because of the area this family lived in at that time, the custom for the first-born varied according to his wishes. Therefore, Esau could sell his birthright to Jacob, the second-born brother, denoting that he despised the birthright and no longer valued it as a high privilege or rite of passage, which he did. (Ref. Hebrews 12:15-17)

As these two young men grew into manhood, they each had their own lifestyle. It was not long before the second-born son found favor with his mother and the first-born son was the favorite of the father. The time came that the father became weary of life, his sight was failing him and he knew the time was upon him when he would have to bestow the blessings of the father upon his son who held the birthright, "that in blessing I will bless you, and in multiplying I will multiply your seed like the stars of the heavens, and as the sand which is upon the seashore. Moreover, your seed shall possess the gate of his enemies. And in your seed shall all the nations of the earth be blessed." The father believed his first-born son was his legal heir, however the mother of the two young men knew the truth about both the men, therefore she knew that she must at all costs protect the one whom God had chosen to carry the seed of the Messiah and multiply the seeds of His people. (Remember, God delivered the message to Rebekah, the mother of the twins, who would serve whom.)

I really do want to make this point clear, because for years I have heard the story of these twins in church by many different pastors, some on the Christian Television Channels, and at the Bible College I attended, and the story remained the same. It was said that the second-born was a thief, a deceiver, a supplanter. However, it was not the second-born who was the thief, deceiver, and the liar. It is written (Ref. Genesis 25:21-34) that the firstborn son pushed his way ahead of his weaker brother. It was the older twin who was willful, determined, and headstrong in the womb. It is the way of Christ to humble ourselves and do unto our brother, as we want our brother to do unto us. Wait our turn, be patient. However, that was not the nature and character of Esau. Esau was a bully; he wanted what had been promised to his brother Jacob, and was determined to take it by force. Therefore, because Esau pushed his way to the top, he just took it for granted that his younger cowardly brother, Jacob, would just sit back and let him receive the blessings of the father, even though he was not the one to carry the seeds of promise. In the end, out of a spirit of gluttony, he forgot all about his birthright, because his motive at that time had changed based on the hunger in his belly. "Looking diligently lest any man fail of the grace of God; lest any root of bitterness springing up, trouble you, and thereby many be defiled; Lest there be any fornicator, or profane person, as Esau, who for one morsel of meat sold his birthright. For ye know how that afterward, when he would have inherited the blessing, he was rejected: for he found no place of repentance, though he sought it carefully with tears. (Ref. Romans 9:15)

The Word tells us of the danger of living with a spirit of indecisiveness or being double-minded causing us to get out of God's will based on God's time and order. Therefore, when the two men were grown, their mother (Rebekah) made sure the youngest twin, Jacob, who carried the seed of promise, promised by no other than the LORD, received the blessings of inheritance from their father, Isaac. Remember, the LORD told Rebekah, their mother, that Jacob the second-born was to rule and reign. However, because Esau the first-born was the strongest son, he pushed his way ahead and out of the womb first. Esau was an angry, vengeful child who grew into an even greater enemy of Israel and his seeds of promise. Today that war continues, and the battle over who is the rightful heir to Abraham's promised multiplication principal rages on. Giving note: Jacob (Israel) began his life as a weak coward in the womb, who did not fight for his position as the leader against his brother the bully, Esau. Jacob's nature and character was that of a coward, refusing to protect the seed of the Messiah, preceded his calling as Israel, showing its true color hundreds of years later as the Jews cowered first before, Annas, and Caliphas the Sanhedrin, the scribes and the elders who laid hold of Jesus the Messiah and King of the Jews, when He was brought before the people to be falsely accused based on the testimony of liars who wished to put Jesus to death, yet they found none. (John 18:12-14, Matthew 26:57-62) Innocent of all charges, Jesus was chained like a thief, a liar, a supplanter, and accused of claiming He could do something that they were sure He could not do. "I able to destroy the temple of God and build it up in three days." In fact, the LORD God Almighty through His prophets told them that He would come in the name of Immanuel (Jesus). (Ref. Isaiah 53:1-12, Isaiah 7:14) Therefore, instead of the Jews (His own blood line) standing up for Jesus as Jacob's mother did for him; the Jews threw Jesus under the bus.

Jacob had to wrestle with the LORD because the LORD had to test and try Jacob for him to see he was no longer a coward and that he would hold out until he was blessed and given his new name, Israel. It is too bad that the Jews have such a difficult time acknowledging their Messiah, Jesus Christ. However, I praise His holy name; Israel is standing strong against the line of the bully, Esau.

Obadiah's Prophecy against Edom

The vision of Obadiah: Thus says the Lord GOD concerning Edom, we have heard tidings from the LORD, and a messenger has been sent among the nations: "Rise up! Let us rise against her for battle!" Behold, I will make you small among the nations, you shall be utterly despised. The pride of your heart has deceived you, you who live in the clefts of the rock, whose dwelling is high, who say in your heart, "Who will bring me down to the ground?" Though you soar aloft like the eagle, though your nest is set among the stars, thence I will bring you down, says the LORD. If thieves came to you, if plunderers by night -- how you have been destroyed! -- would they not steal only enough for themselves? If grape gatherers came to you, would they not leave gleanings? How Esau has been pillaged, his treasures sought out! All your allies have deceived you; they have driven you to the border; your confederates have prevailed against you; your trusted friends have set a trap under you -- there is no understanding of it. Will I not on that day, says the LORD, destroy the wise men out of Edom, and understanding out of Mount Esau? And your mighty men shall be dismayed, O Teman, so that every man from Mount Esau will be cut off by slaughter.

For the violence done to your brother Jacob, shame shall cover you, and you shall be cut off forever. On the day that you stood aloof, on the day that strangers carried off his wealth, and foreigners entered his gates and cast lots for Jerusalem, you were like one of them. Nevertheless, you should not have gloated over the day of your brother in the day of his misfortune; you should not have rejoiced over the people of Judah in the day of their ruin; you should not have boasted in the day of distress. You should not have entered the gate of my people in the day of his calamity; you should not have gloated over his disaster in the day of his calamity; you should not have looted his goods in the day of his calamity. You should not have stood at the parting of the ways to cut off his fugitives; you should not have delivered up his survivors in the day of distress. For the day of the LORD is near upon all the nations. As you have done, it shall be done to you, your deeds shall return on your own head. For as you have drunk upon my holy mountain, all the nations round about shall drink; they shall drink, and stagger, and shall be as though they had not been. In Mount Zion there shall be those that escape, and it shall be holy; and the house of Jacob shall possess their own possessions. The house of Jacob shall be a fire, and the house of Joseph a flame, and the house of Esau stubble; they shall burn them and consume them, and there shall be no survivor to the house of Esau; for the LORD has spoken. Those of the Negeb shall possess Mount Esau, and those of the Shephelah the land of the Philistines; they shall possess the land of Ephraim and the land of Samaria and Benjamin shall possess Gilead. The exiles in Halah who are of the people of Israel shall possess Phoenicia as far as Zarephath; and the exiles of Jerusalem who are in Sepharad shall possess the cities of the Negeb. Saviors shall go up to Mount Zion to rule Mount Esau; and the kingdom shall be the LORD's. (Obadiah 1:1-21)

Word of Wisdom -- To all who have not been taught the truth about (Jacob) Israel, search *the Principles of Truth*, and if you have believed a lie, consider repenting for unrighteous judgment.

14. Principle of Seed

What do you think it would be like to be a seed? I think it is much like the human body! We all have a shell, we are different colors, different textures, different thickness, we serve different purposes, yet we all have life within a shell. We all need light, love, food, and water. The male seed, through a process of multiplication called procreation, or bringing forth

God's creation, must fertilize the female egg. For we know that life within humankind is brought about only through the breath and the blood. In plants this process is called pollination. We have heard of seeds of corn being found in the pyramids in Egypt that were thousands of years old and when planted they sprouted and grew. In the plant kingdom, life is brought about by soil, water, and light. Jesus uses *the seed, time and harvest principle* as a parable that is vital to the understanding of the entire Word of God. It is one of the very beginning concepts of learning. Everything begins in seed form, including humankind. A woman is said to have an egg, the male has the sperm. The egg has the very same description of a seed; both must have a warm, moist environment, which is protected before life begins to stir within the shell. This understanding comes from revelation of the truth buried deep within the shell of knowledge.

Word of Wisdom -- The Word of God is a seed within the heart; protect it, guard it with your life, knowing it is your life.

Types and shadows of the Father and the Christ are found hundreds of years before the only Begotten Son, Jesus was born.

Abraham and Isaac: We come on the scene to find Abraham in a state of concern. He and Sarah had been married a lengthy time, and they had not been blessed with a son. A son born in his household was needed in Abraham's time to pass on the seed line and heritage, therefore Abraham went to the LORD. (Ref. Genesis 21:12, Genesis 26:24) No, he did not go to a doctor or Planned Parenthood clinic, he went to the LORD. The LORD of seed time and Harvest told him, "This one shall not be your heir." That statement seemed strange to me, because Abraham did not have an heir born in his household and that was his concern. We see the LORD telling him that the one born *to him* would be his heir, not just one's born in his household. (Ref. Genesis 15:1-6) Reading on in the 15th chapter of Genesis we find the LORD had warned Abraham, however Abraham did not listen to the Word of the LORD to him, because we find him taking his legal wife Sarah's advice, to go into the bed of her servant girl, Hagar. However, Sarah, Abraham's legal wife was to be the mother of his child, not a servant girl. Now what it sounds like is that she had her own dwelling, however Hagar was a servant in Abraham's household. That union produced a bastard son they called Ishmael. (Ref. Genesis 16:1-4) Here we begin to see the curse of the bastard son. Bastard in Hebrew is *mam-zare'* From an unused root *mian --*to *alienate*; a *mongrel*, that is, born of a Jewish father and a heathen mother: - bastard.

During the accountings in the Old Testament, it is noted that we will frequently find a man having many wives and many concubines and children born to all of them. It is also here that we see *the Principles of God's perfect will and His permissive will.* God's perfect will was for one man to have one wife and the two should become one flesh. (Ref. Ephesians 5:13) They were then permitted to have children and their seed was to multiply and not before. The Apostle Paul addressed the issue of multiple wives and clarified it as the lust of the flesh. He ordered or commanded putting a stop to the practice of polygamy/multiple marriages among the Christians, based on God's foreordained plan for man and His perfect will. (Ref. 1Corinthians 7:1-4) A scripture that is seldom discussed in marriage seminars or amongst the Christian Church is found in Genesis 2:24, "therefore, shall a man leave his father and his mother, and shall cleave unto his wife: and they shall be one flesh." This must have been prophetically spoken by Adam; for neither Adam nor his wife Eve had a natural father and mother to leave. *Or did he?*

When Sarah conceived Isaac, he was to be brought forth out of Abraham's loins and Sarah's womb. Moreover, God told him that when Isaac was born, he was to take him outside, look toward the heavens, and count the stars, if he was able to count them. And God said to him, so shall your seed be. (Ref. Genesis 15:13, 14)

They that sow in tears shall reap in joy. He that goes forth weeping, bearing precious seed, shall doubtless come again with rejoicing, bringing his sheaves with him. (Ref. Psalms126:6) Seeds sown into Him (the Lord Jesus Christ) will multiply and bring forth as the sands of the sea.

▶ **It only takes One Bad Seed**

Three strangers strike up a conversation in the airport lounge in Bozeman, Montana, awaiting their flights. One is an American Indian, passing through from Lame Deer. Another is a cowboy on his way to Billings for a livestock show. And the third is a fundamentalist Arab student from the Middle East, newly arrived at Montana State University. Their discussion drifts to their diverse cultures. Soon, the two Westerners learn that the Arab is a devout, radical Muslim and the conversation falls into an uneasy lull. The cowboy leans back in his chair, crosses his boots on a magazine table, and tips his big sweat-stained hat forward over his face. The wind outside is blowing tumbleweeds around and the old windsock is flapping, but still no plane comes. Finally, the American Indian clears his throat and softly speaks. "At one time here, my people were many, but sadly, now we are few." The Muslim student raises an eyebrow and leans forward, "Once my people were few," he sneers, "and now we are many. Why do you suppose that is?" The Montana cowboy shifts his toothpick to one side of his mouth, and from the darkness beneath his Stetson says in a drawl, "That's 'cause we ain't played Cowboys and Muslims yet, but I do believe it's a-comin'." Author Unknown

Abraham and Ishmael

Abraham and Ishmael: This could be a very touchy subject; however, everything I have taught on so far is sticky and touchy. Why is that? The Bible has it laid out for us and it is very specific. Maybe we need that old Montana cowboy to explain it in terms that city Christian folks could understand.

God told Abraham that he would have a son who would be his heir and who would be the one to carry the seed of the Messiah. However, Abraham listened to the voice of his flesh that came through his wife. Now I have shown that not all wives speak out of their flesh, and I am sure Sarah was a fine wife to Abraham, however, on this one occasion she missed the mark by eons of time, causing all the seeds to follow her words and Abraham's works into one horrible battle after another, between the seed line of his legal son, Isaac, and his bastard son, Ishmael. Today the line of Ishmael will quickly tell you that they are the children of Abraham. What they fail to tell you is that they were disowned by Abraham and Sarah. Ishmael and his mother, Hagar were sent to the wilderness where their lives changed due to the culture of those who befriended them. (Ref. Genesis 16:1-16, 21:14-21, 22:2-8)

Ishmael was by nature and character an angry, bitter man, whose seed produced nothing but hate and revenge, which brings destruction and death. God said He would make of this child a great nation, because he was of the seed of Abraham. However, God also said regarding Ishmael specifically that he would be a wild donkey of a man; his hand would be against everyone and everyone's hand against him, and he would live in hostility toward all his brothers. (Ref. Genesis 16:12)

Understanding that the world we live in is divided into good and bad, positive and negative, keep our focus on the right road. I would like to take a moment to recommend a book by John Bevere, called **"Good or God? Why Good Without God isn't Enough."** He says he was told by God, that it wasn't the evil side of the Tree of the Knowledge of Good and Evil that Eve was drawn to. It was the good side. Please buy the book it will bless you. I believe God told John Bevere, not because I can prove it in chapter and verse, but because many times I have heard the voice of God. Who can argue with what you personally have experienced, or heard? Then I would say, the burden of proof lies in or on the one who needs the proof.

We really should talk here about that serpent who stirred the pot. In the Bible College I attended, the founder who was one of the college teachers frequently called me a pot stirrer. Had I not understood the natural and spiritual use of a pot stirrer I could have been offended, however I was delighted to be viewed as a pot stirrer in his classes. As a pewter manufacturer, I was privileged to be used to stir the pots of metal, which were being melted down at a very high heat. During the product production, the metal would become contaminated with dust, powder, and other impurities that would sink to the bottom of the pot. If the contaminants were left in the metal, the next time the pot was fired, it would cause the product production to be dirty and impure, and since not all the contaminants could be removed during that firing, the pot was allowed to cool down so that most of the contaminants would sink to the bottom and harden until the next time we turned up the heat. Once the metal melted, the pot stirrer would take the ladle and rake the contaminants "draught" off the bottom of the pot, so it would rise to the top being exposed to the eye of the pot stirrer. In hand, the ladle then raked off the contaminants and discarded them in a bucket to be sent to the refiner. Isn't it wonderful that God can use animals of all types to do the work of the pot stirrer, exposing, and cleaning the draught out of His people so what is produced is the cleansed fruit of His Spirit rather than the contaminated fruits of the flesh?

The serpent was one of God's created beasts of the field. When God gave Adam the privilege of naming all the animals, etc., he named them all based on their nature and character, including the serpent. I have often wondered what my instructor saw in my nature and character that gave him the knowing that God had favored me as a pot stirrer. It is evident what Lucifer saw in the serpent.

A little further down in the book we are going to devote a section on how the name gives way to the nature and character of God's creation, because that is vital in understanding our predestined journey. Since Adam knew the nature and the character of the serpent, he knew or should have known the serpent was a beast that could not to be trusted. Early on in my journey I began to pray for the gifts of understanding and knowledge. I did not know enough then to pray for the spirit of discernment, however, I have since sought that gift also. For without them God's people perish. When the earth brought the serpent up out of the soil, it had four legs and was identified in the same order as the cattle. These beasts of the earth were called creeping things that God saw was good. (Ref. Genesis 3:14) God's created beasts were not given a free will; they were to be in subjection to Adam-male and female, who were placed on the earth to rule over them. Note here that animal life has a will. However, it is not a free will. Therefore, when Lucifer (whose nature and character is to kill, steal, and destroy) appeared in the spiritual realm, he did not appear as a visible creature, instead he appeared through the bodily form of the serpent. Remember, Lucifer was cast out of Heaven because he allowed iniquity to possess his immortal being; moreover, he wanted the praise and worship from the souls (Stones of Fire) that lived within the loins of the Father on His holy mountain in a place called Eden.

Lucifer, being in spirit form, needed a body he could control, remembering that creation has a natural side and a spiritual side it was not difficult for Lucifer to obtain authority given to Adam-male and Adam-female by the Father, when He placed the creation in subjection to them. All he had to do was ask his father and it was as we see granted. And since the nature of the serpent, was to deceive and beguile it fit right into Lucifer's plan. I may not be the wisest cookie in the jar, but this I am wise enough to know, "nothing happened in the Word of God by accident." And I am wise enough to believe that since God is the same yesterday, today and forever. He probably did not change the pattern when the man possessed with devils met up with Jesus in the country of the Gergesenes. There the demons could and did request from Jesus to be allowed to leave the natural body and spirit of the possessed man and go into the natural bodies of the swine where they took over the spirit or breath of the swine, at which time the swine gave up their spirits to death. (Ref. Matthew 8:28-34) Therefore it was nothing for the spirit of Lucifer to order the body of the serpent to open his mouth, for it is through the mouth, at birth, that the spirit of life was blown, and then for the spirit of Lucifer to crawl or fly in. Adam-male and Adam-female were well acquainted with the nature of the serpent. Remember Adam named it, "serpent." Now I know you are going to need a book, chapter, and verse for this one. However, I cannot provide you with one. What I can provide you with is theory.

Word of Wisdom -- It is written that it is not what goes into the mouth that defiles the man, it is what comes out of the mouth.

Since Lucifer now has a mouth and a voice, he used the words that would beguile Adam-female later known as Eve. It only took a little white lie to set the course of life on a path that was totally opposite of what the Father had foreordained and planned for humankind. Would that Adam-male and female have used the spirit of discernment! It would be wonderful if we all ask for the spirit of discernment to be the driver in our decision-making progress.

Just a note of clarification, Lucifer, Satan, the devil, or whatever you prefer to call him, has no power or authority over you. He has to have permission from the Father to even bother you and you have to open the door, window, or your mouth and let him in, and you have to open your mouth and let him out. Today, Lucifer is subject to the Godhead, for when Jesus was in the grave, His Spirit was in Heaven with the Father but His Soul was in hell, taking the keys (all power and authority) away from Satan/Lucifer, so even he is not to blame for any of the bad things we say, we do or that happen to us. It is written that what you bind on earth will be bound in heaven, and what you loose on earth will be loosed in heaven. (Ref. Matthew 18:18) Therefore it is a matter of using the authority to bind and loose that sets us free from his grips. Charles Capps has a wonderful little book called, "Speaking the Word." I highly recommend it.

Then Lucifer ordered the serpent to open his mouth, and out came the words that would beguile Adam-female, later known as Eve. It only took a little white lie to set the course of life on a path that was totally opposite of what their Father had foreordained and predestined as His plans for humankind.

Another one of God's perfect plans that, through the mouth of the serpent, has been corrupted is *the principle of reproduction/multiplication.* All of God's created life was to reproduce after (like kind) itself, God never put genetically modified plants and animals, etc., into His original plan of reproduction, and since we know God is the same yesterday, today, and forever, we know God did not change His mind along the way, if He had, He would have told us. (Ref. Hebrews 13:8)
I have to say that I personally believe that all artificial intelligence (AI) is demonic and should not be believed or trusted.

The Antichrist

Once upon a time there was a young man who I believe might have been set up. The word set up means he was predestined to his calling in life, and I am certain that he had to have chosen his calling, because no human being would have chosen his destiny without believing there was a cause greater than that seen, when the man known as Jesus called him to come follow Him.

Predestinate, in the Greek, means to *limit in advance* (figuratively *predetermine*), determine before, ordain, predestinate. A primary preposition; "fore," that is, *in front of, prior* (figuratively *superior*) to. In compounds it retains the same significations: above, ago, before, or ever, to mark out or bound, to appoint, decree, specify, declare, determine.

Remember in Chapter 2 we explained the difference between predestined and foreordained.

It is written, "And we know that all things work together for good to them who love God, to them who are the called according to His purpose. For whom He did foreknow, He also did predestine *to be* conformed to the image of His Son, that He might be the firstborn among many brethren. Moreover, whom He did predestined, them He also called: and whom He called, them He also justified: and whom He justified, them He also glorified." (Ref. Romans 8:28-30)

The man named Judas Iscariot was predestined to obey the call to follow Jesus. Judas was one of the twelve disciples given and received all the gifts of authority to the Kingdom of Heaven by Jesus. Judas was, as I said, predestined by God. No, it is not God's fault, because by Judas's free will of choice he was foreordained and predestined to his destiny. Remember prophecy had to be fulfilled.

He chose before he was formed in his mother's womb, to follow Jesus throughout the three-and-one-half years of his time on earth as one of the twelve disciples of the Messiah. Jesus was predestined to save the world from the predestined hell that awaited all of humankind prior to Jesus' obedient, humble life, surrendered unto the Father on our behalf. And it was Judas's choice to betray the Master, Teacher, and friend, who was the Messiah. Remember we are given a free will; therefore, we have the power of choice right up to our very last breath. Judas walked with Jesus and learned not only in theory but also in experience everything he needed to know about the duties of the Messiah. There was a reason for that; think about it, there is a reason for everything we do just as Jesus did everything, He saw His Father do. Ultimately, we all have a motive, and we do nothing without a motive.

Islam's Belief in Al-Qadr (predestination) says that God knew the fate and destiny of everyone on earth. And one should accept this because it is already written in destiny/fate by God.

Both John Calvin and Martin Luther have revelation truths regarding predestination which are worth reviewing on the Internet if it interests you.

However, in this author's viewpoint, because they do not have all the pieces of the puzzle, they are both dangling at the end of the string. Islam does not believe in Jesus Christ as the Messiah, therefore there is only the bottom for them because there is no string to hang on to.

We believe God has only one road back to Him. He is the beginning and the end, the Alpha and the Omega. We begin with Him and it is His perfect will that we end up back with Him. However, because He is a God who does not want anyone to live in His garden who has to be coerced, manipulated, or forced in any way, He gave all of His created human beings a free will. We were given choices in Eternity Past, He knew us there, and we knew Him. Predestination is a simple way of explaining the journey of the Prodigal Son and his father. (Ref. Luke 15:11-32)

Let me talk here just a moment about motives. The word *motive* in Webster's Dictionary is something that *causes a person to act in a certain way, or to do certain things*. God does not make mistakes. I am telling you this story because it is very disturbing to me when I hear men and women of God, who profess to be Watchmen on the Wall, deliberately, willfully, or out of ignorance, avoid telling the flock of God that the journey they are on is predestined. The church world avoids mentioning why, how, who and what is predestined to destroy them. What is the church world afraid of? Should those who lead the flock not want the flock to be as knowledgeable about the enemy as they are about the Savior? MOTIVE is very important. We protect our children in the natural by warning them about the dangers in life. Should we who are the Watchmen on the Wall not protect the children of God in the same manner?

News flash: we do not understand nor do we have the mind of God. We are to strive daily to think as Jesus thinks so, we can act as He acts, and we are commanded to **_renew_** our minds, which means we did have the knowledge and the understanding of God's mind prior to Lucifer choosing to rebel and defy God's will out of his perverted pride. (Ref. Ephesians 4:23) You see, even pride has a positive side, because it must have come from the mind of God, since there is no other origin that is pure and without perversion. Lucifer has never had the ability to create anything, not even the emotions that center around self. The Father, who is in Heaven, is the only one who is the creator and originator of every thought and emotion, and pride is nothing more than a thought conjured up in the mind. Therefore, we are told to renew our minds, take what we have, strip it of all the dirt, tar, and varnish, get it down to the bare "I am nothing, nobody, I know nothing, I can do nothing" flesh. It is written of Jesus that He was a worm and a no man. (Ref. Psalms 22:6) Therefore, brothers and sisters, humble your pride flesh, and take it down to the worm stage of existence and then begin to apply the truth. I can do all things through Christ who strengthens me. This is **renewing the mind**. (Ref. Philippians 4:13)

Okay, now back to our story. Judas Iscariot was a pawn in the hand of God to bring to pass the death of our Lord and Savior Jesus Christ. I am most sure because I know that Judas was as human as you or me, that he had no clue he was being set up to fulfill the plans and purposes of God, as well as to fulfill his predestined role in God's plans, we know that in Eternity Past Judas was given the choice of following Heavenly Father or Lucifer and he chose Lucifer. God being a merciful God gave Judas a second chance and put him in line to be chosen by Jesus to follow Him. Judas chose at the time to follow Jesus. Because Jesus is no respecter of persons Judas did all the miracles; he was given the ability to heal the sick, cast out demons, and it is written that he even had the ability to raise the dead. Speaking of raising the dead, that is not an ability or a gift given to Lucifer, because only the Creator has the glory anointing to do that, as He is the breath of life. Therefore, feel special -- Jesus gave His disciples, you, and me the ability to raise the dead. Please do not lay hands on me if I am found dead -- I am ready to go be with my Lord.

Judas Iscariot opened the door of his heart to greed for sure. After all, he was the holder of the treasury. Just like Lucifer, Judas took whatever he wanted, even though it did not belong to him and he begrudged the way Jesus gave to others. Moreover, as we know one potato chip is never enough, just as one sin is never enough. We hunger for more, even if more is bad for us and we know it will continue until it destroys us. The order of God was in line with prophecy and it was the right time, so Jesus told His disciples at dinner (communion) one warm spring night that one of those whom He loved and trusted was going to betray Him. (Ref. Luke 22:15-23) Oh, I am sure that all the disciples become concerned and began to check their consciences. "Is it me?" they asked themselves, and since they had been warned not to judge the motives of others, they knew they must only check themselves for the sins that could so easily lead them to fall into the web of deception. Once Jesus set their minds at ease by disclosing the one who had lost his hope, Judas ran from the room and began to plan and plot the course of Jesus' betrayal. (Ref. John 13:10-30)

I remember many times acting out a deed simply because my motives had been exposed. Thinking, they know, so let's get on with the program. Given that our conscience is seared with the hot iron of self-righteous judgment, we have no fear of the LORD, and the stench of sin has become way too familiar when we smell it, we will in word and deed fall into the same shoes as Judas. After Judas allowed Lucifer to possess his body, soul and spirit, and he had done the dastardly deed of leading the enemy to Jesus and identifying him by kissing him on the cheek, Judas, lost all hope in being good enough for the Kingdom in Heaven, so he took his life into his own hands. Remember, even in suicide God has the upper hand. God is the only one who can give the breath of life, and He is the only one who can take it. No, it did not need to end that way. Judas could have humbled himself, repented before God and he would have been forgiven. Judas was sorry, he was sick inside for what he had done, and he gave back the money, but just being sorry is not enough, it is only a good deed. However, we have to acknowledge our sin before God, repent and turn from our evil ways. It is never enough to just say, I am sorry. Lucifer's spirit was within Judas, so that might have been his justification; however, I know by what the Word of God says, that was not an option for Judas and just saying we are sorry is never an option for us. So instead of humbling himself and repenting, he showed himself a coward and went to his death by hanging himself, **a death of disgrace**.

It is clear that when Judas took an offense against the Messiah and all that He stood for, Satan/Lucifer's spirit entered into Judas. It is also written that Satan entered into the serpent who tricked Eve to eat the forbidden fruit from the forbidden tree. Now we see for the second time in all of the scriptures that Satan/Lucifer has taken another one of the Father's created beings captive by entering into his body. It is written then that Judas became the son of perdition. (Ref. Luke 22:3) It is also written that Judas, who had now become (the devil) the antichrist in spirit, went out from them to await his time, as did the antichrist spirits of the others that followed his leading. Just as Judas's father, Lucifer, did in Eternity Past when he was banished from the Holy Mountain of God, one-third of the host of angels followed him.

It is believed by this author, that the other disciple of Jesus the Messiah did not know that the antichrist, the deceiver, Judas was in opposition to the plan and purpose of the Creator and was one of them. Today the church is full of Judas's; they live in our homes, eat at our tables, and pray at our altars. The author of this book as a Christian believer, knows without doubt and is convinced based on the Word of God that just as the glory of God raised Jesus from the dead in His perfect time and order, the glory of God will raise Judas Iscariot, body, soul, and spirit from his eternal home in Hell to rule and reign as the Antichrist for the set time known as the tribulation period on earth. Noting that just as Jesus Christ was not a fleshly mortal body after resurrection; neither will Judas Iscariot be fleshly, even so he will appear to be flesh and will deceive many. Instead of life and light running through his veins, it will be darkness and death. Then it is written that Jesus Christ and His Bride will descend from Heaven and will send the entire satanic head back into hell for one thousand years. This time is called the Millennium (Ref. Revelation 20:1-3) I will not go any further than this in the progression of Eternity Future for the sake of time. We will be praying about a second book, after this book is received and the seeds of desire for more are growing.

Yes, folks, it is written and has been a mystery to so very many Christians. Now search the scriptures, all of you who believe, pastors, and scholars, that you be not deceived.

There is a difference between the anti-christ spirits and the Antichrist. The anti-christ spirits are those who followed Lucifer out of Heaven prior to creation. They are already at work in the world, opposing and resisting all that is of God. Many false christs and prophets are forerunners of the Antichrist, oppressing and bringing havoc to the men and woman of God. At the appointed time, Antichrist will appear upon the earth as a resurrected human being, having great power to work miracles and wonders, speaking blasphemies against God and deceiving many. (Ref. 1John 2:22, 1 John 4:3, 2 John 1:7)

The Antichrist with his monstrous nature will set forth the mystery of iniquity and tyranny for the season, until God brings judgment upon his seat of power and authority. Also, the world and man's works are destined for the judgment of God. God will not be slack concerning His promise of judgment. Although there are scoffers among us, because we are in the last days, this will not prevent God from fulfilling His WORD. *"Because we are in the end of this dispensation, men are lovers of themselves, covetous, boasters, proud, blasphemers, disobedient to parents, unthankful, unholy, without natural affection, trucebreakers, false accusers, incontinent, fierce, despisers of those that are good, traitors, heady, high-minded, lovers of pleasures more that lovers of God."* (Ref. 2 Timothy 3:2, 1 Timothy 1:9)

It behooves us to know the truth, for we are in the days of seducing spirits and doctrines of devils. The Word of God has not left us ignorant concerning the things that are to come, for as children of light, **we are forewarned to be forearmed**.

The seed of the Antichrist has its origin back in the Garden of Eden, where the serpent tempted Adam-female to disobey the command of God.

Here was the entrance of sin into the human race. However, even as God spoke words of judgment, He held forth a hope and the promise of a Redeemer—Jesus Christ.

❁ HIS ORGIN:

First, He (God) spoke of the serpent's seed. ANTI-CHRIST: This is the first mention in the New Testament of him. (Ref. John 6:70, 71) This is the beginning of a perpetual quarrel between the Kingdom of God and the kingdom of the Devil among man; war is proclaimed between the seed of the woman and the seed of the serpent. There is a continual conflict between grace and corruption in the ears of God's people. Satan, the Devil, the Serpent, the Dragon, assaults, buffets, sifts and seeks to devour God's people. The woman's seed, Jesus Christ, was to bruise the head (head, speaking of authority and power) of the serpent, whereas the serpent's seed was to bruise the heel of the seed of the woman. This was fulfilled when Judas Iscariot betrayed Jesus into the hands of the enemy, and when Jesus went to the cross;

He bruised the head of the serpent. Although the Antichrist has not yet been revealed, we see the spirit of Antichrist, the seed of the serpent working in the earth today.

[Note: an apple is the fruit of the apple tree, right? If we cut open the fruit/apple, we will find many seeds. The seed does not look like the fruit, yet it carries its nature and character. The seed is a representation of the fruit, which is a representation of the tree, which is a representation of the roots.] (Ref. Genesis 3:15)

So many words with so many explanations!

Ephesians 1:5 having predestinated us unto the adoption of children by Jesus Christ to Himself, according to the good pleasure of His will.
Ephesians 1:11 In whom also we have obtained an inheritance, being predestinated according to the purpose of Him who worketh all things after the counsel of His own will:

Jesus answered them, have not I chosen you twelve, and one of you is a devil? He spoke of Judas Iscariot *the son* of Simon: for he it was that should betray him, being one of the twelve. (Ref. Luke 22:3)

Judas lived and walked with Jesus and observed Him throughout most of His earthly ministry, yet Judas Iscariot had at times rejected Jesus in his heart and had opened himself to the Devil. Recognizing the Devil's presence, Jesus exposed the betrayal devil that dwelt in His disciple. In due season, the final disloyal act was committed—Judas betrayed his master. Overcome by remorse at his dastardly deed, Judas went out into the night and hung himself.

The body of the Antichrist has its origin in the person of Judas Iscariot. Satan needs a body to work through, as God had a body to work through in the person of His Son, Jesus Christ. The body God prepared within the womb of the Virgin Mary was called Jesus. When God sent the angel Gabriel with a message to Mary, He was fulfilling the Eden prophecy about the coming of the woman's seed. Being overshadowed by the power of the Almighty God, the divine seed of Christ, the Word, entered into that body in its prenatal state. (Ref. Luke 1:31-35)

It is written, behold thou shalt conceive in thy womb, and bring forth a son, and shalt call his name JESUS. He shall be great, and shall be called the Son of the Highest: and the Lord God shall give unto him the throne of his father David: And he shall reign over the house of Jacob forever; and of his kingdom there shall be no end. Then said Mary unto the angel, how shall this be, seeing I know not a man? And the angel answered and said unto her, The Holy Ghost shall come upon thee, and the power of the Highest shall overshadow thee: therefore, that holy thing which shall be born of thee shall be called the Son of God. (Ref. Matthew 1:18)

It is written -- I have come in My Father's name and you do not receive Me, if another comes in his own name, him you will receive. (Ref. John 5:40-47)

⚙ BODY OF SATAN:

Even so, since Satan was in spirit form, he needed a body to enter into, the body of Judas Iscariot. Before Judas betrayed Jesus, Satan, Lucifer, or the Devil had access to Judas's body because of the condition of his soul (mind, will, and emotions) and spirit. Since we know Satan can only imitate the action of the Godhead, it is also possible that Satan could have sought out a woman with child in one way or another and corrupted that seed, for Judas was also the fulfillment of the Genesis prophecy in that he was the seed of the serpent. I have no specific scripture to substantiate this belief; I do believe that the principle shown regarding the immaculate conception of our Savior stands as valid in principle for this teaching. Remember, Satan has no new revelations or abilities, he cannot create, all he can do is imitate the LORD, who is the Originator.

Just a thought for you biblical scholars who might want to consider Bible principles. *Bible Principles are Bible facts.* These *Principles are Bible Truths* that have a common thread running from Genesis through Revelation, many of which fall under the cover of God's hidden mysteries.

We know that from the account in the book of Jeramiah, "before I (God) formed you in the belly I knew you; and before you came forth out of the womb, I sanctified you, *and* I ordained you a prophet unto the nations." (Ref. Jeremiah 1:4, 5)

Therefore, God knew Judas and his destiny, God knew Judas before he was formed in his mother's womb and God knew he was to fulfill the prophecy regarding the betrayal of Jesus, and the man of sin we know as the Antichrist.

We have no other record of Satan himself in spirit form entering into any other human other than Judas Iscariot. Jesus established this fact when He recognized that one of the twelve disciples was a devil; that is, he was not possessed by a devil, but he was a devil. (Ref. John 6:70, 71) In the Greek this word devil is "diabolos," which means in English "adversary, usually translated Satan." On this occasion, Peter had undertaken to speak and declare the faithfulness of the disciples unto their Master (Jesus Christ), but Jesus corrects him by revealing that Judas not only possessed by a devil, but he was a devil, or the seed of the serpent. Again, we find this statement concerning Judas, "Then entered Satan into Judas surnamed Iscariot, being of the number of the twelve." Judas Iscariot partook of the feast of the Passover with Jesus and the disciples, even dipping his hand into the dish, symbolizing his loyalty and unity with Jesus. He had even permitted the Lord to bow in humility before him to wash his feet. After receiving the sop (bread and wine) from the hand of Jesus, Satan entered into him to possess him with a prevailing prejudice against Christ and His doctrine and to incite him to the covetous desire of the wages of unrighteousness. (Ref. John 13:10-30) **Judas now declared himself openly to be a devil, the son of perdition.** Thus, Judas' body became the property of Satan, he became Satan's body. Jesus turned Judas over to Satan to do and to be what he chose; (Ref. Luke 22:21-24) likewise, when Judas is resurrected and becomes Antichrist, he will give himself completely to the control of Satan, Devil, Serpent, and Dragon. This is where we see the manifestation of the Serpent's seed, or Satan's body.

The man of sin denotes flagrant wickedness. Not only is he addicted to the practice of wickedness, but he also promotes and commends sin and wickedness in others. The only person called the son of perdition in

Scripture is Judas. Jesus prayed to His Father, "While I was with them in the world, I kept them in thy name: those that thou gavest me I have kept, and none of them is lost but the son of perdition; that the scripture might be fulfilled" (Ref. John 17:12.) Since the Word of God declares that the Antichrist is the son of perdition and that the one named Judas Iscariot is the son of perdition, it is evident that the Antichrist is Judas resurrected from the dead. Now once again, I have no specific scripture that names Judas as "the Antichrist." However, we find this in principle form and believe that Judas will be or maybe has been raised from the dead in seed form from the grave. That principle is found in (Ref. Genesis 4:9) -- and the LORD said unto Cain, where is Abel thy brother? And he said I know not: *Am* I my brother's keeper? And he said, what hast thou done? **The voice of your brother's blood cried unto me from the ground.**

Later on, we see that Adam knew (had sexual intercourse) with his wife Eve again; and she bore a son, and called his name Seth: For God, said she, **hath appointed me another <u>seed</u> instead of Abel,** whom Cain slew. (Eve did not refer to her son Seth as a son, instead she referred to him as a seed, which she appointed or gave up unto God.) (Ref. Genesis 4:25)

Seed here in Hebrew is *zera figuratively fruit, plant, sowing time, posterity*: -carnally, child, fruitful, seed, (-time), sowing-time.

Cain must have known in his subconscious mind or was totally under the influence of Satan that Abel carried the seed of Jesus Christ through his bloodline. That was why he killed him. Or is that just too farfetched to believe. And what about Esau, he pushed his way ahead of his brother Jacob in the womb because he must have known that there was a promise awaiting the one who received Isaiah's blessing, (remember, MOTIVE played a big role in the outcome). Yet we say how could they have known; they were not yet born. (Satan tried to destroy the seed of Jesus from Genesis; he is still at it today, which is another reason Christians should seek the spirit of discernment.) However, God preserved that bloodline seed by resurrecting it and implanting it in Seth. With God all things are possible. This is the first resurrection miracle -- of the seed of Christ Jesus. The second resurrection was His body and the Resurrected Blood.

Perdition means destruction, depth going to his own place, perdition, the bottom of it. Perdition is used in connection with the bottomless pit.

The Word of God declares that Judas went to his own place in natural death, that he took part in the ministry and apostleship, from which he by transgression fell, and that he will go back to his own place in spiritual death. Thus, his place has been declared to be the place of perdition in the bottomless pit. (Ref. Acts 1:25)

During the tribulation, the Antichrist, as the son of perdition, devotes himself to the total destruction of many people (spirit, soul, and body) before he returns to perdition. Judas, the Antichrist, came from perdition and he will return to perdition (HELL). (Ref. 2 Thessalonians 2:1-17)
The Antichrist is called the wicked one. The name wicked means lawless one. A lawless person is one who refuses to come under subjection to God's laws. With his diabolic power, the Antichrist, the lawless one, opposes the divine dominion and power of our Lord Jesus Christ. He actually thinks in his deceitful mind that he has power to contradict and conquer the very Throne of God. The Antichrist is also called the beast. (Ref. Revelation 17:11-18) (Ref. 2 Thessalonians 2:8)

It is written that they worshipped the dragon which gave power unto the beast: and they worshipped the beast, saying, who is like unto the beast? (Ref. Revelation 13:4) Remember when Jesus was led into the wilderness he was attack by the beasts.

The name beast signifies the brutality, filthiness, and irrationality of the nature of Antichrist. It also tells us how contrary the Antichrist will be to the nature and dignity of man. These, then, are the names that describe the Antichrist: man of sin, son of perdition, the wicked one, and the beast. He is a man with a sinful, destructive, wicked, beastly nature.

It is written that when they saw the beast that was, and is not; and shall ascend out of the bottomless pit, and go into perdition: that they whose names were not written in the book of life from the foundation of the world, that dwell on the earth shall wonder, when they **behold the beast that was, and is not, and yet is**. And the beast that was, and is not, even he is the eighth, is of the seven, and goes into perdition (the bottomless pit). (Ref. Revelation 17:8-11) (Ref. Revelation 11:3-7)

Now that we have answered the questions of the Antichrist, and where he came from, I would like to talk a moment about where he is going to set up his kingdom. Patrick and I spent our honeymoon in the country of Israel. Twenty-eight wonderful days, and in all of our travels we both agree Israel was the most awe-inspiring.

⚙ MYSTERY, BABYLON

And upon her forehead was a name written, MYSTERY BABYLON THE GREAT, THE MOTHER OF HARLOTS AND ABOMINATIONS OF THE EARTH. (**This is speaking of Old Jerusalem**) And I saw the woman drunken with the blood of the saints, and with the blood of the martyrs of Jesus: and when I saw her, I wondered with great admiration. "And the angel said unto me, wherefore didst thou marvel? I will tell thee the mystery of the woman, and of the beast that carrieth her, which hath the seven heads and ten horns." Old Jerusalem or Mystery Babylon will ride upon the back of the Antichrist, she will reign over all the kings of the earth, and because she was the one who crucified Jesus Christ, the true Messiah she will be judged with the hell fire (hot and cold) icy cold breath of the wrath of God's vengence. (Ref. Revelation 17:5-7)

And cried when they saw the smoke of her burning, saying, what city is like unto this great city! And they cast dust on their heads, and cried, weeping and wailing, saying, alas, alas, that great city, wherein were made rich all that had ships in the sea by reason of her costliness! for in one hour is she made desolate. Rejoice over her, thou heaven, and ye holy apostles and prophets for God hath avenged you on her. And a mighty angel took up a stone like a great millstone, and cast it into the sea, saying, thus with violence shall that great city Babylon be thrown down, and shall be found no more at all. And the voice of harpers, and musicians, and of pipers, and trumpeters, shall be heard no more at all in thee; and no craftsman, of whatsoever craft he be, shall be found any more in thee; and the sound of a millstone shall be heard no more at all in thee; And the light of a candle shall shine no more at all in thee; and the voice of the bridegroom and of the bride shall be heard no more at all in thee: for thy merchants were the great men of the earth; for by thy sorceries were all nations deceived.

And in her was found the blood of prophets, and of saints, and of all that were slain upon the earth. (Ref. Revelation 18:18-24) Even the blood of her Messiah, Jesus the Christ was splattered on her bricks, and the ground she sets upon soaked it up.

Many scholars believe Mystery Babylon to be Rome and the Pope to be the Antichrist. However, Rome was not the city of sin that God referred to as His wife, Rome is not where Jesus was crucified, and Rome was not the city that Jesus wept over. The author of this book does believe the Pope of today could well be one of the false prophets. He does not have the credentials, the power, or the authority of the Antichrist. Just as Jesus the Son of God, called Judas as a full grown man to come out from amongst the others who were Jews, to come follow Him, the author, believes the Lord will call Judas who has been prepared out from amongst the others who have been called and possibly chosen, He will establish him in his position, and it is our prayer that the called and chosen of our Lord Jesus Christ will be wiser and awake watching for their Lord and Savior and will know by the spirit of discernment who he is. NO SURPRISES

Jesus tells John, "Why do you marvel, why are you surprised at what you are seeing now when you have seen it all along?" Those who cultured and sat upon the throne in old Jerusalem are the ones who are wicked and corrupt. The entire Torah, the Scrolls which are the writings of Moses and the Prophets resided behind the walls of the city and yet they rejected and crucified Jesus, the Son of God, their Messiah, and many Jews reject Him today as their Messiah.

The Antichrist who will sit on the seat of the true Messiah is a counterfeit; he will usurp the place of Jesus Christ, our Heavenly Bridegroom, just as Jerusalem has usurped the place of the true *bride*. God the Father spoke of Old Jerusalem as His wife; however, she became a harlot, and her wickedness surpassed that of Jezebel. The angel, still pulling back the veil of darkness from John's understanding, concluded the matter with words in

Revelation: "And the beast that was, and is not, even he is the eighth, and is of the seven, and goeth into perdition."

Who opposed and exalted himself above all that is called God, or that is worshipped; so that he as God sat in the temple of God, shewing himself that he is God? Remember you not, that, when I was yet with you, I told you these things.

Word of Wisdom -- He that hath an ear, let him hear what the Spirit saith unto the churches; To him that overcomes will I given to eat of the tree of life, which is in the midst of the paradise of God.

Prophetic fulfillment of the Apostle Paul's words to the Thessalonians: In the past twenty years there has been a great falling away, churches closing their doors, pastors quitting the ministry. Now do you think that they might have missed their calling and were never called to the ministry of pastoring to begin with? I believe that, because what God begins God completes and it is not about the situations going on in the world. The Apostle Paul tells us that he faced more obstacles than any other and God never gave up on him. He said at the end of his life that he finished the race well. That could be my perception. However, how do you quit something that you are given without your permission? Oh wow, maybe you pastors would rather say you never chose the fivefold ministry giftings. Well, if you didn't choose them or it, who did? Moreover, if you are unable to finish well, whose fault, is it? Oh, and what about those of us who have had the seed of life placed in our womb? Is this not the very same principle? Life is life, be it the seed of the spirit or the seed of the flesh. Let no man deceive you by any means.

It is written by the Apostle Paul, now we beseech you, brethren, by the coming of our Lord Jesus Christ, and by our gathering together unto Him, that ye be not soon shaken in mind, or be troubled, neither by spirit, nor by word, nor by letter as from us, as that the day of Christ is at hand. Let no man deceive you by any means: *for that day shall not come*, except there come a falling away first, **and that man of sin be revealed, the son of perdition.** (Ref. 2 Thessalonians 2:3)

I was also taught in the church that the falling way was going to happen after the great revival of the Church. I have also listened to prophetic messages by many great men of God, like David Wilkerson, Smith Wigglesworth and others who would contradict the timing of this great revival. Today after an extensive study through the book of Revelation, I am convinced the great revival will not come to the world until after the rapture of the overcomers. Most of the Church believes the rapture will include the entire body of believers, however the book of Revelation confirms there will be more than one rapture. There will be those who are believers, men and woman who sit in the church Saturday or Sunday, whatever day you wish to go to the house of the believers to worship God, who are not what the Word of God calls overcomers and they will be left behind. Yes, they very well may have accepted Jesus Christ as their Savior, but based on the lifestyle they choose to live every day, including Sunday, they may not be overcoming anything.

Therefore, how can they be called overcomers? Remember the *Left Behind* series; were they truth or fiction? Those who are left behind are men, women, and children all over the world and they will know what has happened, they will know because the Spirit of God that is within them will bear witness of the truth that God was real, is real, and will always be real, and the Word of God did not lie to them or deceive them. Man may have lied, and man may have deceived, but God never lied or deceived man. He has never kept any secret from man; that is, the man who believes and receives the truth.

◎ BOTTOMLESS PIT – Sea

The resurrected body of the Antichrist has its origin from the bottomless pit or the sea.

In the book of Revelation, we read that God will give power unto His two witnesses, and they shall prophesy a thousand two hundred and threescore days, clothed in sackcloth. These are the two olive trees, and the two candlesticks standing before the God of the earth. And if any man will hurt them, fire will proceed out of their mouth, and will devour their enemies: and if any man will hurt them, he must in this manner be killed. (Ref. Revelation 11:3) (EYE FOR AND EYE) no lengthy trial or investigation, simple huh? These two witnesses will have power to shut heaven that it rains not in the days of their prophecy: and have power over waters to turn them to blood, and to smite the earth with all plagues, as often as they will. And when they shall have finished their testimony, **the beast that ascended out of the bottomless pit** shall make war against them, and shall overcome them, and kill them. Probably like ISIS, by cutting off their heads.

In the book of Revelation, we see there will be many *after* the resurrection of the bridal party (church) at the first coming of Jesus Christ who will be saved. They are also known as the overcomers (Ref. Revelations 6:9-11), having overcome the beast, his image, his mark and his number.

Nature and Character

Name in Hebrew gives us the meaning of one's nature and character, be it human, animal, or plant.

The first order of business for God and Adam to do was to name all the animals and plants. The name is reflective of its nature and character. In the beginning of time the animals, be they the fowl of the air, fish of the sea or the beasts of the fields had a nature, when God made them or had them come up out of the earth that He had put into order.

And out of the ground the LORD God formed every beast of the field, and every fowl of the air; and brought them unto Adam to see what he would call them: and whatsoever Adam called every living creature, that was the name thereof. (Ref. Genesis 2:19)

The word nature is derived from origin. The source of all animals and plants originated in the mind of God. They were birthed out of the earth, and in the end of their lifespan they will return to the earth. Plants differ from animal, as they have to stay attached to the source (earth) to live. Animals do have a soul [mind, will, and emotions] and that soul is their attachment, and they will return to their source, the mind of the Creator. Likewise, man originated in the mind of God, however man did not come up out of the earth, he was formed from the ash and dust that lay on the surface or the top layer of the earth. His body will return to the earth; however, his spirit and soul is designed to stay attached to the Creator, or source of his origin. We have a natural and spiritual umbilical cord. At the natural birth of a child, the cord that is the bloodline to the biological mother is cut. The spiritual umbilical cord is attached to their father (the father of the world). Christians have been told and it is written that we are to be in the world but not of it. We have shown the umbilical cord must be cut, freeing us from the world at the time of our spiritual birth; It is then that there is the cord attachment that binds, which is attached to the heart of the Father God, our Originator, attached to the heart of the man, woman or child who receives His Son as their Savior and Lord. At that time a blood transfusion it supernaturally done. (Ref. James 4:4) "Ye adulterers and adulteresses, know ye not that the friendship of the world is enmity with God? Whosoever therefore will be a friend of the world is the enemy of God."

The Jews absolutely refuse to eat the blood of animals (beasts) because it carries not only the DNA but also the seed line of that animal, and they did not want to become as it was in the natural form. Thinking that the natural form and attributes of a pig, cow, sheep, or goat is transferable to humans. In the world of demonic practices, the drinking of animal and human blood is commonly done to gain their strength and power, nature and character. Have you not heard or said, "You act just like a pig"?

Definition of nature and character is the particular combination of qualities belonging to a person, animal, thing, or class by birth, origin, or constitution, native or inherent character such as one's characteristic, disposition, temperament, biological functions or urges.

Nature and character are the laws or principles that guide the universe or an individual (***Webster's College Dictionary***). Often times, God personifies our attitudes and disposition of our carnal and fleshly natures in the forms of the animals that God created through visions or dreams in our night season.

For a few definitions of individuals' names with the correlation of nature listed, see the study guide in the back of the book.

The Awakening

Word of Wisdom -- "To silence a preacher from preaching judgment is like being awoke from sleep by a fire alarm, and just silencing the alarm, and going back to sleep." Author Unknown

One morning not long ago, Patrick told me a man whom he had become dear friends with had passed away and he wanted to go to his wake. *Oh great, now I have another question*, I thought. Therefore, I asked him, "What do mean, you want to go to his wake?" He smiled at me with his understanding eyes, "You mean you do not even know what a wake is?" "Yes, I mean I do not know what a wake is!" Again, he smiled and said, very parent-like, "It is a memorial for a dead person. You remember my dad did not want a wake."

So, is it an awakening, yes, the person is dead, but how do you wake up the dead? Great, we are going to learn how to operate in a well overdue gift that Jesus did frequently throughout His ministry. We are going to get to raise a dead man.

Smith Wigglesworth (1859-1947), who is known as the apostle of faith, moved in true healings and miracles and even raised people from the dead, according to many reports. Shortly before he passed into glory, he prophesied:

"During the next few decades there will be two distinct moves of the Holy Ghost across the church in Great Britain, (North American continents). The first move will affect every church that is open to receive it; and it will be characterized by the restoration of the baptism and gifts of the Holy Ghost.

"The second move of the Holy Ghost will result in people leaving historic churches and planting new churches. In the duration of each of these moves, the people who are involved will say, `This is a great revival.´ But the Lord says, `No, neither of these are the great revival but both are steps towards it.´

"When the new church phase is on the wane, there will be evidence in the churches of something that has not been seen before: a coming together of those with an emphasis on the Word and those with an emphasis on the Spirit.

"When the Word and the Spirit come together, there will be the biggest move of the Holy Ghost that the nations, and indeed, the world have ever seen. It will mark the beginning of a revival that will eclipse anything that has been witnessed within these shores, even the Wesleyan and Welsh revivals of former years."

Prophets and apostles of old have been our watchmen on the wall, yet we choose to ignore their words of wisdom and knowledge given them by the Holy Ghost. Smith Wigglesworth, C. S. Lewis, Watchman Nee, David Wilkerson, and countless others have been our eyes, ears, noses, mouths, and hands, yet they have been stored on the shelves, as are the principles left behind in the pages of the Old and New Testaments.

David Wilkerson is noted for telling us, "If we do not see what is coming in the future, it is because of sensuality or apathy. If you are a pastor, teacher, evangelist, prophet, or apostle and refuse to sound the alarm you are not worthy of your calling." We as the men and women of the Gospel of Christ should know the day and hour is nearby. The five virgins may have had oil in their lamps; however, they were found in a state of sleep, therefore they were only one step ahead of the five who had procrastinated, and their lamps were dry. Their spiritual sensor was blind or had been turned off. The word slumber indicates they were slothful. (Ref. Proverbs 6:9-11) They were unable to distinguish between good and evil. They were in a state of deception due to all the counterfeit teaching that had been pumped into them and they did not know the truth. They were afraid to bark against evildoers, which were sent by Satan to kill, steal, and destroy their chances to be in the *bride*. I know most pastors teach that the five with the oil are at the finish line, however that is where the *bride* of Christ has positioned herself to be faithful, for the Word of God tells us that the *bride* of Christ is awake, watching, and waiting for her Bridegroom, she is not asleep, she is pressing toward the mark of her highest calling, she stays at the finish line, her wick is trimmed, her lamp lit and she is on her knees in humility and surrender before Her LORD of LORDs. The five virgins whose lamps were full of oil heard the call of the *bride* and awoke quickly, making themselves ready for the Bridegroom's arrival. These are those that are referred to as the five wise virgins. Yet they were not found in obedience, their lamps were not lit and their wicks were not trimmed, for the word tells us in verse 13 to watch for we do not know the day or the hour when our Bridegroom will come. It warns us against slumbering (Ref. Matthew 25:1-13). The Apostle Paul said as he neared the finish line that he had run the course and finished well. Here we see all the virgins were asleep when the bridegroom neared. The signs of the times are all around us. The earth and God's natural creation are crying for a revival that will shake the entire world. Instead of God's people humbling themselves in complete unity to His greatness and glory and loving our neighbors as ourselves, we find the earth shaking and the rocks crying out. May God help us to stand as watchman on the wall, for if we do not scream at the top of our voice that He is the LORD and King and give Him all praise, honor, and glory, we will have failed Him, and if we do not teach the truth, we will allow the young and old believers to drift into sin and apathy and the blood of the souls of man will be on our hands.

Word of Wisdom -- set your heart now; do not wait for difficult or perilous times to come upon you.

We will not address the tribulation period, which is after the rapture of the overcoming saints, except to say there will be many people left behind who know about Jesus. They know who He is, and when the rapture takes place, they will be struck with fear, and many at that time will receive the Lord Jesus Christ as their Savior and Lord then they will refuse the mark of the beast and be slain. (Ref. Revelation 6:9-11) were the souls of those who had been slain for the Word of God and for the testimony which they held.

CHAPTER 9

15. The Bridal Party
Created by Him and for Him

Word of Wisdom – "Write, blessed are those who have been called to the marriage supper of the Lamb. And He said to me, these are the true sayings of God. He had a name written, one that no one knew except Himself. And He had been clothed in a garment dipped in blood, and His name is called The Word of God. I am your fellow servant, and of your brothers who have the testimony of Jesus. Worship God, for the testimony of Jesus is the spirit of prophecy." (Revelation 19: 9, 10, 12, 13,)

Jesus promised each of the seven churches in the book of Revelation that they would receive a special reward *if* they were overcomers. Each of the seven churches are a picture of the spiritual stature of the Lord Jesus Christ. Therefore, *if* they overcame the obstacles that hindered them, cleaned up their act, and repented, they would lay hold of His resurrection life. Christ's *bride*, will have overcome their moral appetite of the flesh, the pride of life, surrendered her will, plans and purposes for His, and will be presented at the wedding supper of the Lamb as a victorious overcomer. (Ref. Revelation 2, 3, 19:7-9) The scriptures tell us that there will be many who say, "Lord, Lord," when they are brought before the Lord, and it is a sad thought, however, the truth is, He will tell them that He never knew them and to depart from Him, (Ref. Luke 13:25-27 NKJV) then He will order His servants to cast those into the lake of fire. These are those who have played church, pretended to be Christians, and in their perception believed that because the Father sent His Only Begotten Son into the world because He loved them, they had the free pass; the override, the rules pass, so with pride and arrogance, they walked right up to the Heavenly Father and His Only Begotten Son who did die for them, and addressed Him as Lord, not LORD, big difference and a very costly, unforgiven mistake. Then there are those who will be invited to the marriage supper of the Lamb and there will be many who have their garments of salvation "white robes and white raiment" on, and yes, these are those who are guests at the wedding. (Ref. Revelation 3:5, 4:4) However, they will not rule and reign with Jesus Christ as His *bride* during the Millennium [one thousand years] in the New Jerusalem. Remember, there is room for all. There is a new earth and many heavens. I would love to teach on this and may do so if I ever am prompted by God to write another book.

There is a King in Heaven who has a son who is going to get married. The King sent his servants out to invite all the friends of the bridegroom, and to let them know the date and time so that they could prepare themselves. He told them that when they came, he had prepared a great feast of his own personal meats, his very best, most tender lamb, and finest oxen were being killed just for their pleasure. So come to the marriage and enjoy. However, the groom's friends made light of the invitation, they were too busy, one to his farm, another to his business. Moreover, the friends treated the servant of the king very poorly. Therefore, when the servant returned to report the state of affairs of the groom's friends and how poorly they were treating them, the king became very angry and he sent his armies to destroy those who had claimed to be friends, when in fact, they were not friends at all; therefore, the king even had their city burned. Then he told his servant that the wedding was ready but those who had claimed to be the groom's friends were not worthy, so they should go out to the humble, the poor, the meek, and the lowly and ask them to come in to share in the food and party for his son. Soon the hall was filled with guests, however when the king came in to see the guests, he saw there was a man who did not have on a wedding garment. When the King confronted the man, he acted surprised. After all, it had been the custom of the church to dress any old way and that was good enough for them, why was it not good enough for the king? When the King saw the arrogance of the man who was not dressed in his wedding garments, he told the servant to bind him hand and foot and to take him out into the darkness, and there he would go into eternal hell. (Ref. Matthew 22:2-14) Yes, many were called but few were chosen.

I know the majority of the Christian church-going believers have been taught that the church is the *bride*; however, the Word tells us each individual who receives Jesus Christ as their Lord and Savior are the body and the body is the church. The Word never tells us that the Lord Jesus Christ is coming back for a building or that we are to have a building, made with man's hands. That was acceptable in the Old Testament dispensation; however, Jesus Christ does not dwell in a building. The Word tells us He dwells within the body of man. So where do you think the *bride* came from? It is a subject not taught in truth by the Church. The *bride* comes from among the believers. We must understand that we have the opportunity here on this earth to grow up into a fully matured stature, as did Jesus Christ, so that we can not only attend the wedding of the bridegroom and the *bride*, we can be the *bride*. (Ref. John 3:29) Being the *bride* is enough to motivate me to choose to die daily to my old soulish nature and character, so that when the last amen is said, I will be one who will see His face; and His name will be written on my forehead.

16. Eternity Future

His Perfect Will and His Plan for all of humankind

He that goeth forth and weepeth, bearing precious seed, shall doubtless come again with rejoicing, bringing his sheaves *with him*. (Ref. Psalms 126:6)

My quest for truth has taken me in many directions, as have so many who have begun new movements with strange doctrines. Note here I said I seek only the truth, not some fad or strange doctrine. Therefore, when I got far enough down the path the Lord would show me, based on the witness of the Holy Ghost and the Spirit of Jesus Christ within me, if I was falling into deception. Then I had to choose to either humble myself and turn back to the beginning, where hunger began and I got off on the wrong path, or I had to stick my head in the sand of pride and press deeper into darkness. Sadly, many Christians have their heads in the sand and their butts in the air and they do not know the difference between truth and deception. Friends, we can all get off into a doctrine that leads to death and destruction, or a doctrine with no earthly or eternal means, and we can all humble ourselves, get off the fence of indecisiveness, repent, turn from our earthly mindset, and do whatever it takes to walk in peace under God's grace.

The mindset that all is good sounds so very good. However, it reminds me of a pile of leaves that got there by accident. This is the fall season as I write this book, and the leaves are falling all around us. I am continually sweeping and raking, and then the wind comes up from the north or south or east or west, picks up the leaves, and swirls them up and down, to and fro, round, and round. If I close my eyes, I can picture the cross with a complete ring around it. We are born, we die, and then what? I do not believe the leaves got into the pile by grace, I do not believe they arrived there by accident. I know that all the scriptures, from the very first word in Genesis to the very last word in Revelation, are given by the inspiration of God for me so that I will grow and mature and leave a legacy of love, light, faith, hope and truth. Therefore, to get there I ask my Lord, "What is your perfect will and plan for all humankind?" Remembering that I do not believe anything is by accident; I looked down at that pile of leaves and knew that any man or woman who is double-minded will end up going in a million directions and receive nothing.

Jesus left the disciples with His bucket list, many of which are not being taught in our local churches by the new modern grace-based pastors, because teaching the Word Jesus taught the multitude when He told them they must hate (let go of) all those individuals and things, including themselves, was not the word that would draw the crowd or bring in the money for projects they had in their bucket lists. Many of the pastors of the 20th and 21st centuries believe that the Word of God has been fulfilled, by Christ, and does not apply to the Christians in our day and time. So many of the old doctrines and principles have been forgotten and replaced by new doctrines, so what we are ending up with is a bucket load of man's ethnic and religious traditions and rituals that have gotten mixed up with the truth [thus saith the LORD]. In the end, what God laid out for us is so convoluted that it is impossible to separate the truth from the lies, making the simplistic truth of the matter very complicated.

It Could Only Exist in the Imagination

Because I am from the baby boomer generation, I did not grow up with television or Internet, and getting to go to the movie house was maybe done once a year. It cost us five cents of our allowance money we had earned from doing chores around the farm. Life in those days was so very different, and yet I would go back in time anytime. When I began the process of movie going in the 1980s, I would say, "What imagination." I had not yet learned that the imagination comes from the realm of the soul, and I had not yet found where the soul came from or had been, so the hunt was on. (Ref. Romans 1:16-32)

I still have many questions, yet I see how God has answered so many of them. Today as I look into my basket of questions, I find there are so many jewels of understanding and knowledge that were not there in the beginning of my journey of asking and seeking for God's mysteries -- which God has answered. Most are so simple, so transparent, and with each one answered that one explains many unanswered questions, if we will just think with a godly mindset.

Word of Wisdom -- *Possessing an open mystery* box most often means, we have gotten out of the box, peeled away the ceiling, expanded the walls, then recognized we had lived in the mystery all along.

This morning, I had a call from an old and treasured friend. Our conversation went quickly to the things of God, given that is one of the things we have in common. She began telling me about her adventures into the Sudan in Africa, and how the people there were having to beg for food, yet they were working with their hands, doing a job that was laborious and very time-consuming. It was intriguing to hear that these girls were working without the expectation of being paid for their labors. It seemed to me that the girls were afraid or intimidated to request monetary payment from the lady who brought the work for them to finish without a wage. I asked her if she took the same work to girls who were having to beg for food and expected them to work without some sort of reimbursement, be it money or food, did she think the girls would accept that? She said no because she is a white lady and viewed in the eyes of the Africans as a person with money. Therefore, because the lady who brought the work for the girls was black that changed the mindset and expectations of what was right and what was wrong. I shared with my friend that maybe her job there was to help them in the area of their imagination. The mindset is a big factor in our belief system. She told me that the congregational church she is attending has a new pastor, and last Sunday his message had transformed her mindset. He taught on circumstances having a name. "Really?" I said, as she told me I should know that cancer is a circumstance and that is its name. The revelation she received was that she has to change the name of the circumstance. Great thought, if I can change the way I perceive a circumstance, or situation, by changing its name, then the nature and character of the circumstance will have to be different.

Now is this truth or fiction, reality or pretend? So, I told my friend I was writing a book and I had just looked up the word "nature," and I asked to read the meaning to her. It was one short paragraph from the *Webster's Dictionary*. At the time I did not agree with the phrase she had given me, "Circumstances have a name," nor was I denying it had merit and could be truth. The definition of nature showed that cancer has an origin. To change that circumstance of this name, I have to find its origin. To me, this is as simple as study and prayer. Once I find the answer, I want to make sure it is by revelation knowledge and understanding and not by human (medical) reasoning. Today I understand that to change the circumstance I have to call all circumstances be they sickness, or infirmities after its root name, "EVIL." If I get a pimple I refer to it as evil, I do not have to wait for Cancer to test my faith.

As we have worked through our many questions from Genesis thorough Revelation, we have found that everything originates in God. He is the beginning and there was nothing before Him. We did not begin in a pond of muck as a tadpole, we did not evolve from a cell in the muck to a furry monkey or ape. These too are circumstances with names. I am not the man who had the mindset of evolution, so I really cannot say where he got his revelations; however, I know that they could not have been from God, who is the Origin of creation. Therefore, there are many circumstances whose name and origin are not evil. That takes me back to Eternity Past and choices. Most all our situations, and circumstances can be answered when we understand where they began.

Believing the Word of God in all truth is not easy when Lucifer has perverted our imagination. After all, his mindset is based on death and darkness, his purpose is to kill, steal, and destroy all truth. As said before, truth and perception are two different matters, yet both can be within the same mindset. Truth is from the spirit and perception is from the soul.

Changing our mindset requires changing who is in control of our imagination. Releasing the control lever and letting the one who is the Originator take back the lever will change the circumstance, and in turn change the name of that circumstance or situation, be it in the natural or spiritual realm. Words are cheap until they have substance. Like I am frequently reminded, "Actions speak louder than words." We will be held accountable for them all.

Moving forward: we are questioning how the television movie producer or screenwriters could possibly come up with such, pardon me, trash. How could they imagine the worlds beyond, and the worlds before? I have a difficult time imagining the world in reality today. As I would go on long solitary bike rides in the countryside, I would talk to God and in turn He would talk to me. One day, God told me who I was before I came to this earth and I was put into the shell of a body that was being formed in my mother's womb. Oh yes, I was surprised, because I was saved or born again or accepted Christ as my Savior in the summer of 1971, to be exact July 1971, in Interlaken, Switzerland. Fast forward to 1995. I had been to many Bible preaching-teaching churches, and listened to many men and woman of God who could give me addresses, dates and times in the Bible, yet had never told me that I existed before my mother's egg and father's sperm met head on, and you may very well be hearing or reading this for the very first time in your life also. So, do not fall into that oh too-well-known category called a "cynic or skeptic." You are reading this book because it is time you knew whose fault it is that you live in Africa, you are of the black race of people, you have a house made of mud, and you have no money, or you are of the red race and are not only a chosen people you are a cursed people, and you are always at war with each other and others, or you are of the yellow race and your eyes are slanted for you are people of light, you have great intelligence and find it easy to invent, and you are small and live in very crowded conditions, or you are white and your color is deceptive because it is very diversified, not because you are from America but because there is no such race as pure white. Many from the so-called white race from the nations of the European, Russian, English, Swedish, from the Netherlands, Spain, or the other nations that produce people with light colored skin humans. You are one that is hungry for knowledge and understanding, you are a people that are giving and generous sometimes to a fault, you are on the end of the string and seem to always have your nose in others business, it is called the god syndrome. Let me make it a little clearer, maybe you are Chinese or an Indian from India, or an Indian from America, or the white race from all over the world, an African, a dark skinned American, or Hispanic from the South American parts of the world. Or maybe you are a woman whose father sexually abused you from the time you were five or ten and he ruined your life forever. Or maybe you live in Denver or Chicago and you were abandoned when you were two or three years old and shipped from foster home to foster home. Or just maybe you are of the seed of Abraham and know you are a Jew. What I am saying is, it does not matter who you are, where you are from, the color of your skin, or what has happened to you, the story remains the same. You see God is not partial to anyone anywhere. His story never changes. Each one of His creations has their own fingerprint, identity, and story, each fit who and what we are. However, we were all Stones of Fire, equally formed and of equal origin before creation, before the first tower. Our entire future changed at the tower of Babel. Get the picture? Let me lighten this up just a little. A couple of years ago the Lord took me up to heaven in a vision, like the Apostle Paul said, "in the body or out of the body I do not know". The atmosphere was very light, almost a transparent blue, and there were lots of colored flowers, they were all very large. As I looked at the flowers, I saw what looked like grayish forms, they were almost colorless. I could see right through them. As the form moved behind the flower the form turned from that grayish look to the color of the flower. The Lord reminded me that there would be neither male or female, bond or free, the Lord said, "there will be no color." Separation and division began after the tower of Babel. OH no, now what will we fight over, no males, no females, no races, no color, no difference in statue just the reality, we are what and who and where we chose to be in Him.

How many towers, do we the people ooh and aah over not, realizing that every tower in our lives are the temples and towers (of pride) naturally and spiritually that have brought separation between us as God's created people? Do you wonder why God allowed, permitted the Twin Towers to fall? It was not an accident or just an act of terrorism, even though terrorists carried out the act. God was trying to get the United States' attention. He uses people, the elements of weather, pestilence like mosquitoes, and plagues to draw His creation back to Him, destroy all the idols, and worship the one and only true living God. We today have man as our idol. Look at the television screen as you pick out all those "heroes" you idolize. Our world is full of them; they are in the sports world, the music world, the theatrical world, the business world, and even the religious world. Yes, God is calling for a revival. That will not happen until all the idols are torn down and burned, and we the people who call ourselves Christians fall prostrate on our faces in repentance, as Nineveh did thousands of years ago. Repentance requires change, not lip service. That is mockery and it has got to start in the "church" with individuals that are sincere and sold out to the Lord. Until the Church understands they are idolatrous they will remain as Ninevites. It was not until Jonah landed on their shore that they saw and heard what they were and through acknowledging their idolatry and evil ways they were changed and the fear of the LORD fell upon them. You see the reason they were in idolatry and evil was because there had been no fear of the LORD. However, because God is faithful to Himself, He created and prepared that great fish, who listened to its maker and swam to the bottom of the sea and obeyed the LORD completely. He obeyed God's order and His time, and he spit Jonah out according to God perfect plan, purpose, and will. The scriptures tell us that then "the FEAR of the LORD" fell on the entire nation of Nineveh, then they repented and turned back to Him.

I have listened to and even met Joyce Meyer in person [I say that I met Joyce in person because our meeting was prophesied in Africa the year before]; she is a beautiful lady inside and out. Her story is one that has opened many doors for her, and "Ashes to Beauty" put her on the map. Why? Because it is her life. We may have begun as ash and dust, for it is written that we will return to ash and dust, however in the meantime, I am convinced by revelation that I am no accident and I chose every step of my Eternity Present journey on the way back to my Eternal Heavenly Father. I know the Resurrected Blood of His Only Begotten Son, Jesus Christ paid my passage, and I must allow the Holy Ghost, who I am also convinced by revelation is my Eternal Mother, (no this is not doctrinal; however, it is a principle) to take me by her side as the hen does with her little brood of chicks and protect me until I grow up into the full matured stature of my Lord and Savior Jesus Christ, whom I have chosen as my Eternal Bridegroom. Then she will lead me back to my Eternal parent and home. Who would have ever dreamed parenthood was planned, set up, by the master parent and Father, who provided the very best counselors, a book of instructions, and guidelines?

One morning in early April 2004, God spoke to me and said, "I am sending you to Africa to train pastors to be pastors." I had never been to Africa, I had never been a pastor, and I was not to my knowledge a teacher. I was however in a Bible college that was mission purposed. I made an appointment with the school director, and after about ten minutes of small talk, I asked the director how the school felt about women going on missions. The director was an older man, yet younger than me, so I felt we were on the same wave link. However, when he gave me the rundown in short order of the school's desired requirements, I knew that since I was an older woman who was single and had no church or other outside support, I should not expect any financial or other support or encouragement from the school I was attending or the mission's department the director was head over. I knew my calling was one that was not common and would not be favored by the male world of the Christian sector, at least that sector.

In 2006, my calling was a reality. I landed in Entebbe, Uganda on August 1, 2005. During the days to follow, as I sought God for direction, I realized how important my time alone on my bicycle was over ten years prior. He told me to walk the back paths, and as I walked, we talked and our relationship of trust was cemented in as the foundation for a ministry that to this day is alive and well. Expectation ran high at that time because of all the money that had been brought into Uganda to fund the hundreds of projects that the Western world felt sure would pull the country of Africa out of its impoverished state. One afternoon, after several pastors left the home I so graciously had been offered, I went to my room, and in frustration I climbed up on my bed where I cried out to God for direction. All of the pastors who came to see me wanted money to fund the projects that they needed and wanted to start, or funding for those projects that had been started, like food for the chickens that had been given to them, or fencing to keep in the cow that had been given to them. I heard the Lord say to me, "I did not send you to Africa to fund or feed their projects, I sent you to Africa to teach them. You will feed them and fund them out of the seed bank within you."

What a load that was off me. A week later, I was in my first leadership conference, deep in one of the villages, where I taught for six to seven hours straight for three days. That hit off the ministry of discipling, teaching, and training hundreds of African men and women in the ministry. As the months evolved into a year, and my face was not so white and unfamiliar, I found that I was being chased down the streets in the marketplaces in Uganda and Rwanda by men and woman yelling, "It is her, it is her." They thought I was Joyce Meyer, her billboards with her picture and the upcoming event were hanging right there in front of me, and even though I did not physically look anything like her, except I was white and my hair was short, I had become familiar to these people and had developed a reputation. I knew it was not my looks they were seeing, as I passed by their places of business and worship. It was my style of ministry and teaching, and I had been told many times that we carried the same anointing. I realized that a woman I did not know, just because of the anointing we carried, was blessing me. She had such a huge ministry in those two countries and her personal testimony and her ministry opened so many doors for me.

I loved Joyce's enthusiasm for the Word of God and her ministry to the mind, will, and emotions of humankind. I appreciate the doors she as a woman has opened for woman like me all over the world. Parenthood comes in many different forms, as does idolatry. My prayer for all Christians everywhere is to check your heart, your closet, your wardrobe for anything that might look like an idol, and lay it in the fire bin. One of the reasons America is cursed is because we have sacrificed our children to Molech. Not only in the womb, but in the arena of education. Our culture, traditions, lifestyle and free belief system which are in opposition to God's plans, purposes and will for His creation.

Just as I was blessed by Jesus Christ because of the anointing of Joyce Meyer, many Americans are cursed because of the anointing of those whom they worship and idolize. Pride, arrogance, and self-reliance fill the stadiums every weekend. The spirits of competition, envy, and greed drive men and women to succeed and be on the top of the pinnacle of the tower that God is going to bring down. Church would not be church if it was in the field under a tree or in a simple home. The individuals in the presidential elections have spent billions of US dollars funding their agendas on how great they think they are, and how we need to elect one of them as our newest idol… Oh my God, forgive us, for we are not in the right mindset. You, LORD our Father, Lord, King, Leader, Teacher, Master, and Friend.

CHAPTER 10

23. PLANNED PARENTHOOD

Plan or **planned** so to formulate a scheme, or program. Predestination.

Parent is any organism that produces or generates another, mother, father, ancestor, or fore-father, being the original source, pertaining to an organism, cell or structure that produces another.

Hood is a state, condition, or quality of being...Hood, a covering, an extended part.
definitions from: *Webster's College Dictionary*

Planned -- predestined
Parent -- original source
Hood -- covering

First God placed the anointed cherub, which was a spiritual being as the covering hood over the Stones of Fire, which we see are the souls. God could not have given this position to the cherub which was appointed by God unless He was sovereign (original source) over him. God is seen in the role of our Father parent because of His nature and character.

The Father who is in Heaven purposed and planned (predestined) the care and wellbeing of all His creation, which in reality all comes from His mind. Yes, the Father has all five senses and functions out of them, just as He wants to teach us to do in the natural and then the spiritual realms.

There is a COUNTERFEIT plan, a COUNTERFEIT parent, and a COUNTERFEIT hood. This book has shown you from the "beginning," which is the first principle given man as a directional guide from our Heavenly Father. In the beginning, God's plan was perfect, as was all that He created, right through the sixth day of Creation. That is why on the seventh day, which is the number of completions, He could rest, and the rest is history.

Here I would like to speak to all of you reading this book. We have finished the course and I am sure that if you are reading this, you have jumped over many hurdles and scaled many mountains of unbelief, skepticism, sarcasm, and criticism, because your desire was to finish well as you cross the finish line and hear the words, "Well done, my good and faithful servant." I am also sure there are a few readers who in their perception have convinced themselves that they are doing the world a service by playing God and have not considered the outcome of that dream. I spoke occasionally of dreaming in the context of this book, and praise God, I always woke up and found myself right where I was before I began that journey in my dream state. I would say aloud, "Praise God, I was only dreaming," because if it had not been a dream and the situation had continued down the road it was traveling, the outcome would have been anything but good. We never think a couple of drinks of alcohol will turn our world upside down, destroy our families, ruin our jobs and destroy our body and soul but then comes the day when we are alone, lying in a puddle of our own vomit, homeless, jobless and dying of cancer, reality is a very difficult road to travel. Or that first puff on the cigarette never a thought that emphysema will come to us, even though we open the door and invite it in, when over and over we hear the testimonies from others begging us not to begin something that will take us down a road leading to dependency on the counterfeit, or even worse a premature death because of its side effects. Cigarettes are not only dirty, they make your house, car, clothes, hair, and everyone, including your children, stink. Cigarettes are toxic to the inside of your body, to the air you inhale and the air you exhale. Alcohol and Tabacco will eat up your bank account, your dreams, as well as your body. Yet unlike my dream, you are not going to just wake up from the horrible effects that your choice to drink and smoke will cause for you. Speaking of never thinking something could never come to you, the stench of hell should be a visitor you never want to meet.

Playing God destroyed Lucifer, destroyed his seed, and destroyed everything he viewed as his. Playing God opened the door when he walked into the presence of God, as he took his morning stroll, and because the real, genuine, loving parent saw and seized that valuable opportunity to redirect and correct the direction His created son Job was going. God used His servant Lucifer as the spoon in which God poured the antidote "humility, mercy, Truth," and gave Lucifer the clearance to pour it down Job's throat. Our Father in Heaven is the best father ever, He forgives. If the book of Job was not for your doctrine, correction, discipline, direction, and instruction, it would not be in the sixty-six books of the Torah, Word of God....

▶ Abortion

As a person who loves to spend time in the kitchen, I have learned to love meats, cheese, vegetables of all types and fruits. You say what does that have to do with abortion??? I saved the very best for last. The icing on the cake or the desert. The beginning of Predestined Journey we learned the importance of the Family Unit.

There is only one real and genuine reason for "abortion" and that is to PREVENT something that is not (wanted) planned and purposed, by the Originator; the Source, the Creator from ever getting started in the beginning. Are you listening? Abortion is an action word. If you want to abort any action, do it FIRST IN THOUGHT. Take responsibility for YOUR choices, do not scapegoat your bad behavior off on others, be it the doctor, nurse, friend, or even yourself, none of the above named are the originator, only the LORD can fill that role. It is easy to erase or change a word written on the computer, because we can just backspace, or hit delete, but our bodies do not have an erase or backspace key, and even though we are programmed to feel regret, and realize that what is on the screen is not what we wanted to say or to happen, we should have thought about the consequences before we put the words or thoughts out there and allowed them to become an action.

However, listen to me…Jesus is a God who is able to erase our words and our behaviors, if we will just give Him the eraser. Repent, lay all your burdens at the foot of the cross, and He will gather them up in the same hands that created you, and wrap them in a blanket of His love. He washes all our past thoughts, words, and deeds white as snow and sends them into the sea of forgetfulness. Abortion is only legal and works when you abstain from any thought or action that is not in God's perfect plan and will for you. When it comes to the action of aborting a life be it the day the sperm and egg unite or in one of the three gestational stages it is murder. It may be in your body however, it is not your life, and it does not belong to you. As explained in the meat of this book it is the egg that was yours, however once it becomes a living soul you are only the caretaker not the owner. Abortion is in the eyes of the LORD, who is the Lord of the Harvest is the absolute worst slap in His face which violates His Perfect Plan and purpose for unity of the family.

So let us for just a moment finish this chapter and book with these very valuable and timely words from the Messenger of Wisdom. We should take note and remember that a parent is any organism that produces or generates another, mother, father, ancestor, or forefather, being the original source, pertaining to an organism, cell or structure that produces another. God gave us a free will to choose His perfect will. It is His perfect will that we use His plans and purposes for our ticket. The train is about to leave the station, and depending on the platform you depart from determines your destination. Best wishes for a safe journey. We pray you listen to the voice of God, ask Him for confirmation in your spirit of TRUTH, and if what you have read is difficult for you to believe or comprehend, please, place these principles, and concepts in a little jar and put them on the back burner until the light of truth unscrews the lid and the jar roles off and lands in your space of reason. Then, it will be your time and season to reread it slower, and with the purpose of listening and learning and not just reading.

Predestined Journey Study Guide

All scriptures are taken from the King James Version unless otherwise named.

Definitions from:
The New Strong's Exhaustive Concordance of the Bible 1990 (NSEC)
Webster's College Dictionary –Random House 1991-1997 (WCD)

Bibles used for reference material:
1. King James Foundation Study Bible -- Thomas Nelson (2015)
2. New Kings James Scofield Study System Bible-- Oxford (1909-2009)
3. Spirit Filled Life Bible NKJV-- Thomas Nelson 2552 (1982-2002)
4. Dake's Annotated Reference Bible --Dake
5. God's Word -- word search Bible 10 Software
6. Revised Standard Version Bible
7. Message Bible -- Word search Bible 10 Software

Introductions

Colossians 2:1-23 For I would that ye knew what great conflict I have for you, and *for* them at Laodicea, and *for* as many as have not seen my face in the flesh;
Col 2:2 That their hearts might be comforted, being knit together in love, and unto all riches of the full assurance of understanding, to the acknowledgement of the mystery of God, and of the Father, and of Christ;
Col 2:3 In whom are hid all the treasures of wisdom and knowledge.
Col 2:4 And this I say, lest any man should beguile you with enticing words.
Col 2:5 For though I be absent in the flesh, yet am I with you in the spirit, joying and beholding your order, and the steadfastness of your faith in Christ.
Alive in Christ
Col 2:6 As ye have therefore received Christ Jesus the Lord, so walk ye in him:
Col 2:7 Rooted and built up in him, and stablished in the faith, as ye have been taught, abounding therein with thanksgiving.

Col 2:8 Beware lest any man spoil you through philosophy and vain deceit, after the tradition of men, after the rudiments of the world, and not after Christ.

Col 2:9 For in him dwelleth all the fulness of the Godhead bodily.

Col 2:10 And ye are complete in him, which is the head of all principality and power:

Col 2:11 In whom also ye are circumcised with the circumcision made without hands, in putting off the body of the sins of the flesh by the circumcision of Christ:

Col 2:12 Buried with him in baptism, wherein also ye are risen with *him* through the faith of the operation of God, who hath raised him from the dead.

Col 2:13 And you, being dead in your sins and the uncircumcision of your flesh, hath he quickened together with him, having forgiven you all trespasses;

Col 2:14 Blotting out the handwriting of ordinances that was against us, which was contrary to us, and took it out of the way, nailing it to his cross;

Col 2:15 *And* having spoiled principalities and powers, he made a shew of them openly, triumphing over them in it.

Let No One Disqualify You

Col 2:16 Let no man therefore judge you in meat, or in drink, or in respect of an holyday, or of the new moon, or of the sabbath *days*:

Col 2:17 Which are a shadow of things to come; but the body *is* of Christ.

Col 2:18 Let no man beguile you of your reward in a voluntary humility and worshipping of angels, intruding into those things which he hath not seen, vainly puffed up by his fleshly mind,

Col 2:19 And not holding the Head, from which all the body by joints and bands having nourishment ministered, and knit together, increased with the increase of God.

Col 2:20 Wherefore if ye be dead with Christ from the rudiments of the world, why, as though living in the world, are ye subject to ordinances,

Col 2:21 (Touch not; taste not; handle not;

Col 2:22 Which all are to perish with the using;) after the commandments and doctrines of men?

Col 2:23 Which things have indeed a shew of wisdom in will worship, and humility, and neglecting of the body; not in any honor to the satisfying of the flesh.

The Word of God is Truth!
2 Timothy 3:16, 17 KJV All (every) scripture (document, bill in writing (grave) *is* given by inspiration (to *breathe* hard, that is, *breeze*: - blow) of God, and *is* profitable for doctrine, for reproof, for correction, for instruction (*tutorage*, that is, *education* or *training*; by implication disciplinary *correction*: - chastening, chastisement, instruction, nurture, to *train* up a child, that is, *educate*, or *toil* (*as an effort or occupation*); *line* (by punishment): - chasten, instruct, learn, teach) in righteousness (*equity* (of character or act): That the man of God may be perfect (*equity* (of character or act), this day (hour), hence [-forth], here [-after], hither [-to], (even) now, (this) present), thoroughly furnished) unto all good works (to *equip fully* (a teacher.) (NSEC)

Debar is Hebrew and Log'-os is Greek for our English **word** *which means;* a *matter* (as *spoken* of) of *thing*; a *cause*: - act, advice, affair, answer, any such, because of, book, business, care, tidings, treatise, utterance, word, work. **(NSEC)**
James 1:22, 23 KJV become doers (a *performer*; specifically, a "poet": - doer, poet) of the Word, and not hearers only, deceiving your own selves. For if anyone is a hearer of *the* Word and not a doer, he is like a man studying his natural face in a mirror.
James 1:25 KJV whoever looks into the perfect Law of liberty and continues *in it*, he is not a forgetful hearer, but a doer of *the* work (*toil* (as an effort or occupation); by implication an *act*: - deed, doing, labor, work. This one shall be blessed in his doing.
Revelation 19:9-13 KJV These are the true sayings of God.
Acts 28:24-25 KJV And some believed the things which were spoken, and some believed not.
2 Peter 1:19-21 KJV no prophecy of the scripture is of any private interpretation.
Revelation 22:18, 19 NKJV Warning: Do not to add to or take away from the "TRUTH."
Proverbs 25-29 NKJV Warnings and Instructions

Introduction from the Messenger of Wisdom/the Watchman on the Wall Study Guide
Matthew 7:7 NKJV Ask, Seek, and Find.
James 1:5, 6 & 4:2 NKJV Because you do not ask.

Ezekiel 28:1-19 KJV/God's Word

Chapter 1
1. All God's Secrets are found hidden from the Wise and Prudent
Matthew 11:25 KJV because Thou hast hid these things from the wise and prudent, and hast revealed them unto babes.
Mark 4:33 KJV And with many such parables spake He the Word unto them, as they were able to hear *it.*
Matthew 15:16 KJV And Jesus said, are ye also yet without understanding? Do not ye yet understand?
Luke 8:9, Matthew 13:10-17 KJV The Purpose of Parables
Proverbs 22:19 KJV That thy trust (dependency) may be in the LORD.
Hosea 4:6 KJV My people are destroyed for lack of knowledge: because thou hast rejected knowledge, I will also reject thee.

Bondage to a lie producing unbelief
2 Peter 2:19 KJV of the same is he brought in bondage.
2 Thessalonians 2:10 KJV And with all deceivableness of unrighteousness in them that perish; because they received not the love of the truth, that they might be saved.

Job, the man most judged and misunderstood
Job 42:1-6 NKJV (You said to me) Who is this that darkens and obscures counsel (by words) without knowledge? Therefore (I now see) I have (rashly) uttered what I did not understand, things to wonderful for me, which I did not know.
Job 28:2 NKJV (I had virtually said to You that You have said to me :) Vs: 6 Therefore I loathe (my words) and abhor myself and repent in dust and ashes.

God has no secrets from a humble, righteous man
Job 42:1-3 KJV I know that thou canst do everything, and that no thought can be with-holden from thee.
Proverbs 1:7 KJV The fear of the LORD is the beginning of knowledge.
Matthew 16:8 KJV Oh ye of little faith.

Ephesians 3:7-9 KJV Saul/Paul's conversion and call: And to make all *men* see what *is* the fellowship of the mystery, which from the beginning of the world hath been hid in God, who created all things by Jesus Christ:

Romans 1:16-32 KJV For I am not ashamed of the gospel of Christ: <u>*so that they are without excuse: Because that, when they knew God, they glorified him not as God, neither were thankful; but became vain in their imaginations, and their foolish heart was darkened. Professing themselves to be wise, they became fools.*</u> Reference (**2Cor 10:5, Luke 1:51, Proverbs 6:18**) Vein imaginations.

Matthew 4:1-11 KJV Jesus said "It is written again, thou shalt not tempt the Lord thy God.

God will fill my Treasure Chest

Matthew 13:44-46 KJV The Kingdom of Heaven is likened unto hidden treasures.

Proverbs 8:17-24 KJV I love them that love me; and those that seek me early shall find me. Riches and honor *are* with me; *yea*, durable riches and righteousness. My fruit *is* better than gold, yea, than fine gold; (Gold in Hebrew--*incised* or (active) *incisive*; a *trench* (as dug), *gold* (as mined), a *threshing sledge* (having sharp teeth); (figuratively) *determination*; also *eager*: - decision, diligent, (fine) gold, pointed things, sharp, threshing instrument, wall) and my revenue (well) stricken [in age] than choice silver (sense of reason. I lead in the way of righteousness, in the midst of the paths of judgment:

1 Thessalonians 4:6 KJV The dead in Christ.

Proverbs 8:21 KJV That I may cause those that love Me to inherit substance; and I will fill their treasures.

Proverbs 8:2-12 KJV The ways of Wisdom.

Proverbs 8:19-21 KJV My fruit is better than gold, yea, than fine gold; and my revenue than choice silver. I will fill their treasures.

James 1:3-8 KJV Knowing this, that the trying of your faith worketh patience. A double minded man is unstable in all his ways.

2. Pride is the Root Cause

Proverbs 16:18 NKJV Pride goes before destruction and a haughty spirit before a fall.

1 Samuel 17:28 KJV I know thy pride, and the naughtiness of thine heart; Pride questions the motives of the heart and stands as an unrighteous judge.

Exodus 23:1 KJV Thou shalt not raise a false report: put not thine hand with the wicked to be an unrighteous witness.

2 Timothy 4:8 KJV the Lord, the righteous judge.

Obadiah 1:3 RSV The trouble with Esau is pride. Pride is the root of all human evil, and pride is the basic characteristic of what the Bible calls the flesh that lusts against, wars against, the Spirit.

Romans 2:15 KJV who show the work of the Law written in their hearts, **their conscience also bearing witness.**

John 18:37, 38 KJV Pilate said to Him, Are you a king then? Jesus answered; you say it that I am a king. To this end I was born, and for this cause I came into the world, that I should bear **witness to the truth.** Everyone who is of the truth hears My voice. Pilate said to Him, what is truth?

Hebrews 10:15, 16 KJV the Holy Ghost also is a witness to us;

John 7:7-19 NKJV My doctrine is not Mine, but His who sent Me.

3. Repentance, Forgiveness, and Restoration
Repent and you shall be forgiven, forgive and it shall be forgiven you.
1 John 2:12-17 KJV *little children*, fathers (*MATURE ONES*), and *young men*, because your sins are forgiven you for his name's sake and because ye have overcome the wicked one.

Job 42:7 KJV Job's friends.

Job 42:10-12 KJV Jehovah added to Job all that *had been his*, to double.

Deuteronomy 30:1-3 KJV the blessing and the curse.

Matthew 5:31, 32 KJV Marriage is sacred and binding.

Mark 10:2-9 NKJV A spiritual writ of divorce.

Deuteronomy 24:1 NKJV A natural writ of divorce.

Proverbs 22:6 NKJV Train up your child in the way they are to go.

Proverbs 3:1-35 NKJV Guidance for the Young.

Chapter 2
4. Eternity Past
The First Garden of Eden in His Holy Mountain
Doth not wisdom cry? and understanding put forth her voice?
1 Peter 2:1-12 KJV Wherefore laying aside all malice, and all guile, and hypocrisies, and envies, and all evil speaking's, as newborn babes, desire the sincere milk of the word, that ye may grow thereby: If so be ye have tasted

that the Lord *is* gracious. To whom coming, *as unto* a living stone, disallowed indeed of men, but chosen of God, *and* precious.

1 Peter 2:5 KJV Ye also, as lively stones, are built up a spiritual house, in the scripture, Behold, I lay in Sion a chief corner stone.

1 Peter 2:11 KJV Dearly beloved, I beseech you as strangers and pilgrims, abstain from fleshly lusts, which war against the soul (Stone of Fire).

Lucifer's first mistake
Ezekiel 28:11-19 God's Word

Shepherd of the flock (Covering)
Lucifer begins as God beloved, created cherub and ends as ashes upon an earth of darkness.

Ezekiel 28:14 KJV *__Thou art the anointed cherub that covereth__*; (*Shepherd*) and I have set thee so: thou wast upon the Holy Mountain of God; thou hast walked up and down in the midst of the **Stones of Fire** (souls of man i.e. the flock) Thou *wast* perfect in thy ways from the day that thou wast created, till iniquity was found in thee. O covering cherub, from the midst of the "Stones of Fire."

Lucifer, The accuser
Job 1:6-12 KJV Then Satan answered the LORD, Doth Job fear God for nought?

All that was left was the Ash
Job 42:6 KJV *Therefore I despise myself, and repent in dust and ashes.*
Pride—**Ezekiel 31:8-9**, Redemption -- **Ezekiel 36:28-33,**

CHAOS IN THE HOLY MOUNTAIN
When the Caregiver is away, the Stones of Fire become unruly be it in Eternity Past or Eternity Present.

The Stones of Fire were left without a covering.
Joel 2:1-24 KJV so shall they run. (*Souls without a shepherd*)
Matthew 9:36 KJV But when he saw the multitudes, he was moved with compassion on them, because they fainted, and were scattered abroad, *as sheep having no shepherd.*)

Joel 2:5-14 KJV Like the noise of chariots on the tops of mountains shall they leap and there was CHAOS IN THE HOLY MOUNTAIN.

Joel 2:32 KJV whosoever shall call on the name of the LORD shall be delivered:

The Little Red School House

1 Peter 4:17 NKJV The time has begun.

Jude NKJV Warnings and Instructions.

Revelation 20:11-15 NKJV Judgment according to their works.

Ecclesiastes 11:9 NKJV God will bring thee into Judgment.

Matthew 12:36 NKJV They shall give an account.

Time for School, called the Master

Matthew 11:25 NKJV At that time Jesus answered and said, I thank You, O Father, Lord of Heaven and earth, because You have hidden these things from *the* sophisticated and cunning, and revealed them to babes.

1 Samuel 9:1-27 KJV The Children of Israel did not want the LORD to be their Master so they chose a human master Saul.

Romans 8: 29 KJV Predestined (Ephesians 1:5, 11)

Romans 8:18-22 NKJV All of creation grown.

Revelation 4:11 NKJV For you created all things and by Your will they exist.

Chapter 3
5. Eternity Present
The Second Garden of Eden

Genesis 1&2 Days of Creation

 God Creation:

God Created the Heaven and the Earth.

Genesis 2:4, 6, 7 KJV the day that the LORD God made the earth and the heavens.

Acts 17:24 KJV God that made the world and all things therein.

Genesis 1:1-18 KJV In the beginning God created the heaven and the earth.

Genesis 1:19-26 KJV And the evening and the morning were the fourth day. God created the fish of the sea, the fowl of the air, and the beasts of the field. Then they created man the fifth and sixth day.

Genesis 1:27-31 KJV So God created man in His *own* image, in the image of God created He him; male and female created He them.

Genesis 1:10 KJV And God called the dry *land* Earth; and the gathering together of the waters called He Seas: and God saw that *it* was good.

The seas are referred to in the masculine he Seas and according to the Strong's Concordance the Hebrew word for seas has nothing to do with salt.

Matthew 5:13 KJV ye are the salt of the earth: but if the salt has lost his savior, wherewith shall it be salted? It is thenceforth good for nothing, but to be cast out, and to be trodden under foot of men.

Mark 9:49, 50 KJV for every one shall be salted with fire, and every sacrifice shall be salted with salt.

Salt (*salt*; figuratively *prudence*:)is good: but if the salt has lost his saltiness (*salt-less*, that is, *insipid, to become (come into being), used with great latitude (literally, figuratively, intensively, etc.) impudent*: Have salt in yourselves, and have peace one with another. (NSEC)

(**John 19:34** KJV But one of the soldiers with a spear pierced his side, and forthwith came there out blood and water) and out of Jesus eyes flowed tears as he wept for God's people (**Luke 19:41** KJV And when he was come near, he beheld the city, and wept over it,).

Now to answer my question and hopefully yours. Where did the salt in our bodies and the salt in the seas come from? *I believe it came from the eyes of God as he knelt down and scooped up the sacrificed ash of the anointed cherub before the foundation of the world as we know it, into his hand, he looked at it knowing what had been and what was going to be and a salty tear fell from His eye, giving the moisture need to create the form of a man...* Science Fiction you say. Yet you watch that trash on television every day, you fill your children's minds with it every day and you find this hard to believe. Well, tell me, where did the salt in your body come from? I do not have all the answers however I am searching for the truth not fiction or the counterfeit.

✓ 1. Time

Exodus 12:17 KJV Directions given by -- - Ordinance; Hebrew an *enactment*; hence an *appointment* (of time, space, quantity, labor or usage): - appointed, bound, commandment, convenient, custom, decree (-d), due, law, measure, necessary, ordinance (-nary), portion, set time, statute, task. (NSEC)

Colossians 4:5 NSFL Walk in wisdom toward those that are without, redeeming the time.

Opportune time, set time, appointed time due time, definitive time, quantity, or extent of time.

Ecclesiastes 3:1-11 KJV To *everything there* is a season, and a time to every purpose under the heaven.

✓ 2. Order

Genesis 1 -- All of the Creation was (ordered by God) an *arrangement*, that is, (figuratively) mental *disposition*: - preparation. (NSEC)

Genesis 4:4 KJV -- -- Respect -- -- or the lack of respect.

Genesis 4:5-7 KJV why is thy countenance fallen?

Romans 8:27-30 KJV He also lays the order according to His predetermined plans, and purposes.

Exodus 26:30 KJV Made from the hands of man.

Moses was commanded by God to set the Tabernacle in order according to the (pattern) *structure*; by implication a *model, resemblance*: - figure, form, likeness, pattern, similitude.

2 Kings 20:1 KJV Thus saith the LORD, Set thine house in order;

Job 33:5 KJV If thou canst answer me, set *thy words* in order before me, stand up.

Matthew 20:16 KJV The last shall be first -- -many are called but few are chosen.

6.   [A.] Body, Soul, and Spirit
▶ Covering for the body

Genesis 3:7, 10, 21 KJV the Glory of God, Leaves, and animal skins.

1 Peter 2:24 KJV Jesus took ours sins in His own body on the tree.

1 Thessalonians 5:23 KJV And the very God of peace sanctify you wholly; and *I pray God* your whole spirit and soul and body be preserved blameless unto the coming of our Lord Jesus Christ.

▶ Covering of the Soul, and Spirit was the created "body"

Genesis 2:7 KJV And the LORD God formed man of the dust of the ground, and breathed into his nostrils the breath of life; and man became a living soul.

James 2:26 KJV For as the body without the spirit is dead

Ephesians 4:23 KJV And be renewed in the spirit of your mind; And that ye put on the new man, which after God is created in righteousness and true holiness.

Romans 12:2 KJV And be not conformed to this world: but be ye transformed by the renewing of your mind, that ye may prove what is that good, and acceptable, and perfect, will of God.

2 Corinthians 4:16 KJV For which cause we faint not; but though our outward man perish, yet the inward *man* is renewed day by day.

Mark 16:18 KJV if they drink any deadly thing, it shall not hurt them;

[B.] Five Senses
Body, Soul, and Spirit

Touch (Hand) -- the instrument of Affection -- so that we can Worship.

Hearing (Ear) -- To him that hears let him hear; why so that he can remember (Memory) what the Spirit said, so that he can Reverence the LORD. [First Commandment]

Smell (Nose) -- Conscience -- Hope deferred makes the heart sick.

Taste (Mouth) -- Reason -- Prayer, thy will be done.

Sight (Eye) -- Imagination -- Faith, may your faith sustain you.

Chapter 4
7. Rod of Correction

Proverbs 29:15 KJV The rod and reproof give wisdom: but a child left to *himself* bringeth his mother to shame.

Acts 7:7 NKJV And God said, "I will judge the nation to whom they shall be in bondage," and "after these things they will come out and will serve Me in this place."

A Relationship with Requirements

Proverbs 10:17 KJV He is in the way of life that keeps instruction/correction.

Degree of growth in the natural and the spiritual

Isaiah 28:9 NKJV Whom shall He teach knowledge? And whom shall He make to understand doctrine? *Those* weaned from the milk and drawn from the breasts.

1 Peter 2:2-5 KJV As newborn babes, desire the sincere milk of the word, that ye may grow thereby.

Ephesians 4:15 KJV But speaking the truth in love, may grow up into him in all things, which is the head, *even* Christ:

Man's Responsibility in God's Plan: Prophets, Apostles, Pasters, Teachers, and Evangelists.

Psalms 68:18

Immorality: immoral quality, character, or conduct, sexual misconduct. (WCD)

Galatians 5:19, 2 Corinthians 12:20, 21, Ephesians 4:17, 18, Titus 3:3, Colossians 3:5-8 KJV

God the Provider

Genesis 2:7, 8, 15,16 KJV Of every tree of the garden thou mayest freely eat.

Genesis 2:9 KJV "El Shaddai" The God of many breasts.

Genesis 17:1 KJV The LORD Jehovah appeared to Abram.

Joel 2:15 KJV gather the children, and those that suck the breasts.

Chapter 5
8. The Counterfeit
Obadiah 1: 1-21 KJV Esau

Who is your master?

Greek -- tsore, tsore; a rock; Tsor, a place in Palestine: - Tyre, Tyrus. (NSEC)

Exodus 21:5, 6 KJV his master shall bore his ear through with an aul; and he shall serve him forever.

Luke 14:25-26, KJV If anyone comes to Me and does not hate.

Hebrew 12:5, 11 KJV My son, despise not thou the chastening of the Lord.

Counterfeit affections

Romans 1:27-31 KJV or this cause God gave them up unto vile affections:

Proverbs 30:17 KJV The eye *that* mocketh at *his* father, and despiseth to obey *his* mother, the ravens of the valley shall pick it out, and the young eagles shall eat it.

The Antidote to the Counterfeit
Water Baptism in the Name of Jesus Christ
Acts 2:36-39 KJV Repent and be baptized, every one of you, in the Name of Jesus Christ.

Knowing your true identity
Understanding that the Counterfeit is an imitation, it is twisted, it may look like, taste like, & smell like, however, the components are not true to the true principle.
The antidote to the counterfeit can be found in principle throughout the Word of God. It will allow you to grow up into the full stature of Jesus Christ.
Key 1) Study to show yourself approved unto God.
 A. Rightly Divide the Word of Truth
 B. Meditate on God's Kingdom Principles (to be and to do His Perfect Will)
Key 2) Order of God's Perfect Will and Plan for your life
Key 3) Fear of the LORD
Key 4) Understanding Your Spiritual make-up
A. Your relationship with God
1. Will give you the ability to rightly divide the truth from fiction.
2. Will empower and enables you to overcome the lies and attacks of the enemy.
Philippians 1:21-23 NKJV To die is gain.
1 Corinthians 15:31 NKJV We must die daily.

The living stone/seed
Luke 6:48 KJV for it was founded upon a rock.
A Rock of Offense
Isaiah 8:14-15 KJV Jesus is our rock of offense to the counterfeit rock.
Tyre, (prince of the underworld, the rock, Lucifer) is the counterfeit rock
John 14:6 KJV Jesus saith unto him, I am the way, the truth, and the life: no man cometh unto the Father, but by me.
Isaiah 28:16 KJV Therefore thus saith the Lord GOD, Behold, **I lay in Zion for a foundation a stone, a tried stone, a precious corner *stone*, a sure foundation**: he that believeth shall not make haste.
Matthew 6:7 KJV Keep asking, seeking, and knocking

Chapter 6
9. You knew or you should have known

Isaiah 7:14 KJV <u>Therefore the Lord himself shall give you a sign</u>; Behold, a virgin shall conceive, and bear a son, and shall call his name Immanuel.

It was no accident or coincident that Mary was a virgin and that she conceived as prophesied many years before the virgin Mary was even born.

John 17:4-7 KJV I have glorified Thee on the earth: I have finished the work which thou gavest Me to do. Now they have known that all things whatsoever Thou hast given Me are of Thee.

2 Timothy 3:15 KJV And that from a child thou hast known the holy scriptures, which are able to make thee wise unto salvation through faith which is in Christ Jesus.

Romans 1:32 KJV <u>Who knowing the judgment of God</u>, that they which commit such things are worthy of death, not only do the same, but have pleasure in them that do them.

1 John 3:1-2 KJV Behold, what manner of love the Father hath bestowed upon us, that we should be called the sons of God:

10. Will it be Heaven or Hell

Proverbs 15:11 KJV Hell and destruction *are* before the LORD: how much more then the hearts of the children of men?

Revelation 1:18 KJV *I am* He that liveth, and was dead; and, behold, I am alive for evermore, Amen; and have the keys of hell and of death.

Matthew 10:27, 28 KJV Jesus teaches the Fear of the LORD

1 John 5:1-6 NKJV Faith is the overcoming principle in the world's conflict.

▶ Who is your father?

Ephesians 2:2 KJV **The spirit that now works in the children of disobedience.**

John 8:42-45 KJV If God were your Father

John 14:6-31 KJV Believest thou not that I am in the Father, and the Father in Me?

John 14:20-29 KJV At that day ye shall know that I am in My Father, and ye in Me, and I in you.

Isaiah 64:8 KJV The Father is called **LORD___JHWH or Jehovah.**

Isaiah 45:21 KJV The Son is called **Jehovah.**

Act 4:12, Act 1:5 KJV "And there is salvation in no one else; for there is no other name under Heaven [Jesus Christ] that has been given among men, by which we must be saved."

Isaiah 11:2 KJV The Holy Ghost is called JHWH,

Noting here: that there is a difference between the Holy Spirit, which is the Spirit of the Lord, and the Holy Ghost which Jesus told the disciple could not come until after His death, burial, and resurrection. Jesus told them in the book of Acts just prior to His ascension that they would be baptized with the Holy Ghost not many days hence, referring to His transfiguration. **Acts 2:38**

John 14:30 KJV Hereafter I will not talk much with you: for the prince of this world cometh (Satan), and hath nothing in Me. But that the world may know that I love the Father; and as the Father gave Me commandment, even so I do. Arise, let us go hence.

John 3:16 NKJV Who so ever believes.

Revelation 21:2 NKJV Jesus, the Father, and Husband.

▶ **Persecution from a Judas**

John 15: 20, 21 KJV Persecution of the Messenger of Wisdom/ Watchman on the Wall

Remember the word that I said to you, the servant is not greater than his master. If they have persecuted Me, they will also persecute you. If they have kept My saying, they will also keep yours. But all these things they will do to you for My name's sake, because they do not know Him who sent Me.

Matthew 14:3-12 KJV Beheaded for speaking the truth. It is not lawful for thee to have her.

1 Peter 5:1-6 NKJV Since Christ has suffered, why should we not suffer?

2 Timothy 3:5-14 NKJV Having a form of godliness, but denying the power thereof.

God possessed me

Proverbs 8:22-24 KJV The LORD possessed me in the beginning of his way, before his works of old.

The word possess in the Hebrew means to *erect*, that is, *create*; by extension to *procure*, especially by purchase (causatively **sell**); by implication to **own**: - attain, buy (-er), teach to keep cattle, get, provoke to jealousy, possess (-or), purchase, recover, redeem, surely, verily. (NSEC)

Jeremiah 1:4 KJV Before I formed thee in the belly, I knew thee.

11. Family Reunion
▶ **Of like kind -- Unity**
Proverbs 30:27 KJV The locusts have no king, yet go they forth all of them by bands;
John 1:1-16 KJV In the beginning was the Word, and the Word was with God, and the Word was God.
Galatians 5:5-26 KJV For we through the Spirit wait for the hope of righteousness out of faith.
(Faith and Works)
2 Thessalonians 1:11
Philippians 2:12
1 Thesalonians 1:13
Romans 2:7
John 6:27-29
The Curse
Romans 1:25-29 KJV Who changed the truth of God into a lie?
Proverbs 29:21 KJV He who pampers his servant from childhood will have a son in the end. (Welfare)

Chapter 7
12. The Web of Deception
ONCE SAVED ALWAYS SAVED, NO NEED FOR REPENTANCE, JUST LIVE AND LET LIVE, ALL WILL END WELL. True deception!!!
Proverbs 17:3 KJV The LORD tests the heart.
Job 21:8-24 KJV Their seed is established in their sight with them, and their offspring before their eyes.
Job 21:22 KJV Shall *any teach God knowledge?* Seeing he judgeth those that are high. (PRIDE) One dieth in his full strength, being wholly at ease and quiet.
1 Peter 2:1-25 KJV For ye were as sheep going astray; *but are now returned* unto the Shepherd and Bishop of your souls. (Don't live in Hypocrisies)
The Spirit of Ingratitude

Mark 10:17-22 KJV And he was sad at that saying, and went away grieved: for he had great possessions.

Proverbs 13:12 KJV Hope deferred makes the heart sick.

It's just your perception

God is not to blame

John 11:35 NKJV Jesus wept.

Liquid prayers: spiritual brokenness, tears of compassion, tears of sorrow, tears of victory, tears of repentance, tears of desperation, tears of travail or giving birth (spiritually speaking).

Psalm 126:1-6 KJV They that sow in tears shall reap in joy. He that goeth forth and weepeth, bearing precious seed, shall doubtless come again with rejoicing, bringing his sheaves *with him*.

Galatians 3:13 KJV Christ hath redeemed us from the curse of the law.

Cursed according to Strong's means to go against, to stand firmly, frequently denotes *opposition*, *distribution* or *intensity*. In other words, a curse is a willful act, deed, or word that is in opposition against the perfect plans and purposes of God. *down* (in place or time)

Chapter 8
13. Multiplication Principle

Genesis 1:11 KJV And God said, Let the earth bring forth grass, the herb yielding seed, *and* the fruit tree yielding fruit after his kind, whose seed *is* in itself, upon the earth: and it was so. And the earth brought forth grass, *and* herb yielding seed after his kind, and the tree yielding fruit, whose seed *was* in itself, after his kind: and God saw that *it* was good.

Genesis 1:28 KJV And God blessed them. And God said to them, be fruitful, and multiply and fill the earth, and subdue it.

Romans 8:1-18 KJV ye have received the Spirit of adoption, **New Testament believers who are circumcised in the flesh or in the heart (spiritual heart) are under the blood of Jesus Christ, by faith not by works.**

14. Seed Principle
Genesis 1:29 KJV And God said, Behold, I have given you every herb bearing seed, which is upon the face of all the earth, and every tree, in the which is the fruit of a tree yielding seed; to you it shall be for meat.

Abraham and Isaac

Job 21:8 KJV Their seed is established in their sight with them, and their offspring before their eyes.

Isaiah 53:10 KJV Yet it pleased the LORD to bruise *him*; he hath put him to grief: when thou shalt make his soul an offering for sin, he shall see *his* seed, he shall prolong *his* days, and the pleasure of the LORD shall prosper in his hand.

Luke 8:11-15 KJV Now the parable is this: The seed is the word of God.

Luke 8:12 KJV The soil and the seed.

1 John 3:9 KJV Whosoever is born of God doth not commit sin; for his seed remaineth in him: and he cannot sin, because he is born of God.

► **It only takes One Bad Seed**
Genesis 16:1-16 KJV Genesis 22:2-8, Genesis 21:14–21

► **Predestination/ Predestined**
Ephesians 1:11 KJV being predestinated according to the purpose of him who worketh all things after the counsel of his own will:

Romans 8:29-30 KJV For whom he did foreknow, he also did predestinate The word foreknow in the Greek is prog-in-oce'-koto know beforehand, that is, foresee: - foreknow (ordain), know (before).

The word predestinate in the Greek is pro-or-id'-zo to limit in advance, that is, (figuratively) predetermine: - determine before, ordain, predestinate. (PARENT)

The Father knew us beforehand, before the creation of mankind and He predestined us to be conformed which means in the Greek *jointly formed*, that is, (figuratively) *similar*: - conformed to, fashioned like unto His Only Begotten Son Jesus Christ. The word clearly states that we were before we were formed in our mothers' wombs predestined to live in oneness with the perfect will and plans of our Heavenly Father. We were to eat of the Tree of Life which is the Son's realm, by which we would acquire all wisdom, knowledge and understanding and then we would be allowed to partake of the Tree of the Knowledge of Good and Evil, with is the Father's Realm, for it is only the right of the Father to judge between Good and Evil. Yet we read that Solomon because he had a full measure of natural wisdom, judged fairly between good and evil.

Judas Iscariot

Do you think that the Father did not know who Judas Iscariot was when Jesus chose him as one of His disciples?

Matthew 27:3-10 KJV Then Judas, which had betrayed Him, when he saw that he was condemned, repented himself, and brought again the thirty pieces of silver to the chief priests and elders. And gave them for the potter's field, as the Lord appointed me.

The Status of the Anti-Christ

1 John 2:18 KJV Little children, it is the last time: and as ye have heard that antichrist shall come, even now are there many antichrists; whereby we know that it is the last time.

Greek Strong's Concordance -- -an-tee'-khris-tos an opponent of the Messiah: - antichrist. *an-tee'* A primary particle; *opposite*, that is, *instead* or *because* of (rarely *in addition* to): - for, in the room of. Often used in composition to denote *contrast, requital, substitution, correspondence,* etc. Christos *khris-tos'anointed,* that is, the *Messiah,* an epithet of Jesus Christ.

John told them that in the last days there shall come one who is opposite in nature and character of the Messiah,

1 John 2:22 KJV
1 John 4:3 KJV
2 John 1:7 KJV
2 Timothy 3:2-4 KJV But evil men and seducers shall wax worse and worse, deceiving, and being deceived

HIS ORGIN:
Genesis 3:15 KJV
John 6:70, 71 KJV
2 Thessalonians 2:1-5 KJV Let no man deceive you by any means: for *that day shall not come*, except there come a falling away first, and that man of sin be revealed, the son of perdition;
Philippians 1:28 evident token of perdition.

BODY OF SATAN:
John 17:12 KJV
Genesis 4:25 KJV
Seed here in Hebrew is zera῾ *zeh'-rah seed*; figuratively *fruit, plant, sowing time, posterity*: - carnally, child, fruitful, seed (-time), sowing-time.
Revelation 13:4 KJV
Revelation 17:8-11 KJV
BOTTOMLESS PIT – Sea
Revelation 11:3-7 KJV The resurrected body of the Antichrist has its origin from the bottomless pit or the sea.

Nature and Character
God Jehovah, love, joy, peace, mercy, longsuffering, forbearance, kindness, goodness, faithfulness, eternal, everlasting, provider, Father, husband
Jesus, forgiving, savior, master, teacher, mediator, shepherd, bridegroom
Holy Ghost, comforter, revealer
Genesis 2:19 KJV And out of the ground the LORD God formed every beast of the field, and every fowl of the air; and brought *them* unto Adam to see what he would call them: and whatsoever Adam called every living creature, that was the name thereof.
Serpent or snake, - Deceit and Guile **Genesis 3:**1 -- Hebrew meaning *whisper* a (magic) spell; generally, to *prognosticate*: - certainly, divine, enchanter, (use) enchantment, learn by experience, indeed, diligently observe.
Daniel 7:1, 2 KJV Daniel had a dream and visions of his head upon his bed: then he wrote the dream, *and* told the sum of the matters. Daniel spake and said, I saw in my vision by night, four great beasts, lion, bear, eagle and leopard.
Lion is symbolic of domineering, rules without mercy **Genesis 49:9**
Leopard - Stocking Spirit, A spirit that is a predator, it lies in wait for its victim. **Isaiah 11:6**
Bear - Carnal Reasoning, Forceful **1 Samuel 17:34 and Revelation 13:2**
Eagle - Accusation **Leviticus 11:13**

The Awakening
Isaiah 56:10 KJV His watchmen are blind, they are all ignorant, they are all dumb dogs, they cannot bark; sleeping, lying down, loving to slumber.

Ephesians 2:8-10 KJV For we are His workmanship, created in Jesus Christ unto good works, which God hath ordained that we should walk in them.

Chapter 9
15. The Bridal Party
Joel 2:16 KJV (The entire bridal party)
Revelation 19:9, 10 KJV The *bride* is arrayed in her garments. Fine White Linen which indicates her deeds of Righteousness.
Revelation 3:5 KJV Clothed in white remnant. His name will be found in the Lamb's Book of Life. These are the guests of the bridegroom and the *bride*.
Revelation 4:4 KJV Clothed in white robes. These are the 24 elders that minister to the *bride* and Bridegroom around the throne of God.

Created By Him and For Him
Colossians 1:16, 17, KJV For by Him were all things created, that are in Heaven, and that are in earth, visible and invisible, whether they be thrones, or dominions, or principalities, or powers: all things were created by Him, and for Him: And He is before all things, and by Him all things consist. And He is the head of the body, the church: who is the beginning, the firstborn from the dead; that in all things He might have the preeminence.
For it pleased the Father that in Him should all fullness dwell.
1 Corinthians 15:35-44 KJV The resurrection/degrees of glory.

Revelation 22:4 KJV And they shall see His face; and His name *shall be* in their foreheads.
Matthew 24:29-31 KJV The LORD'S call to His bridal armies, blow the trumpet in Zion and sound the alarm in My Holy Mountain.
Joel 2:1, 2, 11 KJV for the Day of the LORD cometh
Joel 3:1-14 KJV The day the bridegroom and bridal armies returns to earth, what a day that will be.

16. Eternity Future
His Perfect Will and His Plan for all of Humankind
Romans 8:28-31 KJV And we know that all things work together for good to them that love God, to them who are the called according to His purpose.

For whom He did foreknow, He also did predestinate to be conformed to the image of His Son, that He might be the firstborn among many brethren. Moreover, whom He did predestinate, them He also called: and whom He called, them He also justified: and whom He justified, them He also glorified. What shall we then say to these things? If God be for us, who *can be* against us?

Revelation 1:8 KJV I am Alpha and Omega, the beginning and the ending, saith the Lord, which is, and which was, and which is to come, the Almighty. **Revelation 2:7** KJV He that hath an ear, let him hear what the Spirit saith unto the churches; To him that overcometh will I give to eat of the Tree of Life, which is in the midst of the paradise of God. **Revelation 2:11** KJV He that hath an ear, let him hear what the Spirit saith unto the churches; He that overcometh shall not be hurt of the second death. **Revelation 2:16, 17** KJV *Repent*; He that hath an ear, let him hear what the Spirit saith unto the churches; To him that overcometh will I give to eat of the hidden manna, and will give him a white stone, and in the stone a new name written, which no man knoweth saving he that receiveth it. **Revelation 2:25-29** KJV But that which ye have already *hold fast* till I come. *And he that overcometh, and keepeth my works unto the end, to him will I give power over the nations:* He that hath an ear let him hear what the Spirit saith unto the churches.

Revelation 3:5, 6 KJV *He that overcometh, the same shall be clothed in white raiment; and I will not blot out his name out of the Book of Life*, but I will confess his name before My Father, and before His angels. He that hath an ear, let him hear what the Spirit saith unto the churches. **Revelation 3:11-13** KJV Behold, I come quickly: hold that fast which thou hast, that no man take thy crown. Him that overcometh will I make a pillar in the Temple of my God, and he shall go no more out: and I will write upon him the name of My God, *and the name of the city of My God, which is new Jerusalem, which cometh down out of Heaven from my God*: and *I will write upon him* My new name. He that hath an ear, let him hear what the Spirit saith unto the churches. **Revelation 3:19-22** KJV As many as I love, I rebuke and chasten be zealous therefore, and repent.

Behold, I stand at the door, and knock: if any man hear My voice, and open the door, I will come in to him, and will sup with him, and he with Me. To him that overcometh will I grant to sit with Me in My Throne, even as I also overcame, and am set down with My Father in His Throne. He that hath an ear let him hear what the Spirit saith unto the churches.

It could only exist in the Imagination

Chapter 10
17. Planned Parenthood
Plan or planned so to formulate a scheme, or program. Predestination.
Parent is any organism that produces or generates another, mother, father, ancestor, or forefather.
Hood **is** a state, condition, or quality of being......**Hood**, a covering, an extended part. **Webster's College Dictionary**

Words of Wisdom --Journaling is the best way to know when you are on track and when you get off the track.

As you journal your revelations, they will become stones in your treasure chest. Each revelation/seed must be stored away in your seed sack until it is time for you to share it or them. Remember and seek understanding of the seed principle, seed, time, and harvest. (Ref. Luke 8:4-15)

www.ingramcontent.com/pod-product-compliance
Lightning Source LLC
Chambersburg PA
CBHW051147120626

46547CB00012B/972